'In this finely conceived and elegantly structured book Philip Bamber brings an international perspective to bear on the notion of learning as a transformative process that combines reciprocity and dialogue with a willingness to recognise our cultural differences. It is, argues Bamber, only through this process of learning together across local and global divides that we achieve ethical agency in respect of our own life trajectories and moral agency in relation to our treatment of one another. This is an important and timely work that has implications for how we conceive of educational practice in a global and increasingly divided world.'

Professor Jon Nixon, *Honorary Professor of International Education and Lifelong Learning and Senior Research Fellow, Centre for Lifelong Learning Research and Development, Hong Kong Institute of Education*

'This book is a major contribution to the conversation about Transformative Learning in a multi-cultural, global context. The focus on being as well as knowing, on self as well as self-in-relationship, is powerful. The critique of International Service-Learning in terms of the apparently unwitting reinforcement of colonization and ignoring systemic causes of injustice is discerning and useful. Weaving the ethics of virtue into the discussion of transformation is profound. I was moved and inspired by this work.'

Professor John Dirkx, *Professor, Higher, Adult and Lifelong Education, Michigan State University, USA; Editor,* Journal of Transformative Education

'This is a timely and compelling book that offers faculty, researchers, and practitioners a richly layered and deeply theoretical framework for understanding the complex process of transformative learning. The expanded conceptualization of transformative learning as a multidimensional and relational journey of becoming an authentic self, derived from a longitudinal study of students' international service-learning experience, is unique and powerful.'

Dr Richard Kiely, *Director, Engaged Learning and Research, Cornell University, USA*

'This publication brims with compelling insights into the pitfalls and possibilities of international service activity and the essential conditions for this to be a transformative learning experience. Philip Bamber has provided a richly detailed map of the ethical and educational challenges of international service activity and a reliable compass to help practitioners and advocates to navigate these.'

Richard Baker, *Head of Education and Youth, Oxfam GB*

Transformative Education through International Service-Learning

Transformative learning is a compelling approach to learning that is becoming increasingly popular in a diverse range of educational settings and encounters. This book reconceptualises transformative learning through an investigation of the learning process and outcomes of International Service-Learning (ISL), a pedagogical approach that blends student learning with community engagement overseas and the development of a more just society. Drawing upon key philosophers and theorists, Bamber offers an integrated, multidimensional approach, linking transformative learning to the development of the authentic self, and analysing the aesthetic, moral and relational dimensions of ISL in an increasingly globalised world. Chapters explore rich empirical data to provide a timely framework and ethical ecology of transformative learning, detailing the challenges facing the approach, and how it can be embedded at the levels of practice, institutional ethos and partnership.

Transformative Education through International Service-Learning will appeal to academics, researchers, teachers, instructors and leaders in the fields of service-learning, international education, character education and in adult learning and education. It will also be of interest to practitioners working in international education, development education, volunteering, service-learning and community engagement.

Philip M. Bamber is Associate Professor in the Faculty of Education at Liverpool Hope University, where he is Head of the Department of Education Studies. He was awarded the International Association of University Presidents' 2013 International Education Faculty Achievement Award for leadership in research and teaching in global citizenship. He is co-editor (with L. Bourke and J. Clarkson) of *In Safe Hands: Facilitating Service Learning in Schools in the Developing World* (Stoke-on-Trent: Trentham, 2008) and is currently Associate Director of TEESNet, the UK Teacher Education for Equity and Sustainability Network. His papers on global citizenship and values in education can be found in *Education, Citizenship and Social Justice*; *Journal of Beliefs and Values*; *Journal of Curriculum Studies* and *Journal of Transformative Education*.

Routledge Research in International and Comparative Education

This is a series that offers a global platform to engage scholars in continuous academic debate on key challenges and the latest thinking on issues in the fast growing field of International and Comparative Education.

Books in the series include:

Transformative Education through International Service-Learning
Realising an ethical ecology of learning
Philip M. Bamber

The Critical Global Educator
Global citizenship education as sustainable development
Maureen Ellis

Investigating Education in Germany
Historical studies from a British perspective
David Phillips

Knowledge Hierarchies in Transnational Education
Staging dissensus
Jing Qi

Global Identity in Multicultural and International Educational Contexts
Student identity formation in international schools
Nigel Bagnall

Teaching in Primary Schools in China and India
Contexts of learning
Nirmala Rao, Emma Pearson and Kai-ming Cheng with Margaret Taplin

A History of Higher Education Exchange
China and America
Teresa Brawner Bevis

National Identity and Educational Reform
Contested classrooms
Elizabeth Anderson Worden

Citizenship Education around the World
Local contexts and global possibilities
Edited by John E. Petrovic and Aaron M. Kuntz

Children's Voices
Studies of interethnic conflict and violence in European schools
Edited by Mateja Sedmak, Zorana Medarić and Sarah Walker

Culture, Transnational Education and Thinking
Case studies in global schooling
Niranjan Casinader

The Changing Landscape of International Schooling
Implications for theory and practice
Tristan Bunnell

Leading and Managing Indigenous Education in the Postcolonial World
Zane Ma Rhea

Multi-campus University Systems
Africa and the Kenyan Experience
Ishmael I. Munene

Education and the State
International perspectives on a changing relationship
Edited by Carla Aubry, Michael Geiss, Veronika Magyar-Haas and Jürgen Oelkers

Conflict, Reconciliation and Peace Education
Moving Burundi toward a sustainable future
William M. Timpson, Elavie Ndura and Apollinaire Bangayimbaga

Citizenship Education and Migrant Youth in China
Pathways to the urban underclass
Miao Li

International Service Learning
Engaging host communities
Edited by Marianne A. Larsen

Educational Borrowing in China
Looking West or looking East?
Charlene Tan

Nationalism and History Education
Curricula and textbooks in the United States and France
Rachel D. Hutchins

Transformative Education through International Service-Learning

Realising an ethical ecology of learning

Philip M. Bamber

LONDON AND NEW YORK

First published 2016
by Routledge
2 Park Square, Milton Park, Abingdon, Oxon OX14 4RN

and by Routledge
711 Third Avenue, New York, NY 10017

Routledge is an imprint of the Taylor & Francis Group, an informa business

© 2016 P. M. Bamber

The right of P. M. Bamber to be identified as author of this work has been asserted by him in accordance with sections 77 and 78 of the Copyright, Designs and Patents Act 1988.

All rights reserved. No part of this book may be reprinted or reproduced or utilised in any form or by any electronic, mechanical, or other means, now known or hereafter invented, including photocopying and recording, or in any information storage or retrieval system, without permission in writing from the publishers.

Trademark notice: Product or corporate names may be trademarks or registered trademarks, and are used only for identification and explanation without intent to infringe.

British Library Cataloguing in Publication Data
A catalogue record for this book is available from the British Library

Library of Congress Cataloging in Publication Data
Names: Bamber, Phil, author.
Title: Transformative education through international service-learning: realising an ethical ecology of education / Philip M. Bamber.
Description: New York, NY : Routledge, 2016. | Includes bibliographical references.
Identifiers: LCCN 2015039171| ISBN 9781138923607 (hbk) | ISBN 9781315684970 (ebk)
Subjects: LCSH: Transformative learning. | Service learning. | Foreign study. | Student volunteers in social service. | World citizenship.
Classification: LCC LC1100 .B36 2016 | DDC 361.3/7—dc23
LC record available at http://lccn.loc.gov/2015039171

ISBN: 978-1-138-92360-7 (hbk)
ISBN: 978-1-315-68497-0 (ebk)

Typeset in Bembo
by Swales & Willis Ltd, Exeter, Devon, UK

Printed and bound by CPI Group (UK) Ltd, Croydon, CR0 4YY

This book is dedicated to Sue and Les Bamber

Contents

Acknowledgements xv
List of abbreviations xvii

Introduction 1

The landscape for transformation 1
A reconceptualisation of transformative learning 4
An ethical definition of International Service-Learning (ISL) 5
A framework for an ethical ecology of transformative learning 6
Overview of the structure of the book 7
Part I: transformative learning 7
Part II: International Service-Learning 9
Part III: transformative learning as the process of becoming authentic 10
Part IV: realising an ethical ecology of transformative learning 10

PART I
Transformative learning 13

1 Towards an integrative model of transformative learning 15

Introduction 15
The transformative dimension of learning 16
Critical, cultural perspectives on education 19
The role of reflection, experience and practice 21
Towards a holistic theory of learning 23
Conclusion 25

2 The knowing, being and doing of transformation 29

Introduction 29
Knowledge: knowing 29
    Connecting different aspects of knowing 29
    Aesthetic aspects of knowing 30

Tacit aspects of knowing 32
Relational aspects of knowing 34
Becoming: being 37
Being as a process of becoming 37
Virtue ethics and being as practice 39
Agency: doing 43
The capability approach 43
Agency and social change 45
Conclusion 47

3 The centrality of authenticity to transformative learning 52

Introduction 52
The authentic self 52
(Authenticity as) selfhood, reciprocity and worldliness 57
(Authenticity as) selfhood 58
(Authenticity as) reciprocity 59
(Authenticity as) worldliness 60
Conclusion 61
Segue 62

PART II
International Service-Learning 65

4 Key concepts and practices in International Service-Learning 67

Introduction 67
Service-Learning 67
International Service-Learning 69
Service-Learning and higher education 74
Service-Learning and faith-based education 79
Conclusion 81

5 Investigating the student experience of International Service-Learning 85

Introduction 85
International Service-Learning at Liverpool Hope University 85
This investigation into the student experience of ISL 89
Narratives of ISL participants 92
Rachel, SOS Tibetan Children's Village, Choglamsar, Ladakh, India, 1993 93
Olivia, Sarata, Transylvania, Romania, 2009 96
Conclusion 101

Contents xiii

PART III
Transformative learning as the process of becoming authentic   103
   Introduction 103

6 Authenticity as selfhood: becoming oneself [integrity]   107

  Introduction 107
  Conditions 108
    Openness with self 108
    Perseverance, resilience and flexibility 110
    Connectivity with self 111
  Processes 112
    Reflexivity and distance 112
    Encountering challenge 114
    Evaluating service 116
    Raising existential questions 118
    Reconnecting with self 119
  Dispositions 120
    Honesty and humility 120
    Being 121
    Reconnecting with time 123
    Personal efficacy 124
  Barriers to integrity 126

7 Authenticity as reciprocity: becoming persons-in-relation [recognition]   131

  Introduction 131
  Conditions 133
    Openness with others 133
    Anticipating reciprocity 134
    Connectivity with others 135
  Processes 137
    Felt sense of the worlds of others 137
    Deliberation and exchange 140
    Shared reflection 142
    Reconnecting with others 143
  Dispositions 146
    Mutual trust 146
    Being with others 147
    Recognising others 149
    Empathy and compassion 151
  Barriers to recognition 152

8 Authenticity as worldliness: becoming other-wise [cosmopolitanism] — 155

Introduction 155
Conditions 156
  Openness with the other 156
  Capacity to critically reflect 158
  Connectivity with the other 160
Processes 162
  Critical reflection alongside immersion 162
  Participatory problem solving 165
  Reconnecting with the other 166
Dispositions 168
  Acknowledging incompleteness 168
  Questioning hegemony 170
  Valuing other ways of knowing 171
  Reconnecting with place 173
  Tackling injustice 174
Barriers to cosmopolitanism 176

PART IV
Realising an ethical ecology of transformative learning — 179

9 Realising an ethical ecology of transformative learning — 181

Introduction 181
Practice 183
  Nurturing the conditions for transformation 183
  The conditions for transformation need to be made and remade 185
  Recognising value orientation 186
  Educating dispositions 188
  The poverty of pre-specifying learning outcomes 190
  The importance of aesthetic engagement 191
Institutional ethos 193
  The student experience 193
  Focus on purpose and process 194
  Institution as role model 196
Partnership 198
  Balancing the multi-faceted nature of transformation 198
  Authentic relationships 199
  A cosmopolitan outlook 202
Conclusion 204

Appendix: Mapping of data collection — 209
Index — 211

Acknowledgements

There are a small number of people without whom this book would not have been completed, not least my own family. My wife Lynda and daughter Lucy have shown incredible love and patience during this time. I am blessed with a wonderful family, including brothers and sisters, and now also nieces and nephews, who in different ways continue to support and inspire.

The pivotal moment that motivated and has sustained this study into the student experience of International Service Learning (ISL) took place in Malawi in 2006. Chief Maliri, a leader of one of the communities in the capital city Lilongwe, told the International Service-Learning project-team I was leading: 'But you are no ordinary citizens, because you have come here to Malawi.' His words provoked me to acknowledge and act upon the insights that I had gained from my own experiences such as ISL.

I would like to acknowledge those I have been most fortunate to live alongside, in educational settings in India, Malawi and Papua New Guinea. In particular: Jolden Dhondup, Migmar Tsering, Ephraim Chinyama, Anton Chisamba, Chrissie D'Costa, Greg and Mari Mambo and their family, Theo Yakam and family, Damian Sam and family, Francesca Kalipapung and family and of course Douglas Hopkos, Basil Pere, Joe Watae and Douglas Rawaiya.

I am also indebted to the staff and students I have accompanied on International Service-Learning experiences. In particular: Jane Cunningham, Graham Moger and David Berg. A special thank you goes to Dave and Sera Rumble, my extended family, who were an unwavering source of support and inspiration during my 26-month VSO placement in Papua New Guinea.

I feel immensely fortunate to have been supported so effectively in developing this research by colleagues at Liverpool Hope University. Special thanks to Wendy Bignold, Bart McGettrick, Ian Stronach, Pro-Vice Chancellor Kenneth Newport and Pro-Vice Chancellor Gerald Pillay for valuing and supporting my work. Thanks are also due to all the research participants for their time and openness.

My understanding of the ideas discussed in this book have been clarified through collegial exchange with friends and scholars at Liverpool Hope University and beyond, including: Sue Cronin, Lorna Bourke, Alison Clark,

Andrea Bullivant, Clive Belgeonne, John Sullivan, Andrew Morris, David Lewin, Beth Green, Jean Conteh, Fran Martin, Doug Bourn, Richard Kiely and John Dirkx. I would particularly like to thank Jon Nixon and Mark Pike for helping me to understand the importance of, and realise, this work. It has been a privilege to share ideas with you.

Abbreviations

HEI	Higher Education Institution
ISL	International Service-Learning
LHU	Liverpool Hope University
NGO	Non-Government Organisation
SALA	Service and Leadership Award
SL	Service-Learning
TCV	Tibetan Children's Village
VSO	Voluntary Service Overseas

Data codes

FG	Focus Group
GI	Group Interview
I	Interview
P	Phase

Permissions

From *To Kill a Mockingbird* by Harper Lee, published by William Heinemann. Reproduced by permission of The Random House Group Ltd. [UK and Commonwealth (less Canada)]

TO KILL A MOCKINGBIRD by HARPER LEE. Copyright (c) 1960 by Harper Lee; renewed (c) 1988 by Harper Lee. Reprinted courtesy of HarperCollins Publishers. [US, Canada, Philippines and open market]

THE MAGICIAN'S NEPHEW by CS Lewis © copyright CS Lewis Pte ltd 1955. Reproduced by permission of The CS Lewis Company Ltd.

From *The Jerusalem Bible* © 1966 by Darton Longman & Todd Ltd and Doubleday and Company Ltd.

Introduction

The landscape for transformation

Our lives, at the start of the twenty-first century, are irrevocably complex. While it is assumed that education must play a part, the form of education to help us navigate this landscape is open to debate. The extensity and velocity of trans-national inter-relationships that now typify global interdependence ensure that individuals and communities are routinely exposed to people, beliefs and events that confound their existing understanding of the world. For the majority of us, a short walk through the centre of our nearest city brings us into contact with a hugely diverse range of cultures and races. Interminable news coverage ensures events from across the planet are experienced by growing numbers in real time, while web-based technology places individuals from contrasting contexts in immediate and direct contact in a way that would have been inconceivable only a few decades ago. The pressing concern, addressed by this book, is how education can support us to make sense of ourselves, each other and this world in a way that reliably and ethically guides our actions.

The emergence of a truly global economy, the revolution in transport and information and communications technology, the reality of climate change and worldwide migration, the end of the Cold War and start of a global war on terror have all served to blur boundaries between individuals and communities, fomenting the opposing forces of integration and fragmentation. The global movement of people has left communities across the globe reconciling the tensions of promoting both diversity and unity: multicultural societies attempt to cultivate commonality while being inclusive of all citizens. Against this backdrop, education has a key role to play in nurturing understanding of ourselves and others: for instance, through the development of intercultural skills, such as the ability to mediate cultural conflicts and misunderstandings in a diverse world.

While technology has compressed the distances between peoples, the war on terror and growth of Islamic State demonstrate that the differences between peoples are sometimes more intractable than ever, threatening the peace of our communities at local, national, regional and international levels. The homogenising might of globalisation has been exaggerated: shared aspects of global popular culture, the universality of mobile technologies, the spread of the English language and the exponential growth of tourism have not served to suppress local beliefs, values and norms. At the same time, our lives are irreversibly intertwined with others, as demonstrated by the causes and effect of climate change: if everyone in the world were to consume natural resources and generate carbon emissions at the rate of average individuals in the UK, we would require three planets, not just one, to support us. Given this landscape of complexity, opportunities for young people to interact first-hand with individuals throughout the world are potentially invaluable in enabling us to come to a deeper understanding of similarities, differences and inter-relationships between people, cultures, places and ideas.

The importance of inculcating a worldwide horizon is not something new: the Stoic philosopher Seneca famously asked his compatriots to 'Look how many broad stretching countries lie open behind you, how many peoples' (Seneca, 2012: 57). Citizens of wealthier nations have, historically, been drawn towards supporting approaches to alleviate poverty outside of their own country, most recently through donations to international aid and international volunteering. International Service-Learning (ISL), the focus of this book, provides one such opportunity for students to use their skills and knowledge to make a distinctive contribution to partner communities overseas and learn from their experience in this different context. ISL has, however, been criticised for promoting patronising and unsustainable educational development, for example through unqualified teachers leading professional development overseas that depends upon teaching resources which cannot be sourced locally. More broadly, efforts by international organisations to support resource-poor communities in developing countries have been accused of reinforcing a culture of dependency and exacerbating the 'poverty trap'. At the same time, globalisation has intensified levels of relative poverty and social exclusion even within the world's most affluent countries. While some privileged groups have been empowered, the UK and USA now find themselves characterised by greater inequality, insecurity and marginalisation than at any time in their histories.

Against this backdrop, Barack Obama proclaimed during his inauguration as President of the United States that 'we are all global citizens now'. It is difficult to comprehend how members of resource-poor communities in either developing or developed countries would identify with this claim. Global citizenship is without doubt a problematic concept in theory and practice (Bamber et al., 2012; Bamber, 2011), and it is not the explicit focus of this book. The term is invoked by individuals and organisations to promote a disparate and sometimes conflicting range of interests. For instance, the term is sometimes used in the media to describe the development of intercultural skills and a loose sense of belonging and responsibility to a global community enacted through acts of charity. At the same time, multinational corporations refer to 'global citizenship' to inflate their green credentials, and the phrase is inscribed on the curriculum vitae of the globetrotting elite. No matter how global citizenship is construed, there is an urgent need to recognise the liquidity and evolution of difference, and cultivate a genuine sense of solidarity and responsibility to others within our own countries and around the world.

This provokes important questions about the role and purpose of education in responding to the crises facing humanity and the planet upon which we all depend. One position is to dismiss such talk as alarmist and irrelevant – a distraction from the core business of education. Those who take this short-term view invoke pressures to increase standards of numeracy and literacy, an already over-crowded curriculum and accountability measures to justify their stance. This approach not only fails to provide a solution to the multiple challenges we face but is fundamentally part of the problem. Indeed, 'without significant precautions, education can equip people merely to be more effective vandals of the earth' (Orr, 2004: 5). The marketisation and commodification of education, discourses and practices relating to performativity and competitiveness in education, the self-serving culture of the individual and the functionality of the knowledge economy are all indicative of ways in which education has separated ourselves from one another. There is an urgent need to re-calibrate our systems and practices of education to not only equip young people for the global economy but for lives in service of the common good.

There are tentative, yet perceptible, movements towards such a re-visioning of education, of which this book is a part. The 2015 World Education Forum at Incheon, South Korea, proposed the post-2015 aim to 'transform lives through education' and, by 2030, 'Ensure inclusive and equitable quality education and promote lifelong learning opportunities for all'. The Incheon Declaration (UNESCO, 2015) shifts the focus of international efforts from 'access to' education, as embedded within Education for All and the education-related Millennium Development Goals, towards 'quality of' education. Furthermore, it concludes the latter is characterised by 'the skills, values and attitudes that enable citizens to lead healthy and fulfilled lives, make informed decisions, and respond to local and global challenges through education for sustainable development and global citizenship education' (UNESCO, 2015). It is no longer enough for developed countries to simply contribute financially to international efforts to improve education, for example through meeting the target of 0.7 per cent of gross national product for official development assistance. The new Sustainable Development Goals demand collaboration among educators internationally to better understand how education as a public good can more effectively nurture peace, tolerance, sustainable livelihoods and human fulfilment for all.

Furthermore, in 2018 the Programme for International Student Assessment will assess the 'global competence' of 15-year-olds across the world, including 'their awareness of the interconnected global world we live and work in and their ability to deal effectively with the resulting demands'. Nevertheless, it is not clear how 'global competence' can be meaningfully measured through international testing. There is a danger that such metrics intensify the focus of education upon short-term observable outcomes rather than longer term changes in behaviour, attitude and practice. In contrast, UNESCO has set out a vision for education for global citizenship that emphasises the holistic aspects of learning the current landscape requires, acknowledging education must move 'beyond the development of knowledge and cognitive skills to build values, soft skills and attitudes among learners that can facilitate international cooperation and promote social transformation' (UNESCO, 2014: 9).

Despite a groundswell of evidence of the need for such 'transformative approaches' to education (UNESCO, 2015), manifestos for 'transformative pedagogy for global citizenship' (UNESCO, 2014) and 'transformative education for critical and active engagement in a globalised society' (Fricke and Gathercole, 2015: 14) provide only cursory analysis of the theoretical perspectives that can illuminate, and must stimulate, such pedagogy and little evidence of what transformative learning looks like in practice. This provides the motivation for this book, which interrogates the transformative dimension of learning through analysis of the student experience of ISL. Drawing upon a five-year research project into an ISL programme at a university in the UK, this book presents a reconceptualisation of transformative learning and an ethical definition of ISL as the foundations for what is described here as an ethical ecology of learning.

A reconceptualisation of transformative learning

> . . . it's incredibly life changing . . .
>
> (Ann, ISL Participant in 1999 in India)

Notions of transformation in education have proved to be seductive and compelling. Since Jack Mezirow introduced in 1975 the notions of 'perspective transformation' and 'transformative learning' into the North American adult education literature, and especially in the last 20 years, research and writing in this area has proliferated. The allure of the notion of transformation coupled with the elegant model presented by Mezirow has ensured that transformative learning theory has received considerable attention in academic discourse and practice in a range of adult educational settings. Mezirow's work provided the basis for establishing the *Journal of Transformative Education* in 2003, which continues to publish material from a diverse range of international academics and practitioners. The 12th biennial International Transformative Learning Conference takes place in October 2016 in Washington, USA, and goes from strength to strength. Nevertheless, to prevent 'transformative learning' simply becoming a 'floating signifier, a buzzword without any clear meaning' (Illeris, 2014: 15), this book attempts to provoke further critical debate around this theory of learning, associated pedagogical approaches such as ISL, and their place within the curriculum.

This book seeks to reconceptualise transformative learning through an investigation into the learning processes and outcomes from ISL. ISL provides a rich context to develop understanding of transformation: in the study upon which this book is based, 24 of the 29 students who completed in-depth interviews chose, like Ann, to describe their experience of ISL as 'life-changing'. This is remarkable given that for many of these students their overseas experience lasted for as little as two weeks. This provides an initial indicator of the intensity and visceral nature of this learning experience, the impact of which endures for many participants beyond their return home. Rather than radically overturning received notions of transformative learning, this book seeks to work within a tradition that takes transformative learning seriously. It draws upon a diverse range of philosophers and learning theorists to develop an expanded conceptualisation of transformative learning with aesthetic, moral and relational dimensions. This holistic conceptualisation looks beyond an epistemological process that involves shifts in worldview and habits of mind towards an ontological process that accounts for changes to the student's ways of being in the world.

The literature in transformative education is mainly preoccupied with the outcomes of transformation without considering the learning processes, which remain elusive. Through investigating the student experience of ISL, this book seeks to redress this imbalance. Groups of conditions, processes and resultant dispositions are identified as being particularly useful for understanding transformative experiences such as ISL. In doing so, this book provides a response to Mezirow's call (2009: 28) for an elaboration of concepts central to a notion of 'integral transformative learning'. Drawing upon empirical data that is longitudinal in nature, it argues that transformative learning is experienced as an ongoing process of becoming. This book is therefore also a timely contribution to debate around virtues in education and how dispositions can be educated (for example see Arthur et al., 2015).

An ethical definition of International Service-Learning (ISL)

> I wanted to give something back. I just really like helping people and not helping in a patronising way, but putting yourself out there, like offering to do things for other people . . . they enjoy you serving them.
>
> (Olivia, ISL participant in 2009 in Romania)

> . . . you go out there thinking I am going there for that reason and that purpose . . . but the experience brings the unexpected . . .
>
> (Coleen, ISL participant in 2007 in Malawi)

International Service-Learning (ISL) is a pedagogical activity that seeks to blend student learning with community engagement overseas and the development of a more just society. ISL is increasingly used as a strategy by schools, colleges, universities and non-government organisations (NGOs) committed to moral as well as academic learning. Programmes tend to be short-term (from two weeks to two months) in duration and have grown as educational institutions and NGOs have sought to develop 'global citizens'. For instance, (I)SL and related initiatives are now promoted by universities in the UK as they respond to reforms in higher education and as they seek to enhance both the student learning experience and their employability. A concern for what I have termed 'service apathy' (Bamber and Pike, 2013) among citizens in general, and college students in particular, along with an awareness of the ramifications of our increasingly individualistic society less concerned with the public good, has also led to growth in service-learning activity (Bamber and Hankin, 2011). Nevertheless, initiatives such as ISL that seek to internationalise the curriculum and nurture global citizenship and intercultural learning remain deeply under-theorised.

ISL is an ambitious endeavour with rich possibilities for personal, interpersonal and social learning. Communities in diverse contexts across the world become sites of learning for students as they participate in programmes that attempt to solve issues relating to poverty and social injustice. It is argued here that this presents a number of problems such as the proclivity to exploit through propagating a form of new colonialism; this demands further interrogation if educators are to avoid exacerbating the social inequities they seek to address. Despite substantial anecdotal evidence of the transformative nature of an overseas experience there is a paucity of research into the exact nature of this learning. An appreciation that the anticipated outcomes for young people do not automatically result from time spent overseas has driven calls for regulation of the international volunteering sector. This book provides a response to calls to develop an ethical framework for activity such as ISL (NIDOS, 2009; Martin and Griffiths, 2012).

This study investigates the transformative nature of ISL as experienced by students at a university in the UK. Through interpreting student descriptions of their ongoing experience of ISL (before, during and after their overseas experience), it analyses features of the transformative learning process in this context and develops understanding of the potential for transformative learning outcomes from what are often relatively short-term experience overseas. It is argued here that ISL activity that promotes rational and instrumental learning represents a deficit model. Furthermore, although ISL is a form of engagement that has the potential to be ethical in character, this book identifies a number of factors that militate against this.

Drawing upon this analysis, the book offers an original and innovative definition of ISL that recognises its transformative potential and ensures its ethical integrity. It is argued that ISL can best be understood as a form of ecological engagement with aesthetic, moral and spiritual dimensions that are enacted through participation in the lives and 'worlds' of those living in different countries, and which enables ethical reflection, enhances personal efficacy and seeks to engender a more just and sustainable society.

A framework for an ethical ecology of transformative learning

This book draws upon a diverse range of theoretical perspectives and also empirical data to link together notions of transformative learning with the concept of authenticity. It presents a framework, or model, to understand transformative learning as the development of the authentic self: an ongoing process of becoming oneself, becoming persons-in-relation and becoming other-wise. The only previous attempt to relate authenticity to transformative process (Cranton and Carusetta, 2004) explicates becoming authentic as a process of individuation that serves to separate the learning self from the broader context and relationships. Authenticity is instead understood here as emerging from an understanding of the relational self. This is different from, although related to, concepts of individuality, identity, autonomy and originality. Understanding transformative learning as a process of becoming authentic provides the basis for the original conception of an 'ethical ecology of transformative learning' that is introduced in this book.

Overview of the structure of the book

The book is divided into four parts. Part I is primarily conceptual and theoretical. Building upon the work of Jack Mezirow and others, an integrated, multi-dimensional approach to transformative learning is proposed, which is linked to the idea of authenticity. Part II provides the contextual background for this analysis of transformative learning: the experience of ISL among students in higher education. In Part III a framework is presented to understand transformative learning as the development of the authentic self: an ongoing process of becoming oneself, becoming persons-in-relation and becoming other-wise. This is exemplified in Chapters 6, 7 and 8 by drawing upon empirical data of the student experience of ISL. Part IV explores in further detail what is meant by an ethical ecology of transformative learning, the challenges facing this approach to education, and how it can be embedded at the levels of practice, institutional ethos and partnership.

Part I: transformative learning

Part I provides the focus and scope for this study of transformative education. It provides the foundations for understanding transformative learning as the authentic self's ongoing process of becoming. This includes the growth of the learning self into the different modes of authenticity: authenticity as selfhood, authenticity as reciprocity, and authenticity as worldliness. This part begins with a conceptual discussion of transformative learning. Rather than explicate a particular model of transformative learning, Chapter 1 draws upon a range of different perspectives to argue that learning has dimensions both ontological (concerned with being) and epistemological (concerned with knowledge and knowing). The work of learning theorists, such as Jack Mezirow, Paulo Freire, David Kolb and others, is critiqued to demonstrate the ways they influence and provide the context for this argument. The proposed integrative model of transformative learning is shown to be grounded in the work of philosophers such as John Dewey, Michael Polanyi and Martin Heidegger.

Through detailed consideration of aspects of knowing, being and doing, Chapter 2 investigates in further detail this account of learning that is both holistic and deeply relational. Whilst acknowledging that it is only in and through relationships that the individual grows and learns, this is primarily an investigation into the journey of the learning self: a journey that is nevertheless completed alongside others. It is argued here that transformative experiences expose the learning self to aspects of knowing, being and doing that cannot be explained on the basis of entirely scientific or rational understanding. These experiences are typified by exchange and engagement rather than transmission. The related learning processes have rational and affective outcomes as students experience shifts in both their habits of mind and being. It is argued that the related ways of knowing, being and doing evince aesthetic, moral and even spiritual dimensions. This view of learning elevates the role of context, interpersonal relationships and the connections between the personal and the social. It is claimed that learning so understood is intrinsically transformative.

Authenticity emerges as a useful concept to understand this account of learning that is both holistic and deeply relational. In particular, Chapter 3 outlines how the learning self's authenticity is enhanced when it encounters the transformative aspects of knowing, being and doing in synergy. Transformative learning, as it is understood here, nurtures neither the 'original-to-be-discovered' nor the 'self-created' authentic self. Indeed, it is argued here that understanding the becoming of the 'authentic self' does not demand abandoning the self but recognising the potential of reconnecting the authentic self with itself, others and the broader context. Given this understanding that the learning self cannot become authentic in isolation, this chapter goes on to provide initial insight into aspects of authenticity that underpin the institutional scenario and specific arena of practice that provides the context for this study: an established ISL programme at a university with a Christian foundation in the north-west of England, UK. This demands recognising how this context is defined relationally: in particular, it will be argued that this context nurtures the authentic self's reflexive relation to self and discursive relation to the particular and general other as well as with the wider world. The concepts of selfhood, reciprocity and worldliness emerge as foundational to a framework to think about authenticity in relation to a particular group of students, who have a particular type of experience of ISL. The detailed analysis of this context will be the focus of Part II. Finally, a segue to Chapter 3 offers initial insight into how understanding transformative learning as a process of becoming authentic relates to a notion of an 'ethical ecology' of learning.

This study has drawn upon theoretical insights, my own experiences of ISL and empirical data at each stage of the research process. Although the detailed empirical analysis follows in Part III, brief excerpts from student transcripts are occasionally included within Part I of this book to indicate how the choices of literature were informed by the data as it was collected. These quotations also serve to provide the reader with initial insight into the relationship between transformative learning and ISL.

Part II: International Service-Learning

The primary purpose of Part II is to interrogate the context of this investigation into transformative learning. Recognising and analysing the interaction between the context in which transformative learning is engendered and the nature of learning itself addresses a limitation of previous research into transformative pedagogy (Taylor, 2009: 4). Chapter 4 therefore begins with an overview of the development of ISL in policy and practice internationally. This will be related to developments in service-learning, citizenship education, study abroad, international education, and educational programmes that seek to nurture global citizenship. First-hand exposure to other cultures opens up an eclectic range of learning opportunities such as language learning, cross-cultural awareness, personal transformation and growth, as well as the creation of a worldwide horizon. Nevertheless, this part will outline how ISL, like other initiatives that seek to provide such transformative experience, presents educational opportunities with complex ethical considerations. This chapter also includes discussion of recent policy and practice in higher education in the UK as it relates to service-learning. This review of the terrain of ISL practice concludes by considering the role of service-learning and community engagement within faith-based education.

In Chapter 5 the contextual spotlight shifts to the particular university and ISL programme that is the focus of this study. Liverpool Hope University (LHU) has a rich tradition of volunteering and, over the last 30 years, over 1,000 staff and students have participated in educational development projects in resource-poor communities overseas. LHU has recently launched an extra-curricular 'Service and Leadership Award' to recognise service in local and global contexts. This chapter begins by scrutinising the links between LHU's mission, as an ecumenical foundation, and the development of ethical international service activity. It goes on to outline how data collection was formulated in terms of four distinct but inter-related phases over a five-year period, from 2006 to 2011. The overseas experience for participants in this study ranged from two-and-a-half to seven weeks in length. The longitudinal nature of this research is further evident in that data was collected from across eight cohorts of ISL participants and includes pre- and post-experience data and interviews with students who had volunteered almost 15 years ago.

Part II concludes with the narratives of two ISL participants. These particular accounts have been selected because they highlight different experiences of ISL, the role of the background and biographies of participating students, and the ongoing impact of volunteering overseas on their lives. These narratives enable the research participants to tell their 'life-changing' stories in their own words. They also provide an initial exposure to the data that provides the basis for Chapters 6, 7 and 8, offering insight into the thematic analysis detailed in Part III and the framework for transformative learning developed here.

Part III: transformative learning as the process of becoming authentic

Part III begins with a short introduction that includes a presentation of the conceptual framework for transformative learning that emerged through the study of the student experience of ISL. It then comprises three empirically based chapters that each include an interpretive analysis of data that seeks to understand the nature of transformative learning in this context. Chapters 6, 7 and 8 explore, respectively, the transformative process of becoming oneself, becoming persons-in-relation and becoming other-wise through participation in ISL. Chapter 6 is oriented towards the development of 'authenticity as selfhood' and how students participating in ISL experience transformative learning as they develop integrity. Chapter 7 explores 'authenticity as reciprocity' and how students participating in ISL experience transformative learning through recognition. This brings into view the various relationships at the core of the ISL experience: amongst the staff and student teams from the UK, children and adults in the communities overseas where the service work is undertaken and also with significant individuals and groups that students meet during their time travelling beyond the project location. Chapter 8 is concerned with 'authenticity as worldliness' and the overarching concept of cosmopolitanism. This elevates the external contextual factors such as socio-economic disparity and historical social injustices that are features of the ISL experience.

Each chapter in Part III will identify the conditions that are necessary for transformation to take place in relation to that particular mode of authenticity, the processes that enable this transformative learning, and the related resultant dispositions. Chapters 6, 7 and 8 each conclude with a discussion of the barriers to transformation in relation to each particular aspect of authenticity.

Part IV: realising an ethical ecology of transformative learning

This final part will synthesise the key ideas developed in this book and explore the implications of this understanding of transformative learning for practice, institutional ethos and partnership. This enquiry has sought to develop knowledge regarding transformative learning and ISL. However, in this final part, practical suggestions will be outlined that will enable educators, communities and institutions to successfully cultivate an ethical ecology of transformative learning in diverse contexts. Implications for theory, policy and practice will be presented, including suggestions for future research. A systematic and comprehensive prescription *for* an ethical ecology of learning is antithetical to the idea of transformative learning developed here. This final part will therefore attempt to orientate educators *towards* an understanding of what may be meant by an ethical ecology of transformative learning and how this may be embedded in practice. Through focusing upon questions of values, purpose and relationships, and in considering the implications for educational programmes and institutions, the book concludes with a series of ambitious proposals for transformative education.

References

Arthur, J., Kristjansson, K., Cooke, S., Brown, E. and Carr, D. (2015) The Good Teacher: Understanding Virtues in Practice Research Report. Birmingham: The Jubilee Centre for Character & Virtues, University of Birmingham.

Bamber, P. (2011) Educating for Global Citizenship. In Gadsby, H. and Bullivant, A. (eds) *Global Learning and Sustainable Development*. London: Routledge, 56–75.

Bamber, P. and Hankin, L. (2011) Transformative Service-Learning: No Passport Required. *Education and Training* 53 (2/3): 190–206.

Bamber, P. and Pike, M. (2013) Towards an Ethical Ecology of International Service-Learning. *Journal of Curriculum Studies* 45 (4): 535–59.

Bamber, P., Bourke, L. and Lyons, M. (2012) Global Citizens: Who Are They? *Education, Citizenship and Social Justice* 7 (2): 161–75.

Cranton, P. and Carusetta, E. (2004) Developing Authenticity as a Transformative Process. *Journal of Transformative Education* 2 (4): 276–93.

Fricke, H.J and Gathercole, C. (2015) *Monitoring Education for Global Citizenship*. Brussels: DEEEP.

Illeris, K. (2014) *Transformative Learning and Identity*. London and New York: Routledge.

Martin, F. and Griffiths, H. (2012) Power and Representation: A Postcolonial Reading of Global Partnerships and Teacher Development through North-South Study Visits. *British Educational Research Journal* 28 (6): 907–27.

Mezirow, J. (2009) Transformative Learning Theory. In Mezirow, J. and Taylor, E. (eds) *Transformative Learning in Practice: Insights from Community Workplace and Higher Education*. San Francisco: Jossey-Bass, 18–32.

Network of International Development Organisations in Scotland (NIDOS) (2009) International Volunteering Organisational Code of Practice. Accessed 4 August 2015 at www.nidos.org.uk/sites/default/files/IV_COP_VolCharter.pdf.

Orr, D. (2004) *Earth in Mind: On Education, Environment, and the Human Prospect*. 10th anniversary edition. Washington, DC: Island Press.

Seneca, L.A. (2012) *Treatises: On Providence, on Tranquility of Mind, on Shortness of Life, on Happy Life*. Memphis: General Books LLC.

Taylor, E.W. (2009) Fostering Transformative Learning. In Mezirow, J. and Taylor, E. (eds) *Transformative Learning in Practice: Insights from Community Workplace and Higher Education*. San Francisco: Jossey-Bass, 3–17.

UNESCO (2014) *Global Citizenship Education: Preparing Learners for the Challenges of the 21st Century*. Paris: UNESCO.

UNESCO (2015) Incheon Declaration. Paris: UNESCO. Accessed 4 August 2015 at https://en.unesco.org/world-education-forum-2015/incheon-declaration.

Part I
Transformative learning

1 Towards an integrative model of transformative learning

Introduction

> . . . it changed everything . . . I came back and completely shifted the job that I wanted to do . . . now I work in the third sector for a charity, and I work within mental health. Part of my job is challenging the preconceptions people have of those with severe mental health problems, and that all came about really because of my ISL experience.
>
> (Katie, ISL participant in 2003 in India)

The idea of transformation is compelling, evoking images of wonder such as a butterfly emerging from a cocoon. It alludes to cataclysmic and dramatic change that is observable through a sudden and significant change in appearance or character. The word and the way it is used has connotations of irreversible change; the crossing of a threshold from which there is no going back. Narratives of personal transformation are seductive and proliferate in Western society: a millionaire works on a placement in a deprived community and begins to reflect on their own values as they learn to associate with the poor; a mother reassesses her role in the family through engagement with a lifelong learning course; an unemployed young man becomes radicalised through the Internet and enlists to fight for extremist religious views; an unruly teenager completes an outdoor residential 'boot camp' and subsequently re-engages with their study at school; the soldier physically debilitated and mentally traumatised by the horrors of war adapts to life after conflict.

Educators are fascinated by such learning that is 'deep', 'fundamental' or 'profound', raising a number of questions, addressed in this book, regarding what is meant by 'transformation' with respect to learning. These questions include; What is transformed through transformative learning and how does this relate to the way we know, act or feel in the world? How can the conditions for transformation be created? Can transformation occur unintentionally or does it require engagement with an intentional act of learning? Are particular events experienced as being transformative or is it that change is gradual and takes place over time? In what ways do we resist transformation or are propelled towards it? In what ways is learning experienced as restorative and transformative, progressive and regressive? What are the ethics of seeking to transform others? Can you transform a life that is your own? In focusing upon that which is transformative do we discredit other aspects of learning?

This chapter seeks to highlight the transformative dimension of learning. It argues that learning is fundamentally holistic and relational and has a distinct moral dimension. It begins by suggesting that Jack Mezirow's conceptualisation of transformative learning must be expanded upon to account for the interaction and balance between epistemological and ontological aspects of learning. This provides the basis, pursued in this book, for an integrated, multi-dimensional approach to learning that has characteristics which are cognitive (concerned with thinking), emotional, affective (concerned with values and feelings), conative (concerned with striving, action and doing) and relational. This conception of learning can be described as transformative not only because it is concerned with how individuals or groups are changed in appearance from one form or character to another but because it also focuses attention upon learning processes that are experienced across these different forms. These ideas are explicated here in relation to established theories of learning, such as constructivism, situated cognition, critical pedagogy and experiential learning.

The transformative dimension of learning

Although the process of learning can be distinguished from the tangible entity of 'learning' itself, understood as a body of knowledge, it is often suggested that learning involves the acquisition or internalisation of knowledge or skills. This resonates with descriptions of 'surface' learning as involving the acquisition of 'information', memorisation or elaboration of existing knowledge and simply adding to 'what we know'. Jack Mezirow's model of transformative learning (1991, 2000) is instead concerned with changing 'how we know' as we reconfigure previously held assumptions or beliefs that frame how we make sense of experience.

For Mezirow, the transformative dimension of learning is related to meaning: in particular, how meaning 'is construed, validated and reformulated' (1991: xii). His theory of learning, building upon and adapting Habermas's theory of communicative action (1981), interrogates the ways we interpret or make meaning of our experiences:

> To make meaning means to make sense of an experience; we make an interpretation of it. When we subsequently use this interpretation to guide decision making or action, then making meaning becomes learning.
> (Mezirow, 1990: 1)

Learning occurs, then, as we use a meaning that we have already made to guide the way we think, act or feel about what we are currently experiencing. Mezirow distinguishes the meaning-making of our everyday lives from meaning-making in transformative learning:

> Normally when we learn something we attribute an old meaning to a new experience. . . . In transformative learning we reinterpret an old experience (or a new one) from a new set of expectations.
>
> (Mezirow, 1991: 11)

This approach to adult learning contrasts its potentially transformative nature with the formative, socialising and acculturating process of learning in childhood. Mezirow predicates his theory of transformational learning on the assumption that most adults are unaware of the origin of their worldview, or lens through which they see, and the reasons behind or justification upon which they base their beliefs, values and actions. The challenge of becoming aware of our worldview can be related to seeing a windscreen that we are accustomed to looking through. Mezirow draws upon the analogy of the Myth of Sisyphus, the Greek king who repeatedly pushed a huge boulder up a hill, only to watch it each time roll back down, to argue that in our adult life we are mostly 'caught in our own history and reliving it' (Mezirow, 1978: 101). Our underlying values, assumptions and beliefs are often uncritically absorbed in childhood through family, school, community and culture. These influence the way we see the world and make meaning of the world as adults and play a central role in our personal development and growth. It is through 'perspective transformation' (Mezirow, 1991: 14) that we become aware of how our presuppositions and assumptions constrain our understanding of the world. This is redolent of Bateson's Learning II and Learning III (1973), Argyris and Schön's double loop learning (1978) and Freire's notion of conscientisation (1970).

Mezirow suggests that our ways of knowing, feeling and believing, which are often uncritically assimilated, provide the frames of reference through which we make meaning and filter experience. Frames of reference (or meaning perspectives) consist of both habits of mind and points of view (Mezirow, 1991, 2000). The former are broad, generalised, orienting predispositions which selectively delimit perception, cognition and feelings by predisposing our intentions, expectations and purposes. The phrase 'habits of mind' alludes to mental drivers that operate below the level of ordinary consciousness and are conditioned and unintended. According to Mezirow, habits of mind are expressed as points of view which comprise clusters of meaning schemes or 'sets of immediate specific expectations, beliefs, feelings, attitudes and judgements' (Mezirow, 2000: 18) that accompany and are articulated within an interpretation. For example, an individual's point of view that they are critical of those fraudulently claiming unemployment benefits is related to an associated habit of mind such as a strong work ethic. Mezirow argued that 'you can change points of view by trying on another's point of view' (2000: 21) but one cannot try on someone else's habit of mind. For example, we can 'try on a point of view' of a subsistence farmer by experiencing a day in their life yet their associated habits of mind are not immediately accessible or simply acquired.

The goals that transformative learning sets itself are both daunting and inspiring. Dirkx argues transformative learning represents 'a heroic struggle to wrest consciousness and knowledge from the forces of unconsciousness and ignorance' (1997: 79). This presents one side of the claim that transformative learning demands learners to 'think for a change' by surfacing, interrogating and overhauling unquestioned assumptions about the world in a process where reason and logic overcome instinct, ignorance and irrationality. The result of the transformative process, and indicator of the relationship between transformation and authenticity, is that students begin to act upon their own 'purposes, values, feelings and meanings' (Mezirow, 2000: 8) as opposed to ones they have uncritically assimilated from others.

This account is consistent with a constructivist view in that it is concerned with how we make sense of our experience through bringing our past experiences to bear. Knowledge emerges from interpretations and experiences that lead to new interpretations and experiences. Mezirow's theory reifies rational, cognitive reasoning and individual transformation:

> Transformative learning is understood as a uniquely adult form of meta-cognitive reasoning. Reasoning is the process of advancing and assessing reasons, especially those that provide arguments supporting beliefs resulting in decisions to act. Beliefs are justified when they are based on good reasons.
>
> (Mezirow, 2003: 58)

Although Mezirow notes that frames of reference have cognitive, affective and conative dimensions (2000: 16), he argues that it is through critical reflection and dialectical discourse (Mezirow, 2003) that our assumptions can be exposed and overturned and our meaning perspectives become 'more inclusive, discriminating, reflective, open and emotionally able to change' (Mezirow, 2009: 22). Unlike King and Kitchener's seven-stage model of developing reflective judgement (1990), Mezirow's theory only implicitly acknowledges the difficulties learners face in developing reflexivity.

The continuous development of more integrated meaning perspectives suggests a rationalisation of society, leading to claims that Mezirow's model is underpinned with a Western cultural bias (Kiely, 2005) that reifies the reflective tradition. Learners do not move inexorably towards an end state of transformed perspective simply by undertaking further experiences. Moreover, emancipatory values are not inherent in any process of learning. Nevertheless, educative practices are instrumental and cannot be seen as value free. Education seeks to lead students towards certain truths. Mezirow's work fails to problematise the nature of power in emancipatory discourse itself, for instance by asking what right do instructors have to promote transformative learning? Dramatic changes in orientation (or perspective transformation) may be brought about by cultural change and brainwashing, coercion and indoctrination, as illustrated by the young man who becomes radicalised by extremist religious views. In closing down the space for critical dialogue where ideas can be contested, meaning perspectives can become impenetrable and impervious to change.

Mezirow's theory presents only one orientation towards education, understood as a course of learning which is transformative. Taylor (2009) identifies two broad theoretical frameworks towards transformative learning that comprise a collection of orientations, namely an emphasis on personal transformation and growth where the unit of analysis is primarily individual (Daloz, Dirkx, Kegan, Cranton, Mezirow, Yorks and Kasl), and a concern for transformative learning that fosters social change as well as personal transformation (Freire, Tisdell). The former group is itself diverse: for example, viewing transformation as a developmental approach (Parks-Daloz, 1999) and also linking learning to spirituality (Dirkx, 2001; Tolliver and Tisdell, 2006). In the latter group, critical reflection is equated with ideology critique whereby learners develop an awareness of power and greater agency (political consciousness) to transform society and their own reality.

Critical, cultural perspectives on education

> . . . it's that clash of cultures and it was like the first time I was like 'wow' people think differently to me and my view of the world isn't necessarily the whole complete view.
>
> (Carol, ISL participant in 2007 in Uganda)

Freire's work on the education of literacy with resource-poor communities in Brazil led him to reject mechanistic, technocratic and instrumental philosophies of education. A progressive educator, he labelled these oppressive forms as 'banking' education that assume 'a dichotomy between man and the world' (Freire, 1970: 62) through which those who consider themselves knowledgeable deposit knowledge with learners as they passively listen to and accept facts.

The concept of 'conscientisation', defined as 'the deepening of the attitude of awareness characteristic of all emergence' (Freire, 1970: 90), is central to Freire's emanicipatory philosophy and has been equated with Mezirow's notion of perspective transformation (Collard and Law, 1989). It occurs as individuals move from a limited awareness of self and societal structures (naive transitivity) to a critical and historical problematisation of society and one's relation to it. They are seen to 'emerge from their submersion and acquire the ability to intervene in reality as it is unveiled' (Freire, 1970: 90). A deepened attitude of awareness is demonstrated as individuals begin to perceive social, political and economic contradictions and develop a critical awareness that enables them to begin to take action against oppressive elements that shape their lives. Through dialogue and problem-posing, learners begin to see their world, their place in it and their ability to transform it in new ways. Through conscientisation learners no longer remain marginalised. These ideas are also evoked in Greene's concept of 'wide awakeness', whereby teaching is an empowering process as learners gain a heightened sense of agency 'to pursue their freedom and perhaps, transform to some degree their lived worlds' (Greene, 1995: 48).

Critical consciousness is at the heart of Freire's educational philosophy. This goes beyond an understanding of 'critical thinking' as understood by scholars concerned with independent and analytic thinking (for example, see Winch, 2006) or the application of logical analysis to attain 'sound' conclusions (Doddington, 2008: 109). Freire and Mezirow both argue that adult education (and therefore, by implication, all education) should lead to empowerment. Freire's notion of conscientisation is primarily focused on the goal of social justice through overturning imbalances of power while Mezirow emphasises the role of rational thought and reflection leading to individual transformation. He accepts that cultural canon, socio-economic structures, ideologies and beliefs about ourselves 'conspire to foster conformity and impede development of responsible agency' (Mezirow, 2000: 8). However, rational thought and reflection that solely aim to discover and liberate a pre-existing, essential self may not only fail to be emancipatory but also operate as a subtle form of self-control (Inglis, 1997: 5). For example, self-help groups ironically reinforce faith in control by pressuring individuals to take control of their own lives through self-inspection, self-surveillance and self-assertion. Brookfield seeks to recapture critical reflection as grounded in the intellectual tradition of critical theory. For him, it involves uncovering, and then investigating, our assumptions in relation to 'power and hegemony that inform practice' (Brookfield, 2009: 126).

Freire was particularly concerned with the false consciousness of the oppressor and emphasises the need to lead the oppressor to see not only how they dehumanise others but also themselves. It was his belief that the conscientisation of both the oppressors and the oppressed would lead to the social transformation of Central American political oligarchies. Transformative education from this orientation is concerned with fostering social change as much as personal transformation. Freire claims that it is through critical reflection that learners discover an awareness of the role of power and their own agency to transform both their own reality and society. Failing to attend to this social dimension, reflection simply changes the individual's assumptions and can become 'an irrelevant and egocentric exercise' (Brookfield, 2000: 148).

These critical-cultural perspectives aim to expose the contested nature of educational practice. In particular, critical theory argues that capitalism, economic inequality, racism, and class and gender discrimination permeate practice and society as a whole. Furthermore, it argues this situation is reproduced as the apparently normal and natural state of affairs (Brookfield, 2005). In relation to formal education, pedagogy and curriculum become enacted without awareness of the political inscriptions embedded within them. Transformative learning must challenge processes that legitimate dominant interests through culture, the media and other social institutions such as schools. The dominant ideology encourages individuals to 'collude in their own oppression' (Brookfield, 2009: 127), and, therefore, the challenge critical theorists face is to understand this situation before seeking to change it. Criticality as understood in this study involves moving towards 'alternative possibilities' (Barnett, 1997: 7) of understanding

The role of reflection, experience and practice

> As we walked into the slum on the way to the school we met a man who asked us what he was going to gain from us being here. I realised at that point . . . the whole project was all about us – and of course he was right. How had I been so stupid, tricking myself into thinking this was something that I was doing for others?
>
> (Jenny, ISL participant in 2007 in Nigeria)

John Dewey's educational theory, initially labelled instrumentalism (1916) but later known as pragmatism, has been hugely influential in the theory and practice of experiential education. The work of Freire and Habermas is rooted in the educational philosophy of Dewey, conceptualising a relationship between learning and experience that is underpinned by a pragmatist philosophy. For example, perspective transformation and conscientisation evoke Dewey's forked-road situation, as experienced by Jenny in the encounter she describes above:

> Thinking begins in what may fairly enough be called *a forked-road* situation, a situation which is ambiguous, which presents a dilemma, which proposes alternatives. As long as our activity glides smoothly along from one thing to another, or as long as we permit our imagination to entertain fancies at pleasure, there is no call for reflection. Difficulty or obstruction in the way of reaching a belief brings us, however, to a pause. In the suspense of uncertainty, we metaphorically climb a tree; we try to find some standpoint from which we may survey additional facts and, getting a more commanding view of the situation, may decide how the facts stand related to one another.
>
> (Dewey, 1933: 14)

Dewey's psychological and philosophical work (1916) informed Kolb's active learning cycle (1984), which includes the four phases of concrete experience, reflective observation, abstract conceptualisation and active experimentation. Kolb (1984) explicates a dialectical relationship between an experience and the translation of this into meaning. The lived experience is recalled and analysed to create mental knowledge structures. The move from the apprehension to comprehension of an experience acknowledges the role of feelings as we acquaint ourselves of things while stating it is our thoughts that enable us to know about them.

This model has been criticised for venerating reflective observation, abstract conceptualisation and active experimentation without exploring the concrete experience upon which these depend (Heron, 1992: 193–6). This problem is exemplified, for example, in Kolb's claim that 'we learn the meaning of our concrete immediate experiences by internally reflecting on their presymbolic act' (1984: 52) and that it is 'through comprehension we introduce order into what would otherwise be a seamless, unpredictable flow' (Kolb, 1984: 39).

Both Kolb and Mezirow clearly separate how we make meaning from our lived experience. For them, experience precedes reflection and only in this latter stage is experience transformed into learning. While Kolb assumes experience to be non-rational and pre-symbolic (Kolb, 1984: 48–52) Mezirow accepts experience is epistemologically, socio-culturally and psychically distorted (Mezirow, 1990: 14–17). In both cases, however, it is assumed that the learner is capable of engaging in abstract critical reflection in which they are separated from their own experiences. This is consistent with the view of constructivism, which recognises the importance of context as a space in which a learner moves but still 'views the learner as fundamentally autonomous from his or her surroundings' (Fenwick, 2000: 250).

This reflective, constructivist approach separates the subject from the environment and views the individual as the central actor in the processes of meaning making. Learning is thereby perceived to be independent and autonomous rather than connected and relational. The emphasis on rational control and mastery that permeates the literature on reflection has been labelled as a 'Eurocentric, masculinist view of knowledge creation' (Michelson, 1996). This view, it is argued, elevates cerebral forms of knowledge and subordinates the emotional, sensual and subjective. Michelson described this discourse on reflection as a new form of colonialism (1996: 449) resulting in a lack of trust in our bodies and feelings.

Theories of situated cognition contest an understanding of learning that focuses on the individual internalising knowledge: whether this has been discovered, transmitted or experienced through interacting with others. Learning is understood here as being grounded in the situation in which the subject participates. Put simply, adults do not learn from experience: they learn in it. Theories of situated cognition attempt to bind together abstraction and experience, reflection and involvement, rational and non-rational activity.

> Knowledge is not a substance to be ingested and then transferred to new situations but, instead, part of the very process of participation in the immediate situation.
>
> (Fenwick, 2000: 253)

Situated learning is an alternative theory of experiential learning that conceives of learning as increasing participation in communities of practice (Lave and Wenger, 1991). It is clearly a more sophisticated theory than that of 'learning by doing' with which it has been equated (Anderson *et al.*, 1996). It theorises social practice to challenge notions of 'surface' learning that dichotomises 'inside and outside, suggests that knowledge is largely cerebral, and takes the individual as the nonproblematic unit of analysis' (Lave and

Wenger, 1991: 47). Furthermore, it 'emphasises the relational interdependency of agent and world, activity, meaning, cognition, learning and knowing' (Lave and Wenger, 1991: 50). This theory of learning places the focus upon the individual within the structure of social practice. The situatedness of the learner cannot be dismissed in knowledge claims, 'but becomes the condition for knowing per se' (Dall'Alba and Barnacle, 2005: 725). Furthermore, by conceiving identities as 'long term, living relations between persons and their place and participation in communities of practice', Lave and Wenger's (1991) theory claims to both decentre the person and arrive at a rich notion of agency in terms of whole persons:

> We think that the two tendencies are not only compatible but that they imply one another, if one adopts as we have a relational view of the person and of learning: It is by the theoretical process of decentering in relational terms that one can construct a robust notion of 'whole person' which does justice to the multiple relations through which people define themselves in practice.
> (1991: 53–4)

Towards a holistic theory of learning

> I have changed as a person.
> (Mary, ISL participant in 2007 in Malawi)

Distinguishing between a pragmatic and phenomenological understanding of experience assists the search for a more holistic theory of adult learning. Simplistically, while the former prioritises the role of reflective discourse, the latter seeks to understand affective aspects of learning. Yorks and Kasl (2002) argue that differentiating between experience as a noun or verb goes to the heart of these perspectives. For example, in pragmatism 'experience has been conceptualised as a noun, a resource that can be catalogued, objectified and reflected upon' (Yorks and Kasl, 2002: 180). Reflecting upon the use of Bateson's levels of learning within reflective practice, Tosey (2006) argues that theories of embodied, contextual and relational learning have become inaccurately invoked within decontextualised inquiry that seeks to bring about particular intentional change. In doing so, the mind is erroneously understood as synonymous with the brain and the knower is separated from the known. This is challenged by this book through re-orienting the human subject as embedded within the world as opposed to being a detached observer of the world.

The role of experience to expose and bring to our consciousness distorted and unchallenged assumptions about ourselves and the world clearly provides a counterbalance to the resilience of ignorance and deception. Surfacing, interrogating and overhauling unquestioned assumptions about the world in a process where reason and logic overcome instinct, ignorance and irrationality is only one way in which learners begin to 'think for a change' (both senses intended). There is an urgent need to explore a conception of learning beyond the psychology of ways of thinking and knowing as outlined by Mezirow, with its focus on the autonomous rational actor, in order to focus on context, relationships and the connections between the personal and social. This demands an approach to learning and education which recognises both the being of the student (ontological learning) and the acquisition of knowledge and skills (epistemological learning).

On this view, the development of the person, as claimed by Mary in the above quotation, is as important as the development of the brain and is congruent with Barnett's claim that learning is a 'human process which has an effect on those undertaking it' (1992: 4). The Transformative Learning Centre in the University of Toronto offers a working definition of an expanded conceptualisation of transformative learning beyond the rational and epistemological:

> Transformative learning involves experiencing a deep, structural shift in the basic premises of thought, feelings and actions. It is a shift of consciousness that dramatically and permanently alters our way of being in the world. Such a shift involves our understanding of ourselves and our self-locations; our relationships with other humans and with the natural world; our understanding of relations of power in interlocking structures of class, race and gender; our body awareness; our visions of alternative approaches to living; and our sense of possibilities for social justice and peace and personal joy.
>
> (O'Sullivan, 2002: 11)

This statement diverges from Mezirow's formulation of transformation of frames of reference in its explicit emphasis on both the role of affect and reason. It elevates the importance of existential change for the learner, as regards their way of being in the world. Yorks and Kasl also extend Mezirow's framework to accommodate ontological aspects of making meaning, defining transformative learning as 'a wholistic change in how a person both affectively experiences and conceptually frames his or her experience of the world' (Yorks and Kasl, 2006: 45–6).

While acknowledging that differentiating West from non-West may constrain our thinking and perpetuate a false dichotomy, approaches to teaching and learning that privilege what are often viewed as a Western conception of 'mind' clearly reinforce notions of the autonomous, independent, individualist self. A socio-centric and collectivist ideal of the self underpins pedagogical approaches, sometimes described as non-Western (Merriam and Kim, 2008), that focus on moral and spiritual development. This includes holistic and relational approaches to learning that incorporate the body, spirit and emotions. This highlights personal and imaginative ways of knowing that are grounded in a more intuitive and emotional sense of our experiences. It demands a shift in focus from decontextualised knowledge and skills to nurturing 'embodied knowing' (Dall'Alba and Barnacle, 2005: 722). While highlighting these distinctions, it is concluded here that the West/non-West dualism does 'little justice to the way learning and thinking tend to progress in the world' (Sen, 2006: 57).

Dirkx advocates the development of an expanded conceptualisation of transformative learning rooted in the 'consciousness of the soul' (1997). Suggesting that the 'ego-based view provides a helpful but only partial understanding of the process of change, self-discovery, and social critique inherent in transformative learning' (Dirkx, 1997: 79), he argues we must understand transformative learning as developing awareness of emotional aspects of experience that also inform our perceptions of the world. He exemplifies the learning process of 'soul work', claiming:

> dramatic opportunities for transformational learning reside in imaginative engagement with the everydayness of our lives . . . encounters with subject matter in adult learning settings provide a rich source of images and fantasies that enable learners to connect more fully and deeply with the text, the self, and their outer worlds.
>
> (2001: 16)

Whilst recognising that transformation cannot be viewed as 'a process of wholly personal reflection, disconnected from broader social currents' (Brookfield, 2003: 148), these ideas do, however, underpin an understanding of critical pedagogy grounded in alternative forms of knowing:

> Knowing and learning are not simply intellectual and scholarly activities but also practical and sensuous activities infused by the impassioned spirit. Critical pedagogy is dedicated to addressing and embodying these affective, emotional, and lived dimensions of everyday life in a way that connects to people in groups and as individuals.
>
> (Kincheloe, 2003: 11)

Developing an integrative model of transformative learning responds to Hart's (1990) call for the themes of contextuality and relationality to become central to attempts to broaden our understanding of emancipatory education. A holistic orientation to transformative learning accounts for the spirit and body as well as the intellect. This post-dualist orientation highlights the 'relational' and 'holistic' aspects of spirituality and, as will be demonstrated in the following chapter, is grounded in the work of philosophers such as Macmurray, Buber and Levinas as well as recent work by Noddings (1984) and Bellah et al. (1985).

Conclusion

The transformative dimension of learning discussed here is concerned more with 'how' we know rather than 'what' we know. Its focus upon 'formation' rather than 'information' is redolent of the etymological meaning of education: both *educare*, meaning to form, and *educere*, meaning to lead out. This shifts attention towards the non-formal and informal learning that characterises the majority of adult education. It is the antithesis of a particular kind of curriculum-driven learning with pre-fixed learning objectives focused on attaining formal certification that seeks to specify and assess the knowledge transmitted to students. It demands an epistemological re-orientation towards the body, relationships, feelings, emotions and affect.

From this view, it is not the separation of the mind and body that makes knowing possible, as Descartes famously asserted, but the fact that they are intimately related. This is suggestive of a reversal of 'cogito ergo sum' – it is because we are that we think, know and act – indicating that knowing, being and doing are each pivotal to this theory of learning. Having argued in this first chapter for a holistic approach to transformative learning, Chapter 2 will interrogate each of its constitutive elements – knowing, being and doing – in turn.

References

Anderson, J.R., Reder, L.M. and Simon, H.A. (1996) Situated Learning and Education. *Educational Researcher* 25 (4): 5–11.

Argyris, C. and Schön, D. (1978) *Organizational Learning: A Theory of Action Perspective.* Reading: Addison-Wesley.

Barnett, R. (ed.) (1992) *Learning to Effect.* Buckingham: Open University Press/SRHE.

Barnett, R. (1997) *Higher Education: A Critical Business.* Buckingham: Open University Press/SRHE.

Bateson, G. (1973) *Steps to an Ecology of Mind.* Chicago: University of Chicago Press.

Bellah, R., Madsden, R., Sullivan, W.M., Swidler, A. and Tipton, S.M. (1985) *Habits of Heart: Individualism and Commitment in American Life.* New York: Harper & Row.

Brookfield, S. (2000) Transformative Learning as Ideology Critique. In Mezirow, J. and Associates (eds) *Learning as Transformation.* San Francisco: Jossey-Bass, 125–50.

Brookfield, S. (2003) Putting the Critical Back into Critical Pedagogy: A Commentary on the Path of Dissent. *Journal of Transformative Education* 1 (2): 141–9.

Brookfield, S. (2005) *The Power of Critical Theory: Liberating Adult Learning and Teaching.* San Francisco: Jossey-Bass.

Brookfield, S. (2009) Engaging Critical Reflection in Corporate America. In Mezirow, J. and Taylor, E. (eds) *Transformative Learning in Practice: Insights from Community Workplace and Higher Education.* San Francisco: Jossey-Bass, 125–35.

Collard, S. and Law, M. (1989) The Limits of Perspective Transformation. *Adult Education Quarterly* 39 (2): 99–107.

Dall'Alba, G. and Barnacle, R. (2005) Embodied Knowing in Online Environments. *Educational Philosophy and Theory* 37 (5): 719–44.

Dewey, J. (1916) *Democracy and Education.* New York: Kessinger.

Dewey, J. (1933) *How We Think.* Boston: D.C. Heath and Co.

Dirkx, J.M. (1997) Nurturing Soul in Adult Learning. *New Directions for Adult and Continuing Education* 74 (Summer): 79–88.

Dirkx, J.M. (2001) The Power of Feelings: Emotion, Imagination, and the Construction of Meaning in Adult Learning. *New Directions for Adult and Continuing Education* 8: 63–72.

Doddington, C. (2008) Critical Thinking as a Source of Respect for Persons: A Critique. In Mason, M. (ed.) *Critical Thinking and Learning*. Oxford: Blackwell, 109–19.
Fenwick, T.J. (2000) Expanding Conceptions of Experiential Learning: A Review of Five Contemporary Perspectives on Cognition. *Adult Education Quarterly* 50 (4): 243–72.
Freire, P (1970) *Pedagogy of the Oppressed*. New York: Continuum Publishing Co.
Greene, M. (1995) *Releasing the Imagination*. San Francisco: Jossey-Bass.
Habermas, J. (1981) *The Theory of Communicative Action: Volume 1*. Boston: Beacon Press.
Hart, M. (1990) Critical Theory and Beyond: Further Perspectives on Emancipatory Education. *Adult Education Quarterly* 40 (3): 125–38.
Heron, J. (1992) *Feeling and Personhood: Psychology in Another Key*. London: SAGE.
Inglis, T. (1997) Empowerment and Emancipation. *Adult Education Quarterly* 48 (1): 119–34.
Kiely, R. (2005) A Transformative Learning Model for Service-Learning: A Longitudinal Case Study. *Michigan Journal of Community Service Learning* 12 (1): 5–22.
Kincheloe, J. (2003) *Critical Pedagogy*. New York: Peter Lang.
King, P. and Kitchener, K.S. (1990) The Reflective Judgement Model: Transforming Assumptions about Knowing. In Mezirow, J. (ed.) *Fostering Critical Reflection in Adulthood: A Guide to Transformative and Emancipatory Learning*. San Francisco: Jossey-Bass, 159–76.
Kolb, D. (1984) *Experiential Learning: Experience as the Source of Learning and Development*. Upper Saddle River: Prentice Hall.
Lave, J. and Wenger, E. (1991) *Situated Learning: Legitimate Peripheral Participation*. New York: Cambridge University Press.
Merriam, S. and Kim, Y.S. (2008) Non-Western Perspectives on Learning and Knowing. *New Directions for Adult and Continuing Education* 119 (Fall): 71–81.
Mezirow, J. (1978) Perspective Transformation. *Adult Education* 28: 110–18.
Mezirow, J. (ed.) (1990) *Fostering Critical Reflection in Adulthood: A Guide to Transformative and Emancipatory Learning*. San Francisco: Jossey-Bass.
Mezirow, J. (1991) *Transformative Dimensions of Adult Learning*. San Francisco: Jossey-Bass.
Mezirow, J. (ed.) (2000) *Learning as Transformation*. San Francisco: Jossey-Bass.
Mezirow, J. (2003) Transformative Learning as Discourse. *Journal of Transformative Education* 1 (1): 58–63.
Mezirow, J. (2009) Transformative Learning Theory. In Mezirow, J. and Taylor, E. (eds) *Transformative Learning in Practice: Insights from Community Workplace and Higher Education*. San Francisco: Jossey-Bass, 18–32.
Michelson, E. (1996) Usual Suspects: Experience, Reflection and the (En) Gendering of Knowledge. *International Journal of Lifelong Education* 15 (6): 438–54.
Noddings, N. (1984) *Caring: A Feminine Approach to Ethics and Moral Education*. Berkeley: University of California Press.
O'Sullivan, E. (2002) The Project and Vision of Transformative Education: Integral Transformative Learning. In O'Sullivan, E., Morrell, A. and O'Connor, M.A. (eds) *Expanding the Boundaries of Transformative Learning*. New York: Palgrave, 1–12.
Parks-Daloz, L. (1999) *Mentor: Guiding the Journey of Adult Learners*. San Francisco: Jossey-Bass.
Sen, A. (2006) *Identity and Violence: The Illusion of Destiny*. London: Penguin.
Taylor, E.W. (2009) Fostering Transformative Learning. In Mezirow, J. and Taylor, E. (eds) *Transformative Learning in Practice: Insights from Community Workplace and Higher Education*. San Francisco: Jossey-Bass, 3–17.
Tolliver, D. and Tisdell, E. (2006) Engaging Spirituality in the Transformative Higher Education Classroom. *New Directions for Adult and Continuing Education* 109 (Spring): 37–47.

Tosey, P. (2006) Bateson's Levels of Learning: A Framework For Transformative Learning? Paper presented at Universities' Forum for Human Resource Development conference, University of Tilburg, May 2006. Accessed 11 April 2012 at www.som.surrey.ac.uk/NLP/Resources/BatesonLevels2006.pdf.

Winch, C. (2006) *Education, Autonomy and Critical Thinking*. Abingdon: Routledge.

Yorks, L. and Kasl, E. (2002) Toward a Theory and Practice of Whole-Person Learning: Reconceptualising Experience and the Role of Affect. *Adult Education Quarterly* 52 (3): 176–92.

Yorks, L. and Kasl, E. (2006) I Know More Than I Can Say: A Taxonomy of Using Expressive Ways of Knowing to Foster Transformative Learning. *Journal of Transformative Education* 4 (1): 43–64.

2 The knowing, being and doing of transformation

Introduction

This chapter elaborates upon the ways in which knowing, being and doing are each, respectively, important aspects of this conception of learning. This argument draws upon a range of influences, including theories of aesthetics (Dewey), care ethics (Noddings, Gilligan), personal knowledge (Polanyi), virtue ethics (Aristotle, Carr), moral aspects of self and identity (Taylor) and the capability approach (Nussbaum, Sen). Although this chapter discusses knowing, being and doing in turn, from the view of learning developed here, these cannot be understood as separated from each other. What is learnt, the way in which it is learnt and how this learning is enacted are all central to the 'becoming' of the 'learning self'. This provides the basis for the argument in Chapter 3 that it is through the integration of transformative aspects of knowing, being and doing that the learning self develops authenticity.

Knowledge: knowing

Connecting different aspects of knowing

This first section will argue that the transformative aspects of knowing are not primarily concerned with the propositional content of formal knowledge but are instead concerned with the aesthetic, tacit and relational aspects of knowing. John Heron's (1992) inclusive but over-hierarchical model of four ways of knowing (experiential, presentational, propositional and practical) can be used to start to redefine the relation between knowing and transformative learning. Experiential knowing, the entry point for all four ways of knowing, is evident when we meet and feel the presence of some energy, entity, person, place, process or thing. It is present in non-linguistic visual symbols that the individual is unable to communicate directly. Presentational knowledge includes music, dance, poetry, movement and mime and 'embraces all forms of myth, fable, allegory, story and drama' (Heron, 1992: 167). Through presentational knowing, language and symbols are used to reveal 'the underlying patterns of things' (Heron, 1992: 168). Presentational knowing is therefore represented by aesthetic relations. Propositional knowing, on the other hand, involves the communication of concepts through discourse that must be grounded rationally and supported by evidence, drawing upon 'logical relations between concepts to represent experience' (Heron, 1992: 169).

The hierarchy embedded in Heron's model privileges propositional above presentational knowing and in so doing undermines the claims to holistic knowing embedded in this theory. Transformative learning takes place as students move back and forth between these categories of knowing. It is not solely concerned with the propositional content of formal knowledge.

> Presentational knowing provides a bridge between the extralinguistic nature of felt experience, which an individual cannot directly communicate, and the ideas communicated through propositional knowing, which is the mode of discourse.
>
> (Yorks and Kasl, 2002: 187)

Through presentational knowing, learners become fully immersed in the felt experience of the lives of others: aesthetic experience bridges worlds, providing a foundation for building empathy and solidarity. It involves learners making sense or meaning pre-linguistically, such as when they discern or intuit presence, motion, kinaesthetic experience and feelings. As individuals detach themselves from their own ways of seeing and being, they can become, as Marcuse theorised, liberated from one-dimensional thinking and being (1964). This provides an opportunity for participants to be 'uncoupled from the streams of cultural givens' (Habermas, 1990: 162) and catalyse both critical thought and critical being, as will be explicated further in the subsequent section on becoming.

Aesthetic aspects of knowing

> I think I only wrote about two emails. It's something that I do now when I'm going away; I kind of cut off and get in to where I'm going.
> (Lucy, ISL participant in 2004 in Malawi)

Moving beyond Heron's hierarchical model, aesthetic theory applied to the educational endeavour would appear to offer us the conceptual tools to enhance our understanding of presentational knowing and its interaction with propositional knowing. Dewey in his later work (1934) espoused a theory of aesthetics that is grounded in the notion of engaged interaction as opposed to passive reception, for 'no experience of whatever sort is a unity unless it has esthetic quality' (Dewey, 1934: 40). Dewey alludes to the necessity of considering multiple ways of knowing, naming 'the esthetic quality that rounds out an experience into completeness and unity as emotional' (1934: 41). Emotion connects our experiences to prior understanding and acts as a 'cementing force' (1934: 42) that consummates an experience. In this view, experiential learning structured around analysing and reflecting upon individual experiences rather than embodied immersion might well be regarded as a deficit model:

> If we are not careful we fix attention upon competition for control and possession of a fixed environment rather than upon what art can do to *create* an environment. . . . It is disastrous because civilization built upon these principles cannot supply the demand of the soul for joy, or freshness of experience; only attention through art to the vivid but transient values of things can effect such refreshment.
>
> (Dewey, 1988: 112)

Dewey lists what he calls the enemies of the 'esthetic' that lead to 'anesthetic' experiences. These include 'the humdrum; slackness of loose ends; submission to convention in practice and intellectual procedure', 'tightness on one side and dissipation, incoherence and aimless indulgence on the other' (Dewey, 1934: 40). In doing so, we are challenged to consider the ways in which potentially aesthetic experiences in everyday life are anaesthetised, such as in failing to engage with unexpected incidents, being interrupted, focusing on preconceived learning objectives, being distracted by technology, laziness in watching and listening and needing to be entertained.

> Zeal for doing, lust for action, leaves many a person, especially in this hurried and impatient human environment in which we live, with the experience of an almost incredible paucity, all on the surface. No one experience has a chance to complete itself because something else is entered upon so speedily. Resistance is treated as an obstruction to be beaten down, not as an invitation to reflect. An individual comes to seek, unconsciously even more than by deliberate choice, situations in which he can do the most things in the shortest time.
>
> (Dewey, 1934: 44–5)

Embodied knowing presents a way of knowing that goes beyond the intellectual and rational. Dall'Alba and Barnacle provide the example of medical education programmes that move beyond the learning objective of acquiring knowledge of symptoms and sickness, and foreground the development of 'appropriate ways of being and acting (in relation to pupils, family members and other education professionals, and other health professionals) towards achieving the best possible health for the person concerned' (Dall'Alba and Barnacle, 2005: 722). This demands understanding the emotional, sensory and embodied dimensions which exist, often beyond consciousness. Theory U (Scharmer, 2009) is an alternative dialogic process, related to becoming self-aware, that offers insight into creating the conditions for accessing and understanding 'embodied knowing'. Sensing, presencing and realising are the three basic aspects of a deep U movement. Sensing requires being able to redirect attention and view the context from another or other perspectives. This involves 'immersing yourself in the reality of the situation until ultimately you become "one with the situation"' (Senge *et al.*, 2005: 88). It requires us, as described by Lucy above, to 'get in' to where we're going. Presencing involves 'being totally present' (Senge *et al.*,

2005: 91) and 'seeing from the deepest source and becoming a vehicle for that source' (Senge *et al.*, 2005: 89). This demands openness with the twin components of 'letting go' and 'letting come'. Letting go involves 'leaving the shores of our uncertainty . . . and overcoming our fear of the unknown' (Scharmer, 2009: 8), while 'letting come' is about being open to change. Finally, realising involves bringing something new into reality in an action 'that comes from a source deeper than the rational mind' (Senge *et al.*, 2005: 91).

Tacit aspects of knowing

> In that environment I was no longer defined by all the things and people that define me at home. I initially felt like I was stripped bare of the things that make me who I am. It was extremely formative.
>
> (Sue, ISL participant in 2005 in South Africa)

> Maybe nothing does change under the sun. Whatever, one thing I know I can have every confidence in is me. I really trust myself. Even in autopilot I like who I am. My intuition guides me in the right direction no matter what!
>
> (Excerpt from the author's diary from Papua New Guinea)

Michael Polanyi outlined a radical position that concluded even scientific discoveries draw upon personal knowledge. For Polanyi, a wholly explicit knowledge would be unthinkable. In stating 'we know more than we can tell' (Polanyi, 1966: 18), Polanyi challenges us to reconsider what we mean by knowledge. For him, the tacit dimension of knowing is grounded in an embodied action of practice: bodily skill, as an expression of tacit knowledge, is at the root of all knowledge. Tacit knowledge is not simply that which cannot be articulated; it is 'a foundation for drawing meaning from other ways of being-in-the-world. It is concerned with the relationship between those explicit and tacit aspects of all practical knowing' (Peck, 2008: 31). For Polanyi, knowledge

> is linked to dwelling and is a direct result of it. Knowledge involves our very person. Through this integrative act we live and we dwell. It is through and by the body that we come to live in our experience as if to dwell with things, concepts and people.
>
> (Peck, 2008: 83)

Central to the structure of tacit knowing are the concepts of subsidiary and focal awareness. The subsidiary, or proximal, is that from which we are attending. It is what is near to us of which we have knowledge that we may not be able to tell. The focal, or distal, is far from us and is that to which we are attending. Through relying on what is proximal we can attend to what is distal. Riding a bike, for example, depends on the interaction between the subsidiary and the focal.

We attend from the particulars such as the feet being on the pedals, gaining balance and moving forward to focusing on the whole: the action of riding the bike. Importantly, if we attend to the subsidiary particulars then we lose the overall meaning of the action, and may struggle to ride the bike. Polanyi therefore concludes, 'It brings home to us that it is not by looking at things, but by dwelling in them, that we understand their joint meaning' (Polanyi, 1966: 18). This is demonstrated by Sue and I in the quotations that lead this section, as we learn to draw upon and trust our tacit knowledge.

The tacit dimension of knowing therefore has two inter-related dimensions: the type of knowing that is extremely difficult, often impossible, to articulate and knowing that is completely internalised. This does not mean the subsidiary state can be equated with the pre- or unconscious (Polanyi, 1969: 194). For example, one aspect of the relationship between the proximal and the distal is the indwelling of knowledge that was perhaps at one point in time explicit and identifiable. This indwelling is similar to internalisation or absorption. Learners experience tacit knowing as knowledge 'becomes' them. Knowledge is no longer external, discrete and explicit but has led to an existential change within them, 'forming part of the bank of tacit knowledge and knowing that all people construct and depend on in their task of becoming' (Le Cornu, 2009: 284). This is an important aspect of meaning making and relates to the inculcation of virtues as will be discussed in the next section on becoming. Le Cornu identifies a key aspect of reflection to be internalisation, described as the transformation of meaning into tacit knowing: 'what was originally discrete and identifiable knowledge "bites" or pieces of information has ultimately been so absorbed into people's beings that it has become tacit – indistinguishable from their very selves' (Le Cornu, 2009: 291).

Polanyi's work can be situated in a larger philosophical discourse about everyday human experience. Polanyi was concerned with philosophical questions regarding epistemology and science, while Heidegger explored ontological questions regarding Being. Both writers were concerned with connections between the knower and the known. For instance, Heidegger distinguishes between two modes of knowing in *Dasein's* (or being's) everyday world: readiness-to-hand (*Zuhandenheit*) and presence-at-hand (*Vorhandenheit*). While the latter is distanced, theoretical and fully present to the mind, the former is active, practical and often pre-conscious and therefore of greater significance to an integrative understanding of transformative learning. Heidegger uses the example of a hammer to illustrate the differences between these modes of knowing, arguing 'the less we just stare at the hammer-Thing and the more we seize hold of it and use it, the more primordial does our relationship to it become' (Heidegger, 1927/1962: 69). In doing so, Heidegger challenges the view that experiencing something in its 'readiness-to-hand' is based upon having made a discovery of it as something which is 'present-at-hand'. This echoes Polanyi's distinction between subsidiary and focal awareness. If we focus on the subsidiary particulars, or what is present-at-hand, we become fixated on the particulars of the hammer and can no longer attend to the hammering itself.

The inter-relatedness between the ready-to-hand and present-at-hand as well as between the subsidiary and focal aspects of the tacit dimension of knowing makes it clear that dichotomising ontological and epistemological learning processes is a wholly inadequate approach. For Heidegger, our knowledge follows from knowing how to do something. Polanyi labels this practical action. It is through our body that we make contact with reality. Knowing as doing takes place before we know that. We do in order to know. Unconscious know-how is tacit knowledge. This demonstrates the deep relationship between knowing and doing. Action 'breathes a life' into knowledge that we can only begin to understand ontologically, as we tacitly act. In this sense doing provides momentum to the process of becoming. This further illustrates the claim made in Chapter 1 that it is because we are that we think, know and act.

A corollary to this argument is that we are related to things primarily through lived experience rather than through discursive knowledge:

> We are in touch in a 'know-how' way with objects, before having any reflective or 'abstract' awareness of their characteristics. The world and its elements are meaningful in some preliminary way and all interpretation is based on a primary 'lived' understanding.
> (Ashworth, 2004: 149)

While absorption describes how people and their 'knowing' become totally integrated (Le Cornu, 2009), raising the ready-to-hand to the present-at-hand involves the reverse process of externalisation. Barnett argues that higher education is 'precisely a process in which the "ready-to-hand" is raised to the "present-at-hand"' (2007: 31). Echoing Mezirow's definition of perspective transformation, he equates a shift from 'ready-to-hand' to 'present-at-hand' with the process of exposing presuppositions as we develop criticality. This relates to tacit knowing in that as one begins to focus on the subsidiary particulars of a specific skill, for example of using a hammer, riding a bike or playing the piano, it is possible to begin to articulate the skills required in a coherent and meaningful way, although undoubtedly some particulars will always remain inarticulable. Barnett relates this process of putting the ready-at-hand under critical surveillance to the Greek description of the 'maieutic' pedagogic process as bringing forth what was already intuitively known.

Relational aspects of knowing

> In the beginning is relationship.
> (Buber, 1953: 22)

> ... the project encourages you to think outside yourself...
> (Becca, ISL participant in 2001 in Malawi)

Having identified the role of the aesthetic and tacit in understanding transformative aspects of knowing, I will now argue for the primacy of relationship. It is through foregrounding relational aspects of knowing that this book extends understandings of critical being as highlighted earlier (Barnett, 2007).

Martin Buber concludes that the self comes into being, fulfilling and authenticating itself not through either itself or the collective but through mutual relationship formed through encounter, dialogue, communication and exchange (Buber, 1961). Among learning theorists, Vygotsky, for example, emphasised the social nature of learning (1978, 1986) through his work on 'sociocultural' and 'sociohistorical' psychological processes. For him, higher psychological functions appear first on the social plane and subsequently on the psychological plane. Vygotsky argued that learners move from 'intermental' to 'intramental' functioning (1986) in that 'the reasoning they can engage in with others to begin with eventually becomes reasoning they can achieve on their own' (Pike and Halstead, 2006: 135). This provides one sense in which interacting and connecting with others socially leads to personal learning.

Learning theories have however traditionally focused attention on how individuals learn, reflecting what has been described as a 'Western' concern with individualism exemplified by autonomous and independent learning. These values have been identified as being representative of 'the underlying problem' of liberalism (Thiessen, 2001: 201). For example, interactive collaborative activities such as group work and discussion have until recently been seen solely as a means to this end. This points towards a need to move beyond the individual as the primary unit of analysis and understand the complex interrelationship between the individual subject and his or her community.

An extensive review of transformative learning studies (Taylor, 2000: 306) highlighted the role of relationship within transformation. The literature highlights that reflection and discourse are not only rationally driven but dependent upon 'trust, friendship, and support' (Taylor, 2000: 308). Trust is particularly pertinent to this study with respect to the notion of ethos, as will be discussed in relation to virtue ethics. According to this view, learning is not an independent act but an interdependent relationship built on trust. For example, pragmatism contends that we know and learn through discourse which is dependent on community, both as a site for conversations to occur and also as an ethic that enables discourse. Concepts and conclusions within pragmatism are always provisional, and open to revision and rejection. Knowledge is contextual in nature and an outcome of discourse. Liu described how the pragmatists' orientation 'shifts our epistemological aspiration from finding objective truth to sustaining a meaningful conversation' (Liu, 1995: 12). Similarly, Palmer claims:

> Without the soft virtues of community, the hard virtues of cognitive teaching and learning will be absent as well. Our ability to confront each other critically and honestly over alleged facts, imputed meanings, or personal biases and prejudices – that is the ability impaired by the absence of community.
> (Palmer, 1987: 25)

Connected knowing, influenced by women's psychology and feminist theory (Gilligan, 1982; Belenky *et al.*, 1986; Noddings, 1984) also emphasises the role of learning embedded in our everyday life. For example, Belenky *et al.* (1986) describe other aspects of making meaning such as 'taking time to learn to attend truly to the object, to wait for meanings to emerge from a poem rather than imposing the contents of your own head or your own gut' (p. 98). Allowing meaning to emerge is central to the methodology underpinning this study of ISL. Saltmarsh argues this approach is consistent with Dewey's pragmatism:

> connected knowing treats education not as something separate from 'life', but as life itself, and education becomes a lifelong process carried forward by an individual provided with the proficiencies to be a self-directed learner. Education is a means to an end, a way of life delineated by civic engagement.
>
> (Saltmarsh, 1996: 15)

From this view, pragmatism is aligned with epistemologies that collapse distinctions between theory and practice, knowing and doing and indeed the knower and what is known (Palmer, 1983; Thayer-Bacon, 2003). Furthermore, Dewey's participatory pedagogy argues that what we learn is interdependent with how we learn, rendering attempts to distinguish between learning processes and outcomes as futile and unnecessary. By associating knowledge with human context in an integral way we come to a conception of knowing and learning as a process of human relationship.

Yorks and Kasl use the phrase 'Learning within relationship' (2002: 185–7) to describe the process of individuals becoming engaged in both their own whole person knowing and the whole person knowing of their fellow learners. This requires 'thinking outside' of oneself as articulated by Becca in the quotation at the start of this section. Buber would contest that this occurs through I–Thou relationships, where individuals encounter each other as equals, rather than in exploitative I–It relations, where individuals objectify and exploit things, including other people. This highlights the importance of mutuality: sharing a felt sense of the other's experience and 'learning within' another's point of view in order to develop empathic understanding.

The context of learning is not simply a particular setting in which learning takes place. It includes the motivations of and interactions between the learner and those with whom they connect. It is in relationship with others that we become knowers and can begin to contribute to the construction of knowledge. This includes the particular individuals and general groups of people with whom we connect, such as family and friends as well as faith-based, cultural, ethnic and local community groups. This demands a greater understanding of the mutuality embedded in learning theory. Relational forms of knowing are, however, not only concerned with the interconnectedness between ourselves and each other, but also with our planet, our cultures, histories and futures. It demands we consider these broader contextual aspects and how they themselves change in relationship to us. As Thayer-Bacon outlines in her discussion of relational epistemologies, 'How people begin to make sense of the world is due to their contextuality, including their own subjective experiences as well as their social setting, and its past' (2003: 7–8). While knowledge and the knower are often separated from the practice or context to which they relate, the focus here on the aesthetic, tacit and relational aspects of knowing implicates the very being of the learner.

Becoming: being

Being as a process of becoming

> To be educated is not to have arrived at a destination; it is to travel with a different view.
>
> (Peters, 1973: 20)

> At the heart of all learning is not merely what is learned but what the learner is becoming (learning) as a result of doing, thinking and feeling.
>
> (Jarvis, 2006: 6)

Having discussed transformative aspects of knowing, this section moves onto exploring the second constitutive element of a reconstructed model of transformative learning: being. Martin Heidegger, one of the twentieth century's greatest philosophers, provides a strong basis for conceptualising an integrative model of transformative learning because he conceives of 'existence' or 'being' relationally. His work involves a hermeneutic turn described by Ricoeur (1981: 53–4) as from an 'epistemology of interpretation' to the 'ontology of understanding'. Consistent with the transformative aspects of knowing outlined in the previous section of this chapter, Heidegger denies the reduction of cognition to the scientific or positivist view. His view is that our fundamental way of being is not rationalist. This insight has profound implications for education where 'knowledge' rather than 'being' is privileged. Indeed, learning hegemonies that equate knowing with *techne*, understood as 'theory without experience' (Dunne, 1999: 50), can be argued to have contributed to a failure to develop educational practices that democratise society (Gibbs and Angelides, 2004: 333).

Heidegger's magnum opus *Being and Time* (1927/1962) provides a powerful philosophical basis for transformative education as a form of engagement and 'being-with' students which acknowledges its aesthetic and relational nature. For Heidegger, we do not engage with the world in a way that 'permits it to be reduced, paraphrased and explicated as aims and objectives, enacted according to designated methods or even understood through systematic reflection' (Pike, 2004: 20). In this sense, approaches to education which make the nature of learning routine, pre-describe learning outcomes, decontextualise the learning from the experience of being, negate opportunities for individuals to make personal sense of their experience and prioritise the acquisition of credits are wholly inadequate. These approaches all risk regarding education as a primarily economic resource, leading to the commodification of learning.

A holistic and relational orientation to knowing demands looking beyond epistemological learning processes that involve shifts in worldview and habits of mind to an ontological process that accounts for changes to our being in the world. In doing so, issues of existence and being are raised to the level of consciousness. As suggested by C.S. Lewis in *The Magician's Nephew*, 'worldview' must therefore be understood as being different from the lens through which people see: 'For what you see and hear depends a good deal on where you are standing: it also depends upon what sort of person you are' (Lewis, 1955: 125). Understanding the being of the learner is to understand the way the learner is in the world. For transformative learning conceived holistically, knowing emerges from a way of being and not vice versa and is redolent of the suggestion that 'we don't think our way into a new kind of living; rather we live our way into a new kind of thinking' (Palmer, 1980: 57). From this view, education is concerned with what we learn to be rather than knowledge we acquire.

Mezirow claims transformation can be epochal as well as incremental (Mezirow, 2000: 21) although empirical research conducted by Parks-Daloz found 'no instance of transformation as the result of an isolated epochal event' (2000: 106). Understanding learning as a finite experience has been identified as a significant flaw in Mezirow's work (Newman, 2012: 44). Incremental change occurring as a sequence of transformations in point of view – for example, about oneself as a learner (such as 'I can understand these ideas') – may cumulatively lead to a transformation in a habit of mind regarding self-concept (such as 'I am a bright, competent person'). An equivalent ontological process would involve a progressive series of transformations in related ways of being culminating in a transformed habit of being. This description of moving towards alternative modes of being could be described as 'critical being' as defined earlier. Nelson Mandela eloquently describes this process of becoming:

> I had no epiphany, no singular relevation, no moment of truth, but a steady accumulation of a thousand slights, a thousand indignities, a thousand remembered moments produced in me an anger, a rebelliousness, a desire to fight the system that imprisoned my people. There was no particular day on which I said, 'From henceforth I will devote myself to the liberation of my people'; instead, I simply found myself doing so, and could not do otherwise.
>
> (Mandela, 1994: 95)

As Mandela found, this ongoing experience of being is not a comfortable experience: it necessarily involves cognitive and affective dissonance that is both felt and embodied. While Mezirow's theory describes how an initial disorientating dilemma leads to self-examination, the high intensity dissonance characteristic of transformative learning can also be equated with the notion of 'border crossing' (Giroux, 2005), highlighting the role of visceral experiences that become manifested in powerful emotions that are difficult to reconcile in the longer term. Similarly, in their explication of a theory of Threshold Concepts, Meyer and Land draw on the concept of liminality as a metaphor for the existence of epistemological obstacles, troublesome knowledge and the state of 'being stuck' as central to the process of coming to new ways of 'understanding, interpreting or viewing something' (2005: 372). This evokes Lather's description of the 'praxis of not being so sure' (1998: 492) and Ellsworth's (1997) exploration of the ontological dimension of the unknown that she argues is unfortunately undeveloped in the field of critical pedagogy.

From this view, transformative learning is likely to be a painful process characterised by anxiety, as will be illustrated in Part III. Elsewhere, such anxiety has been described as '*being* being confronted with itself, as the student wills himself into the world' (Barnett, 2007: 36). Furthermore, Barnett argues that it is the achievement of higher education to enable students to live purposefully with this anxiety. This is consistent with the view that it is through messy, indeterminate situations (Schön, 1983) that learning takes place. Moreover, Dirkx (1997) suggests it is teaching and learning experiences marked by high levels of uncertainty, ambiguity, contradiction and paradox that are the basis for 'soul work' as introduced in Chapter 1. This returns the focus onto moral aspects of a holistic theory of learning, which is concerned with the transformation of self, others and society more broadly. The field of virtue ethics is particularly useful here in that 'it shows precisely how the often distinguished and separated cognitive, affective, social and motivational aspects of moral life may be coherently re-connected' (Carr, 2007: 373).

Virtue ethics and being as practice

Virtue ethics provides a framework to understand the moral aspects of our becoming. It is concerned less with the principled ethics of duty or utility and more with our becoming through the cultivation of inclinations, dispositions and good judgements. Ethics is derived from ethos, which forms the root of the Greek word *ethikos* meaning 'moral character, nature, disposition, habit, custom'. Ethos, pathos and logos were identified by Aristotle as important means of persuasion, or rhetoric. It is worthy of note, given the context of this study to be explored in Part II, that rhetoric, grammar and logic formed the trivium of subjects taught in medieval universities. Ethos continues to be highlighted as an important aspect of education and schooling in particular.

Virtues are the excellences of character that enable someone to achieve the 'good life'. More broadly, they have been described as 'entrenched personal qualit[ies]' which have implications for human flourishing or wellbeing (Pike and Halstead, 2006: 15). Virtues can be categorised in multiple ways. For example, the theological virtues consist of faith, hope and charity alongside the four cardinal virtues of the Christian tradition: prudence, justice, fortitude and temperance. Relating explicitly to learning, Dewey (1933) articulated particular virtues of enquiry that included open-mindedness, whole-heartedness and responsibility. While the term 'epistemic virtues' (Zagzebski, 1996) has been used to describe epistemically valuable characteristics of individuals such as intellectual patience, humility, carefulness and conscientiousness, Lahroodi (2007) claims the social dimension of epistemic virtues must be explored further.

Put simply, according to Aristotle (1925) one cultivates virtue in two ways: as excellences of intellect and of character. The first way is through serious moral reflection upon the human condition and the *telos*, or purpose, of human life. Aristotle's *phronesis* or practical wisdom in action is different from *techne* or skills, where the focus is on the most efficient or effective means of achieving particular ends, because the *phronimos* engages in 'reflection on the moral worth as such of those ends as goals of human flourishing' (Carr, 2006: 172). The other way is through practice: we tend to get better at something the more we do it. Virtues are not developed through adherence to abstract principles but are inculcated through practice. I may become more just or courageous by committing just and courageous acts in the same way that a good athlete or musician becomes a better athlete or musician by repeated acts of athleticism or musical performance. For example, the field of character education is founded upon the Aristotelian principle that 'character is formed in large part through habitual behaviour that eventually becomes internalized into virtues (character)' (Berkowitz and Bier, 2004: 80). This internalisation, as a form of tacit knowledge, results from habits of mind and being which should be understood as things that have to be acquired rather than natural dispositions, inclinations or propensities. From this perspective it could be said that the practice of virtues is equivalent to a person achieving the good life through the well-functioning or performance of its being.

Aristotle's distinction between intellectual virtues (including *techne*, *episteme* and *phronesis*) and ethical ones (such as temperance, courage, fortitude, generosity) is not straightforward since *phronesis* is required to complete each ethical virtue. With respect to the discussion of ethos above, Aristotle identified *phronesis* and *arete* (virtue) as appeals to character or ethos, along with *eunoia* (trust), which underpins relationships between, say, a writer and their audience or a husband and wife. Although Aristotle emphasises that morality is grounded in practice he 'is equally emphatic that full acquisition of the moral virtues of courage, temperance and justice requires the principled reflection of practical wisdom' (Carr, 2007: 373). Cultivation of the virtue of generosity therefore demands developing an understanding of what, when, how and towards whom generosity is well actualised and how much and how often to give so that enough support is provided without creating dependency.

From the virtue ethicist perspective, morality is dependent upon our dispositions or judgements (Carr, 2007: 376), rather than our discernment of a set of beliefs about what is right or good (Carr and Steutal, 1999: 246) or an evaluation of the outcomes of a particular action. It is concerned more with becoming a certain kind of person than following a set of rules or a particular ethical code. Consequently moral education must focus upon the practice of virtues, such as the development of good judgement, when facing ethical dilemmas that do not lend themselves to straightforward solutions and where the implications of actions are contentious and unknowable. This renews focus upon 'ways of being' that, for example, cause individuals to make appropriate, virtuous choices as they encounter any given situation.

How these ways of being are inculcated over time is of particular concern to educators. Although Aristotle argues, for example, that we become just through the doing of just actions, the cultivation of virtues is not simply habituation and does not occur through mindless repetition. Dunne, for example, equates the inculcation of ethical virtues with an inductive process from precepts to concepts that occurs in and through experience. He describes this as commensurate with the transition 'from naïve acts (perhaps only complying with the directions of a parent or teacher) to acts that give expression to a formed character' (Dunne, 1999: 58), underlining the contribution of virtue ethics to our understanding of the transformative aspects of becoming. With respect to *phronesis*, for Sherman (1999), it is critical practice that nurtures the cognitive skills that underpin the making of virtuous choices and action. He concludes, 'In general, wisdom is a matter of seeing the morally relevant occasions for action, and then knowing, sometimes only after explicit deliberation, what to do' (Sherman, 1999: 36).

Understanding deliberation to be a particular form of *phronesis* or practical reasoning (Nixon, 2011: 87–90) demands recognising that *phronesis* is something which we do with others. It highlights relational and collective aspects of virtue ethics and the importance of understanding how individuals flourishing together can contribute towards the public good. While we may reason in isolation from others, practical reasoning or deliberation typically incorporates, in some form, the orientations, views and habits of others. It may be that the process of reasoning together is necessary to decide a collective response, say to an ethical dilemma as outlined above. Furthermore, the practice of deliberation is of value in itself: a form of collective action. In turn it demands dispositions such as responsive understanding, illustrated through perception and attention.

Nevertheless character education, with its theoretical roots in virtue ethics, has been criticised for presenting a view of moral education that fails to take account of relationality. In particular, Noddings (2002) contrasts the relation-centred approach to moral education of care theorists with the agent-centred approach in character education. For example, the notion of inculcating personal virtues alludes to virtues being 'acquired' by individuals as 'possessions' and therefore virtue ethics has been criticised for idealising the 'moral grooming and preening' (Woolf, 2003: 121) of the moral agent. This is also reflected in Nussbaum's definition of practical reason as 'being able to form a conception of the good and to engage in critical reflection upon the planning of one's own life' (Nussbaum, 2000: 78).

Defining virtues situationally and relationally demands consideration of social as well as personal virtues. It would be difficult to deny a role to other-regarding virtues such as kindness and justice within any understanding of human flourishing. Moreover, virtue ethicists recognise the importance not only of others modelling good conduct but also engaging together in practical reason as outlined above. For MacIntyre (1984), virtues are embodied within practice characterised by a particular 'coherent and complex form of socially established co-operative human activity' (MacIntyre, 1984: 187). Flourishing can therefore be seen to emerge through participation in social practices such as the arts, professions and academic disciplines.

At an extreme, relativists may argue that societies, cultures and particular communities have differing opinions on what constitutes a virtue at any one particular time, and consequently understanding of what is virtuous is embedded in time and place. Those who take this view deny the existence of transcultural ethical norms and fail to criticise local conceptions and practices of the 'good' and meaning of life. It can be argued that Aristotle presents an objective account of the human good that is justified irrespective of local traditions and practices. Although clearly not all human beings want the same thing, Aristotle justifies the objectivity of his account in that it derives from 'features of humanness that lie beneath local traditions and are there to be seen whether or not they are in fact recognised in local traditions' (Nussbaum, 1993: 243). Virtue ethics can in this way be justified as a moral project that is 'foundational' in that it transcends 'different cultures and traditions' (Pike, 2011: 357) and, at the same time, recognises difference. This idea will be explored further in relation to agency in the section that follows.

MacIntyre supports an understanding that any particular view of the virtues is socio-culturally conditioned. Furthermore, he argues that the actions we take as part of any particular practice can only be fully understood in relation to 'a life that can be conceived and evaluated as a whole' (MacIntyre, 1984: 205). Accounting for 'the unity of a human life' (MacIntyre, 1984: 216) demands attending to all aspects of our life that form our character since 'the good life cannot be discussed if the sense of that life is lost in its atomization into a series of unrelated acts' (Cafaro, 1998: 6).

> I grow in virtue as I struggle with the continuities and discontinuities inherent in the tradition within which I practice.
> (Nixon, 2004: 119)

The communitarian view that moral formation can be understood as initiation into a set of cultural practices evokes Lave and Wenger's work on situated learning and communities of practice (1991). Clearly, the social tradition and cultural context that frame our understanding of what is virtuous within a particular practice must be accounted for. This means understanding the multiple factors which influence the 'ethos' or ethical environment in which particular practices take place: an important concept in an ethical ecology of transformative learning that will be proposed in the final chapter of this book. Ethos alludes to less tangible aspects of the learning environment (such as the ambience or atmosphere for learning). Within formal education, ethos has been described as the hidden curriculum and is driven by the core values which underpin the institution's life and work. For Eisner, ethos refers to 'the underlying deep structure of a culture, the values that animate it, that collectively constitute its way of life' (1994: 2). Recognising that individuals develop their being through action in and also upon traditions of practice acknowledges the role of individual and collective agency in shifting notions of the 'good' and bringing about social change as demonstrated, for example, in the evolution of the abolitionist movement within societies practising the slave trade in the eighteenth century.

To conclude, this section has highlighted the need for epistemology to embrace ontology: our understanding of knowing must also embrace being. Furthermore, an understanding that it is through the practice of virtues or excellences of character that one becomes virtuous brings into view the important role of agency and doing to our ongoing becoming.

Agency: doing

The capability approach

This final section on the constitutive elements of an integrative model of transformative learning explores the transformative aspects of doing. The previous section outlined how virtue ethics acknowledges the primacy of practice and is concerned not just with individual doing but concerted/collective doing. This highlights the importance of capability: what I can do rather than what I might do and also what we can do together. Martha Nussbaum and Amartya Sen's theory of capability and well-being (Nussbaum and Sen, 1993; Nussbaum, 2000) evolved as an approach to women's development in the context of developing countries and has been hugely influential in reconceptualising approaches to tackling poverty. Moreover, its applications have broadened across a range of disciplines including adult and higher education research.

The capability approach focuses upon what 'people are actually able to do and be' (Nussbaum, 2000: 5). Capabilities, or potential functionings, are understood as the freedoms an individual has to achieve the beings and doings that they have reason to value. Functionings are defined as the beings and doings that individuals actually achieve. We could measure the kind of life someone is leading by assessing their achievement of various functionings. However, echoing Nussbaum (2000), Walker claims that a truly human life is 'characterised by freedom, autonomy and an active agency exercised in cooperation and reciprocity with others' (2006: 91).

Capabilities could therefore be described as freedoms to exercise agency. Evaluating functioning as a proxy for capability is problematic. For instance, Sen highlights the equal functioning but differing capabilities of the affluent person who fasts and the destitute person who is starving: 'the first person . . . can choose to eat well and be well nourished in a way the second cannot' (Sen, 1999: 75). Therefore, a particular capability cannot be inferred from the existence of a particular functioning. For instance, Cousin (2003) provides evidence of mimicry when teaching and assessing the concept of 'otherness', concluding that the learning of 'otherness' can be faked 'without engaging with the concept's personally transformative potential' (2003: 9). At the same time, a lack of functioning does not deny the existence of capability. For instance, a student may have the capability to engage in a critical debate but lack confidence in the presence of particular peers or tutors.

Although some functionings, such as play, loving and learning, 'rely unconditionally upon the freedom of those who to choose to play, love and learn' (Nixon, 2011: 74), if functioning itself is declared as our goal, individuals may be deprived of making choices in line with their own conceptions of the good. In respecting different notions of the good life, educators are therefore primarily concerned with developing capabilities as opposed to the achieved functionings that individuals have reason to value. This demands attending to the conditions for learning. In this view, the educator does not pre-empt what students choose to do with their capabilities. Furthermore, it can be argued the paradox of Education is that its goals can only be achieved when the outcomes are unknown: 'Education as induction into knowledge is successful to the extent that it makes the behavioural outcomes of the students unpredictable' (Stenhouse, 1975: 82). This is redolent of Hannah Arendt's call for educators not to predict the needs of the future and inhibit what cannot be foreseen and instead prepare their students 'in advance for the task of renewing a common world' (1977: 177):

> Our hope always hangs on the new which every generation brings; but precisely because we can base our hope only on this, we destroy everything if we so try to control the new that we, the old, can dictate how it will look.
>
> (Arendt, 1977: 192)

Power relations and social arrangements may inhibit or enhance individual agency in the pursuit of the realisation of functioning. Functioning is therefore one important criterion for assessing agency. Hart (2009) suggests that there are self, other and environmentally oriented constraints which may operate on an individual and give them cause to adapt their preferences for functioning. Indeed, the good human life is dependent upon things that human beings do not control. Nussbaum labels this 'adaptive preferences' (2011: 81–4) and recognises this barrier to functioning by differentiating internal capabilities from combined capabilities. The former are characteristics of persons that are acquired, usually through social interaction, whereas the latter are 'not just abilities residing inside a person but also the freedoms or opportunities created by a combination of personal abilities and the political, social and economic environment' (Nussbaum, 2011: 20–1). Citizens who are denied freedom of speech may only have the internal capability of exercising their thought in line with their conscience (Nussbaum, 2000: 85).

This picture is complicated further when one considers that different capabilities develop relationally rather than on their own. For example, the capabilities of practical reason and affiliation are foundational since, without these, the other capabilities listed by Nussbaum (2000: 78–80) cannot lead to achieved functionings. Of relevance to this study, Amartya Sen's contribution includes the concept of agency freedom (Sen, 1992): the freedom an individual has to turn a range of capabilities into functionings. This demands attending to the agency of an individual to affect others in ways that may either enhance or diminish their own well-being achievement. Nixon goes further, highlighting the importance of reciprocity embedded within capabilities, and claiming 'my capability for justice and friendship towards others is dependent upon the capability of others for justice and friendship towards me' (Nixon, 2011: 73).

The capabilities approach also has an explicit holistic orientation. Nussbaum identifies emotions and bodily integrity as central capabilities for human development (2000: 79). Walker defines emotional integrity within higher education as 'Not being subject to anxiety or fear which diminishes learning. Being able to develop emotions for imagination, empathy, awareness and discernment' (2006: 128). This recognises that emotions should be valued in their own right as important aspects of human flourishing. The implication of this for a virtues-based approach to education is that 'we take seriously that we can become agents of our emotional lives' (Sherman, 1999: 42).

Agency and social change

Capabilities must be seen as fragile and temporary achievements that need to be relentlessly pursued across a lifetime. While recognising that capabilities develop relationally, O'Neill reminds us that 'Connected lives become selectively, variably and sometimes acutely vulnerable lives' (1996: 192). For example, a new job provides support and security yet brings new demands through working with others.

Recognising unexpected consequences highlights the complexity of the endeavour to create capabilities. For example, generosity and charity may support others yet increase their dependency. This highlights the conflicts between exercising virtues such as benevolence and charity, demanding that we recognise that 'the effort to teach ethics as an autonomous subject, abstracted from the particular complex activities that constitute our lives, actually distorts the ideas of these values and norms' (Wallace, 1999: 92). Nussbaum, in her exposition of the fragility of goodness (2001), examined the role of events over which human agents lack control in the formation of virtue. As introduced in the previous section, goodness is reliant upon factors beyond its control. For instance, Hannah Arendt invoked the words of Jesus, 'they know not what they do', to acknowledge the necessity of forgiveness since we can never know the full implications and consequences of our actions (Arendt, 1977: 239).

Situationism provides an account of the contribution of external influences such as institutional factors, culture and environment that impact upon agency. However, rather than overstating the role of such influences and concluding that 'character is dead' (Hunter, 2000), it can be argued that a socio-cultural approach to character and virtue can nurture institutions and organisations that promote virtue and flourishing. Furthermore, Sen recognises the 'deep complementarity' (Sen, 1999: xi) between social arrangements and individual agency in general and the interdependence between the choices and freedoms of ourselves and others. This book provides evidence to support a 'bivalent' approach towards capabilities (Walker, 2003: 182) that accounts for the inter-relationship between individual flourishing and organisational structure that will be explored further in Chapter 8.

This entails acknowledging other-regarding virtues and social aspects of how virtues are practised. For example, Lave and Wenger (1991, 1996) have interpreted Vygotsky's zone of proximal development (ZPD) (1978: 86) in a way that emphasises 'connecting issues of socio-cultural transformation with the changing relations between newcomers and old timers in the context of a changing shared practice' (Lave and Wenger, 1991: 49). This is consistent with MacIntyre's (1984) understanding of traditions of practice as outlined in the previous section. This reiterates the importance of role models, deliberation and collective inquiry as moral ideals. Transformative learning that foregrounds social virtues provides a response to criticism that Vygotsky's ZPD provides 'a model of pedagogy which reduces analysis to teacher-pupil interaction' (Daniels, 2001: 175) and is based upon 'a rather under-theorised conception of context' (Maybin, 2003, cited in Conteh, 2012: 102). Furthermore, in relation to the ways of knowing explored earlier in this chapter, Vygotsky emphasises the role of both the social and the aesthetic within agency, stating 'from the most ancient times art has always been regarded as a means of education, that is as a long range programme for changing our behaviour and our organism' (Vygotsky, 1971: 253).

Sen and Nussbaum's differing versions of the capability approach provide the basis of a theory of justice for humankind. Yet, Nussbaum's universal list of capabilities, by its very nature, is likely to be prescriptively applied in diverse contexts. This is a particular concern in circumstances where her stated universals are viewed as 'deeply rooted in Western philosophy' (Walker, 2003: 184). However, Carr recognises that while there may be different cultural conceptions of virtue and an associated diversity of conceptions of good character, 'ideas of virtue and character are basic to explanations of human agency as such, and they also provide ready cross-cultural currency of moral evaluation' (Carr, 2007: 387). This resonates with the challenge to the perception that moral agency involves conforming to the beliefs of a particular, usually one's own, cultural constituency, since

> to whatever extent morality would seem to involve at least trying to discern a set of correct beliefs about what is right and good, it is upon the

dispositions rather than the beliefs of agents that our moral assessments seem to critically turn.

(Carr and Steutal, 1999: 246)

Nevertheless, acknowledging that there exist different conceptions of the good life and what constitutes a flourishing life demands that we recognise and engage with the similarities and differences across the plurality of our lives. This reiterates the importance of deliberation and practical reason defined by Walker as 'deepening our sense of our own agency through reflective deliberation in and on a plurality of perspectives, and judgement which leads to action' (Walker, 2006: 70). It also demands recognising the institutional and social constraints to realising capabilities that will now be explored further.

Nussbaum's work focuses on a liberal concern for individual flourishing yet clearly affirms the value of relationship, institutional association and society. Her exposition of the capabilities of sociability and affiliation suggest the good life is to be found through participation in the community. Walker, however, goes beyond seeing flourishing as taking place in a social context, and argues for a renewed focus on social justice for the purpose of both individual flourishing and collective solidarities (Walker, 2003: 168). This demands shifting focus from a liberal view of individual autonomy to recognising the mutuality of relationships and the values of institutions and society. Walker, therefore, argues for a critical capability pedagogy which 'may contribute through teaching and learning to societies which are more just, fair and compassionate' (Walker, 2009: 17) through developing student agency and well-being on the one hand and social change towards greater justice on the other. This study attempts to develop understanding of such a pedagogical approach. It demands accounting for the structural constraints that limit freedom not only at a local, national and global level (Hart, 2009: 398), but also for the individual: 'In education, this would mean that our actions for justice need to correct both inequities in education and the structural frameworks that generate them, to change both individual lives and public institutions' (Walker, 2003: 182).

The notion of 'freedom' as evoked by Nussbaum needs to be framed within a broader notion of 'liberation' if it is to challenge the structural inequalities of society. Freire's notion of conscientisation is consistent with a view of transformative learning that requires both critical reflection and action to be part of the same process of praxis (1970: 48): reflection and action upon the world to transform it. This study attempts to understand more deeply the complex relationship between both individual and collective thought and action and their contribution to social change.

Conclusion

In this chapter, a review of a range of eclectic literature from across disciplines has illuminated a tripartite of transformation: the transformative aspects of knowing, being and doing. Knud Illeris, a leading thinker on how people learn, recently produced a one-line definition of transformative learning as 'learning that implies change in the identity of the learner' (2014: 40). Chapter 2 has demonstrated how this book extends Illeris's notion of transformation through incorporating ethical, relational and aesthetic aspects of learning which depend upon interaction with particular and general others. The understanding of transformative learning developed here is also distinct in that it accounts for cultural considerations and draws on empirical data. Like Illeris, this book has used Jack Mezirow's work as a point of departure; however, a reconceptualisation of transformative learning is progressed here through explicitly linking transformative learning to the concept of authenticity, which is the focus of the next chapter.

References

Arendt, H. (1977) *Between Past and Future*. New York: Penguin.
Aristotle (1925) *Ethica Nicomachea* [*The Nichomachean Ethics*]. In Aristotle, *The Works of Aristotle*, Volume IX (trans. W.D. Ross). Oxford: Oxford University Press.
Ashworth, P. (2004) Understanding as the Transformation of What is Already Known. *Teaching in Higher Education* 9 (2): 147–58.
Barnett, R. (2007) *A Will to Learn*. Maidenhead: Open University Press/SRHE.
Belenky, M.F., Clinchy, B., Goldberger, N.R. and Traule, J.M. et al. (1986) *Women's Ways of Knowing*. New York: Basic Books.
Berkowitz, M.W. and Bier, M.C. (2004) Research-Based Character Education. *The Annals of the American Academy* 591: 72–85.
Buber, M. (1953) *I and Thou: The Philosophy of Relationship*. London: Routledge.
Buber, M. (1961) *Between Man and Man*. London: Collins.
Cafaro, P. (1998) Virtue Ethics Not Too Simplified. Paper delivered at the Twentieth World Congress of Philosophy, in Boston, Massachusetts, 10–15 August 1998.
Carr, D. (2006) Professional and Personal Values and Virtues in Education and Teaching. *Oxford Review of Education* 32 (2): 171–83.
Carr, D. (2007) Character in Teaching. *British Journal of Educational Studies* 55 (4): 369–89.
Carr, D. and Steutal, J. (1999) The Virtue Approach to Moral Education: Pointers, Problems and Prospects. In Carr, D. and Steutal, J. (eds) *Virtue Ethics and Moral Education*. Oxon: Routledge, 241–55.
Conteh, J. (2012) Families, Pupils and Teachers Learning Together in a Multilingual British City. *Journal of Multilingual and Multicultural Development* 33 (1): 101–16.
Cousin, G. (2003) Threshold Concepts, Troublesome Knowledge and Learning About Others. Paper presented to the 10th Conference of the European Association for Research on Learning and Instruction (EARLI), Padova, Italy, 26–30 August.
Dall'Alba, G. and Barnacle, R. (2005) Embodied Knowing in Online Environments. *Educational Philosophy and Theory* 37 (5): 719–44.
Daniels, H. (2001) *Vygotsky and Pedagogy*. London: Routledge.
Dewey, J. (1933) *How We Think*. Boston: D.C. Heath and Co.
Dewey, J. (1934) *Art as Experience*. New York: Perigee Books.
Dewey, J. (1988) Art in Education—and Education in Art. In Jo Ann Boydston (ed.) *John Dewey: The Later Works*, Carbondale: Southern Illinois University Press, 2–112.
Dirkx, J.M. (1997) Nurturing Soul in Adult Learning. *New Directions for Adult and Continuing Education* 74 (Summer): 79–88.

Dunne, J. (1999) Virtue, *Phronesis* and Learning. In Carr, D. and Steutal, J. (eds) *Virtue Ethics and Moral Education*. Oxon: Routledge, 49–64.
Eisner, E. (1994) *Ethos and Education Perspectives: A Series of Papers on Values and Education*. Unpublished document. Scottish Consultative Council on the Curriculum.
Ellsworth, E. (1997) *Teaching Positions: Difference, Pedagogy, and the Power of Address*. Columbia: Teachers College Press.
Freire, P. (1970) *Pedagogy of the Oppressed*. New York: Continuum.
Gibbs, P. and Angelides, P. (2004) Accreditation of Knowledge as Being-in-the-World. *Journal of Education and Work* 17 (3): 333–46.
Gilligan, C. (1982) *In a Different Voice: Psychology Theory and Women's Development*. Cambridge, MA: Harvard University Press.
Giroux, H. (2005) *Border Crossings: Cultural Workers and the Politics of Education* (2nd Edition). London: Routledge.
Habermas, J. (1990) *Moral Consciousness and Communicative Action*. Cambridge, MA: MIT Press.
Hart, C.S. (2009) Quo Vadis? The Capability Space and New Directions for the Philosophy of Educational Research. *Studies in Philosophy and Education* 28 (5): 391–402.
Heidegger, M. (1927/1962) *Being and Time* (trans. J. Macquarrie and E. Robinson). Oxford: Blackwell.
Heron, J. (1992) *Feeling and Personhood: Psychology in Another Key*. London: SAGE.
Hunter, J.D. (2000) *The Death of Character: Moral Education in an Age Without Good or Evil*. New York: Basic Books.
Illeris, K. (2014) *Transformative Learning and Identity*. London and New York: Routledge.
Jarvis, P. (2006) *Towards a Comprehensive Theory of Human Learning: Lifelong Learning and Learning Society Volume 1*. London: Routledge.
Lahroodi, R. (2007) Collective Epistemic Virtues. *Social Epistemology* 21 (3): 281–97.
Lather, P. (1998) Critical Pedagogy and its Complicities: A Praxis of Stuck Places. *Educational Theory* 48 (4): 487–97.
Lave, J. and Wenger, E. (1991) *Situated Learning: Legitimate Peripheral Participation*. New York: Cambridge University Press.
Lave, J. and Wenger, E. (1996) Practice, Person, Social World. In Daniels, H. (ed.) *An Introduction to Vygotsky*. London: Routledge, 143–50.
Le Cornu, A. (2009) Meaning, Internalization and Externalization: Toward a Fuller Understanding of the Process of Reflection and Its Role in the Construction of the Self. *Adult Education Quarterly* 59 (4): 279–97.
Lewis, C.S. (1955) *The Magician's Nephew*. New York: Macmillan, Collier Books.
Liu, G. (1995) Knowledge, Foundations, and Discourse: Philosophical Support for Service-Learning. *Michigan Journal of Community Service Learning* 2 (1): 5–18.
MacIntyre, A.C. (1984) *After Virtue: A Study in Moral Theory* (2nd Edition). London: Duckworth.
Mandela, N. (1994) *Long Walk to Freedom*. London: Abacus.
Marcuse, H. (1964) *One-Dimensional Man*. Boston: Beacon.
Meyer, J.H.F. and Land, R. (2005) Threshold Concepts and Troublesome Knowledge (2): Epistemological Considerations and a Framework for Teaching and Learning. *Higher Education* 49 (3): 373–88.
Mezirow, J. (ed.) (2000) *Learning as Transformation*. San Francisco: Jossey-Bass.
Newman, M. (2012) Calling Transformative Learning Into Question: Some Mutinous Thoughts. *Adult Education Quarterly* 62 (1): 36–55.
Nixon, J. (2004) Learning the Language of Deliberative Democracy. In Walker, M. and Nixon, J. (eds) *Reclaiming Universities from a Runaway World*. Maidenhead: SRHE/Open University Press, 114–27.

Nixon, J. (2011) *Higher Education and the Public Good*. London: Continuum.
Noddings, N. (1984) *Caring: A Feminine Approach to Ethics and Moral Education*. Berkeley: University of California Press.
Noddings, N. (2002) *Educating Moral People: A Caring Alternative to Character Education*. New York: Teachers College Press.
Nussbaum, M. (1993) Non-Relative Virtues: An Aristotelian Approach. In Nussbaum, M. and Sen, A. (eds) *The Quality of Life*. Oxford: Oxford University Press, 242–69.
Nussbaum, M. (2000) *Women and Human Development*. Cambridge: Cambridge University Press.
Nussbaum, M. (2001) *Upheavals of Thought: The Intelligence of the Emotions*. Cambridge: Cambridge University Press.
Nussbaum, M. (2011) *Creating Capabilities: The Human Development Approach*. Cambridge, MA: Harvard University Press.
Nussbaum, M. and Sen, A. (eds) (1993) *The Quality of Life*. Oxford: Oxford University Press.
O'Neill, O. (1996) *Towards Justice and Virtue*. Cambridge: Cambridge University Press.
Palmer, P. (1980) *The Promise of Paradox*. San Francisco: Jossey-Bass.
Palmer, P. (1983) *To Know As We Are Known*. San Francisco: Harper & Row.
Palmer, P. (1987) Community, Conflict, and Ways of Knowing. *Change* 19 (1): 20–5.
Parks-Daloz, L. (2000) Transformative Learning for the Common Good. In Mezirow, J. (ed.) *Learning as Transformation*. San Francisco: Jossey-Bass, 103–24.
Peck, D. (2008) *Practical Action: Polanyi, Hacking, Heidegger and the Tacit Dimension*. Saarbrucken: Verla Dr. Muller.
Peters, R.S. (1973) *Philosophy of Education*. Oxford: Oxford University Press.
Pike, M.A. (2004) Aesthetic Teaching. *Journal of Aesthetic Education* 38 (2): 20–37.
Pike M.A. (2011) Ethical English Teaching and Citizenship Education: Promoting Democratic Values or the Tao? *Changing English: Studies in Culture and Education* 18 (4): 351–9.
Pike, M.A. and Halstead, M.J. (2006) *Citizenship and Moral Education: Values in Action*. London: Routledge Falmer.
Polanyi, M. (1966) *The Tacit Dimension*. London: Routledge and Kegan Paul.
Polanyi, M. (1969) *Knowing and Being: Essays*. Chicago: Chicago University Press.
Ricoeur, P. (1981) *Paul Ricoeur, Hermeneutics and the Human Sciences: Essays on Language, Action and Interpretation* (ed. and trans. J.B. Thompson). Cambridge: Cambridge University Press.
Saltmarsh, J. (1996) Education for Critical Citizenship: John Dewey's Contribution to the Pedagogy of Community Service-Learning. *Michigan Journal of Community Service Learning* 3 (1): 13–21.
Scharmer, C.O. (2009) *Theory U: Leading from the Future as it Emerges*. San Francisco: Berrett Koehler.
Schön, D. (1983) *The Reflective Practitioner: How Professionals Think in Action*. New York: Basic Books.
Sen, A. (1992) *Inequality Re-Examined*. Oxford: Clarendon Press.
Sen, A. (1999) *Development as Freedom*. Oxford: Oxford University Press.
Senge, P., Scharmer, C.O., Jaworski, J. and Sue Flowers, B. (2005) *Presence: Exploring Profound Change in People, Organisations and Society*. London: Nicholas Brealey Publishing.
Sherman, N. (1999) Character Development and Aristotelian Virtue. In Carr, D. and Steutal, J. (eds) *Virtue Ethics and Moral Education*. Oxon: Routledge, 35–48.
Stenhouse, L. (1975) *An Introduction to Curriculum Research and Development*. London: Heineman.
Taylor, E.W. (2000) Analyzing Research on Transformative Learning Theory. In Mezirow, J. and Associates (eds) *Learning as Transformation*. San Francisco: Jossey-Bass, 285–328.

Thayer-Bacon, B.J. (2003) *Transforming Critical Thinking: Thinking Constructively*. New York: Teachers College Press.

Thiessen, E.J. (2001) *In Defence of Religious Schools and Colleges*. London: McGill-Queen's University Press.

Vygotsky, L.S. (1971) *The Psychology of Art*. Cambridge, MA: MIT.

Vygotsky, L.S. (1978) *Mind in Society: The Development of Higher Mental Processes*. Cambridge, MA: Harvard University Press.

Vygotsky, L.S. (1986) *Thought and Language* (2nd revised edition). Cambridge, MA: MIT Press.

Walker, M. (2003) Framing Social Justice in Education: What Does the 'Capabilities' Approach Offer? *British Journal of Educational Studies* 51 (2): 168–87.

Walker, M. (2006) *Higher Education Pedagogies: A Capabilities Approach*. Maidenhead: Open University Press.

Walker, M. (2009) Critical Capability Pedagogies and University Education. *Educational Philosophy and Theory* 42 (8): 898–917.

Wallace, J.D. (1999) Virtues of Benevolence and Justice. In Carr, D. and Steutal, J. (eds) *Virtue Ethics and Moral Education*. Oxon: Routledge, 82–94.

Woolf, J. (2003) Contractualism and the Virtues. In Matravers, M., *Scanlon and Contractualism*. London: Routledge, 120–32.

Yorks, L. and Kasl, E. (2002) Toward a Theory and Practice of Whole-Person Learning: Reconceptualising Experience and the Role of Affect. *Adult Education Quarterly* 52 (3): 176–92.

Zagzebski, L. (1996) *Virtues of the Mind*. Cambridge: Cambridge University Press.

3 The centrality of authenticity to transformative learning

Introduction

The search for authenticity in products, experiences and our everyday lives is a contemporary preoccupation. Authenticity has been discussed widely in philosophical literature (Heidegger, 1927/1962; Buber, 1953) and more recently related explicitly to learning (Jarvis, 1992) and teaching (Cranton, 2001; Kreber et al., 2007). Notions of authenticity founded upon introspection or self-discovery that disregard how our selves are socially and historically shaped have been passionately denigrated as jargon (Adorno, 1973) and the idea of authenticity has been reclaimed as a moral ideal (Taylor, 1991). Nevertheless, the only previous attempt to formally relate authenticity to the process of transformative learning (Cranton and Carusetta, 2004) explicates becoming authentic as a process of individuation that serves to separate the learning self from the broader context and relationships.

The previous chapter outlined how an integrative model of transformative learning must comprise the constitutive elements of knowing, being and doing. Drawing on this analysis, the first section of this chapter will argue that the authentic self emerges when the learning self experiences the transformative aspects of knowing, being and doing in synergy, as depicted in Figure 3.1. Given the argument here that the learning self cannot become authentic in isolation, the second section of this chapter will highlight the importance of reconnecting the learning self with itself, others and the broader context. It will introduce the notions of selfhood, reciprocity and worldliness as a framework to think about aspects of authenticity pertinent to the particular context of this study: the experience of International Service-Learning among students from Liverpool Hope University in the UK. Finally, a segue will propose that transformative learning understood as a process of becoming authentic provides the foundations for an ethical ecology of transformative learning.

The authentic self

> Become what you are.
> (Heidegger, 1927/1962: 186)

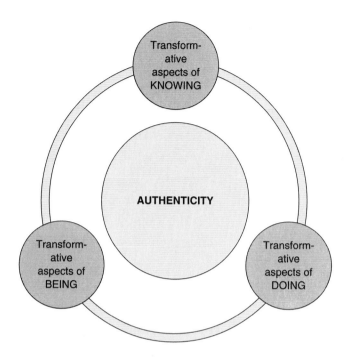

Figure 3.1 The centrality of authenticity

> To the degree that learning is transformative it is what one is meant to be doing in order to become essentially who one is.
>
> (Walters, 2008: 116)

While Polonian and Dadaist notions of authenticity elevate the role of the individual self, this section suggests that the dichotomy of 'original self' versus 'socially constructed self' is false. Building upon the preceding discussion in Part I, it is instead argued here that while the self is original, its origins are relational. We are dialogical by nature. It is through dialogue – mutuality and reciprocity – that we achieve authenticity and thereby become ourselves. Authenticity is therefore understood here as being both different from and related to concepts of individuality, identity, autonomy and originality.

The claim that the authentic self is one that is true to itself is suggestive of it being faithful to something it already is, to its originality, and that only it can discover and articulate. This idea is grounded in an understanding of the self as an essential core (with a singular core essence or single and stable identity as in the humanist ideal of the unified integrated self). Social constructivists and postmodernists reject the possibility of knowing one's true self in this respect and instead see identities as fluid, free-floating, constantly in flux and socially constructed. They argue it is impossible to know oneself outside the socio-cultural background that informs one's life. This leads to an alternative understanding of being true to oneself which sees the self as self-created and as something under ongoing construction, as in Giddens's notion of the 'reflexive project of the self' which he describes as 'the process whereby self-identity is constituted by the reflexive ordering of self-narrative' (1991: 244).

The ways of knowing discussed in Chapter 2 nurture neither the 'original-to-be-discovered' nor the 'self-created' authentic self. Instead, this book supports an understanding of becoming authentic as a deeply relational process. This approach is grounded in the belief that there is something inside us, namely, 'our authentic self, the self we access and express when we are being authentic' that is 'at its deepest level something shaped and defined by society' (Guignon, 2004: 154). Understanding this 'authentic self' does not demand abandoning the self but instead recognises the potential of reconnecting the authentic self with itself, others and the broader context. Consistent with relational ways of knowing, this means acknowledging that our identities are formed in dialogue with others: in agreement or struggle with their recognition of us. We are dialogically constituted since it is in dialogue with other people's understandings of who I am that I develop a conception of my own identity.

> To value individuality properly just is to acknowledge the dependence of the good for each of us on relationships with others. Without these bonds, as I say, we could not come to be free selves, not least because we could not come to be selves at all.
>
> (Appiah, 2005: 21)

The authentic self emerges from an understanding of the relational self. In *Being and Time* (Heidegger, 1927/1962) Heidegger differentiates between authenticity, inauthenticity and everydayness. For him, in living authentically we choose those possibilities that are uniquely our own and become what one already is. This demands both an openness to the truth as well as resistance to social norms and established routines. Our being for Heidegger is characterised by inauthenticity as we have a tendency to 'fall away' from our own being as we fail to confront our own finitude and take 'care' of our own existence or that of others. Inauthenticity is demonstrated by the traditional scientific method as it 'begins with the everyday existence of things and then abstracts or objectifies the phenomenon' (Brook, 2009: 49), as is the case with mere 'presence-at-hand'. Finally, in our *everydayness* our being is distracted by all manner of things as we follow the crowd. This evokes Dewey's description of anaesthetic experiences, the enemy of the aesthetic, as discussed earlier.

> An uprooted understanding of the world, detached from any particular task that might have focused *Dasein* [or being] upon objects in its immediate environment, tends to float away from what is ready-to-hand and

towards the exotic, the alien and the distant. . . . In short, *Dasein* becomes curious: distracted by new possibilities, it lingers in any given environment for shorter and shorter periods; floating everywhere, it dwells nowhere.

(Mulhall, 2005: 107)

Authenticity therefore emerges through immersion in aesthetic experiences. Dwelling is an important characteristic of such authenticity, defined as homeliness, of being oneself in our environment (Heidegger, 1930/2005), and relates to Polanyi's concept of indwelling discussed in Chapter 2. The foundations for Heidegger's notion of dwelling are present within *Being and Time* and more fully expounded in his essay 'Building Dwelling Thinking' (Heidegger, 1951/1971), where he stated: 'To dwell, to be set at peace within the free, the preserve, the free preserve that safeguards each thing in its nature' (Heidegger, 1951/1971: 149). Heidegger, for example, recognises the subject as bound up within the object of its environment and as such 'Learning as dwelling' is also a particularly powerful way of conceiving learning as 'a process through which learners forever weave themselves into the fabric of their natural, social and cultural worlds' (Plumb, 2008: 62). Dwelling provides a useful response to increasing rationalisation that can sever the authentic self from both their own, and other, selves. Students dwell when the learning environment encourages them to interact with what it means to have an authentic understanding of themselves (Ream and Ream, 2005: 593). Similarly, for Polanyi, indwelling is when we rely on the particulars and experience as a whole through focal awareness. It is experienced, like Heidegger's dwelling, through participation and immersion in a comprehensive and meaningful whole. This echoes the aesthetics of Dewey and his identification of the 'unity' of an experience, which is neither exclusively emotional, practical nor intellectual, but instead determined by a single pervasive quality.

This discussion highlights the importance of accessing and understanding our embodied knowing as we become self-aware. A focus on holistic knowing demands considering how we expose and shift both habits of mind and habits of being. Barnett, for example, articulates an ontological substrate to becoming authentic and 'true to oneself', claiming it involves the student being disencumbered by other voices as they enhance their agency and take hold of things in their own way (Barnett, 2007: 42). From this view, understanding should be both embodied in the student and sincerely proposed by the student. These two different ideas are clearly interdependent: 'A student is able to take hold of that which she encounters owing to her being disencumbered and, taking hold, she enhances her state of being disencumbered' (Barnett, 2007: 46). This is redolent of Scharmer's notions of 'letting go' and 'letting come', the twin components of openness that underpin presencing (2009: 8).

Barnett's recent description of being and becoming (2011), although in relation to the institution of the university, reveals the relationship between authenticity and the transformative aspects of being discussed in Chapter 2. He argues that being involves a concern for itself in the world and 'lies behind it, within it and before it' (Barnett, 2011: 61). This points towards the relevant histories and possibilities that the self carries with itself and 'the unity of a human life' (MacIntyre, 1984: 216), as discussed earlier. Becoming involves becoming itself, a 'striving to take itself forward, attempting with all its energies to go in some self-determined direction, even against the swirling waters that would deflect it off its path' (Barnett, 2011: 62). Transformative learning has a role to play in leading us back to who we are, through confrontation with our own being. This process of becoming is an act of creation and construction as well as one of discovery. Barnett, however, claims this is not necessarily experienced as a particular end that is reached, not a shift from 'a mode of being for one kind of life to a mode of being for another specific kind of life' but as comfortableness with being in a state of uncertainty (2007: 39). From this view authenticity must be relentlessly pursued yet is itself never achieved.

Holistic and relational aspects of knowing also support Taylor's act of retrieval regarding the 'moral' ideal of authenticity by embracing the role of unconditional relationships and moral demands beyond the self (1991: 35). He suggests that moral thinking incorporates three axes, including our sense of respect for and obligation to others and our understandings of what makes a full life (1989). In fact, he argues that unless these ideas are embraced, the conditions for realising authenticity itself will be destroyed: to shut out demands emanating beyond the self is to suppress the conditions of significance through which the moral ideal of authenticity can be realised. In particular, his argument dismisses the ethic of self-fulfilment or self-realisation that forges instrumental relationships that subserve personal fulfilment and lead to 'social atomism' (1991: 58). If we are to define ourselves significantly, one of the things we cannot do is deny the horizons against which things take on significance for us.

> I can define my identity only against the background of things that matter. But to bracket out history, nature, society, the demands of solidarity, everything but what I find in myself, would be to eliminate all candidates for what matters.
>
> (Taylor, 1991: 40)

Becoming authentic therefore involves raising existential questions and attending to what matters to us, an important aspect of cultivating virtues as discussed in Chapter 2. This corresponds with Jarvis's criteria for authenticity: that people are being authentic when they choose to act so as to 'foster the growth and development of each other's being' (Jarvis, 1992: 113). This understanding of authenticity as a 'moral' ideal suggests an image of the good life that we ought to desire and that Taylor (1991) claims must move from the margins to centre stage in public debate.

The authentic self emerges through our relationships and connection with others. We are able to critically reflect on our assumptions and develop our own understanding of our own individual selves precisely because of the social practices in which we are embedded. The authentic person has a critical role to play in society, and as such authenticity must, for example like kindness and justice, also be seen as a social virtue. When authenticity is envisioned solely as a personal virtue, those lacking authenticity (for example, those who are out of touch with what they feel or believe and are unable to stand up for themselves) are seen to undermine societies that promote and value authenticity. Reiterating the argument outlined earlier, it is wholly inadequate to conceive of learning or becoming authentic as separated from relationships and context, that is to say, as solely concerned with individual action that leads to individual change.

While agency is often equated with actions and doings, the capability approach shifts our attention towards assessing the freedom and autonomy people have in 'becoming' what people have reasons to become, and as such is related to authenticity:

> What is ultimately important is that people have the freedoms or valuable opportunities (capabilities) to lead the kind of lives they want to lead, to do what they want to do and be the person they want to be.
>
> (Robeyns, 2005: 95)

From this view, the capabilities approach is fundamentally concerned with assisting people to lead authentic lives. Impaired agency can be seen to compromise authenticity. For example, critical theorists such as Adorno (1973) have highlighted the struggle to transform one's own perspective because of socio-cultural barriers that cannot be overcome. This highlights the importance of congruence between an individual's values and actions to authenticity. This demands two related aspects: first getting clear about what one's own deliberations lead one to believe, and second, honestly and fully expressing this in public places (Guignon, 2004; Kreber, 2010: 183). The barrier to achieving this alignment recalls the discussion of capabilities and functionings presented in Chapter 2.

(Authenticity as) selfhood, reciprocity and worldliness

This chapter has thus far argued that authenticity is a feature of the transformative aspects of knowing, being and doing. Furthermore, authenticity is enhanced when the learning self encounters these three aspects of learning in synergy. Of central concern to ISL, the focus of this study, is a learning self that is in relationship with itself, particular others and the wider world. Whilst acknowledging that it is only in and through relationship that the individual grows and learns, investigating the student experience of ISL is primarily an investigation into the journey of the learning self: a journey that is nevertheless completed alongside others. This section introduces the notions of selfhood, reciprocity and worldliness as a framework to think about aspects of authenticity intrinsic to the context of this study: service-learning and higher education in general and ISL at Liverpool Hope University in particular. As Parts II and III of this book will substantiate, these concepts are indissoluble from this investigation into a particular group of students at a particular university who have had a particular type of experience of ISL.

(Authenticity as) selfhood

> Mr Banda asked us 'what was our culture?' and we couldn't answer him. I felt dreadful. We were asking him lots of questions about his culture without having reflected on ourselves.
>
> (Mary, ISL participant in 2007 in Malawi)

A liberal arts inspired education, as offered at LHU, seeks to promote personal development, self-confidence and critical thinking: for example, as students become aware of how they make meaning of the world. The intention is that students become defined by their own expectations rather than others. This occurs for students in higher education as they 'take hold of things in their own way' (Barnett, 2007: 46), a phrase which highlights the creative and ontological aspects of the self becoming itself. This is also intimated in the LHU mission to 'educate in the round' (LHU, 2015): a statement that implicitly recognises the role of feelings and emotions along with the complexity of the lives led by students. This presents a vision for a higher education that has a 'unity of experience' (Dewey, 1934: 10): a pervasive quality which is not solely emotional, practical or intellectual that encourages individuals to break free of their 'everydayness' as defined in the work of Heidegger.

Authenticity as selfhood develops as the I, as it is subjectively perceived, engages with the ways in which it is objectively perceived. This occurs through encountering other people, other places and the unfamiliar: in particular, as illustrated in Mary's account above, through dialogue with other people's conceptions of who I am. This illustrates a feature of higher education and ISL: the nurturing of the reflexive construction of the self. It demands combinations of reflection and action (Dewey, Freire), active learning and attempts to solve 'real world' problems. This is also reflected in the teaching and learning strategy at LHU (Norton, 2009), which contests a compartmentalised view of learning that is concerned solely with individualistic or autonomous learning.

As Chapter 4 will demonstrate, LHU in general and its ISL programme in particular provoke students to question the meaning and purpose of life through engaging with issues of poverty and social justice. They challenge students to reconsider their conceptions of the good life. It is through the interdependence of human identity and our understanding of the good that the authentic self emerges. This is congruent with Taylor's understanding of selfhood:

> My identity is defined by the commitments and identifications which provide the frame or horizon within which I can try to determine from case to case what is good, or valuable, or what ought to be done, or what

I endorse or oppose. In other words, it is the horizon within which I am capable of taking a stand.

(Taylor, 1989: 27)

Attempts to 'make a difference' to the lives of others or put 'others before self' provide horizons of significance that frame the development of (authenticity as) selfhood. These actions bring into view 'a picture of what a better or higher mode of life would be, whereby terms such as better or higher offer a standard we ought to desire' (Taylor, 1991: 16). This aspect of authenticity as selfhood emerges through a social process, for example, as staff and students endeavour to understand the beings and doings that they, and others, choose to value. This enables participants to reflect upon their own assumptions, develop their understanding of their individual selves and, furthermore, align their values and actions.

(Authenticity as) reciprocity

. . . you just did not feel that you were there on the project to deliver something you felt like you were part of them, part of their team.

(Angela, ISL participant in 2005 in Sri Lanka)

The authentic self emerges through and is manifested in our relationships and connections with others. It has distinctly social aspects. The LHU mission statement emphasises the importance of relationships, collegiality and working collaboratively evoking Jarvis's criteria for authenticity: that people are being authentic when they choose to act so as to 'foster the growth and development of each other's being' (Jarvis, 1992: 113). Furthermore, LHU's ambition to be a 'community of communities, collaborating in wider partnerships' (LHU, 2015) is redolent of Boyer's notion of the scholarship of engagement as discussed earlier, highlighting the necessity for universities to take action to address pressing social ethical problems. This contrasts with the portrayal of the university as an ivory tower disconnected from the community which it serves. The vocation and formation of teachers is a primary concern for universities such as LHU and relates directly to the group of students studied here.

Service to others and reciprocal learning are foundational concepts for (international) service-learning practitioners as will be explored in Chapter 4. At LHU, an attempt has been made to embed relationships, reciprocity and mutual learning within ISL provision, as articulated in the guiding principles for this work, which include statements such as 'we believe the needs of partners should be heard and responded to' (Bamber, 2008: xiii). This aspiration has been lived out in practice through the participation of community members in the construction of these guiding principles. ISL in this context nurtures unconditional relationships, as demonstrated by the description of the 'core unit' of participating tutors and students and moral demands beyond the self, such as developing understanding of how to support communities in resource-poor communities. In fact, the work of ISL programmes at LHU, including the development of guiding principles for international volunteering, amounts to the development of a shared understanding of the good life and what is worth doing as described earlier.

Chapter 4 will raise some of the complex ethical questions of which ISL practitioners and researchers must be mindful. The notion of authenticity, understood as reciprocity, provides a lens through which to ask a series of questions related to the ethics of ISL. For example, who are the primary beneficiaries of this activity in practice? Is service-learning, as organised by universities and other educational institutions, self-serving? Does this practice exacerbate existing inequalities and power imbalances? ISL practised as a new form of colonialism comprising exploitative relationships that objectify overseas partners is clearly indicative of inauthenticity and will be explored in the 'barriers to' sections that conclude each of chapters 6, 7 and 8.

(Authenticity as) worldliness

> ... when I did get out there wasn't that much of a culture shock until I arrived back in this country, and that's when it all dawned on me the things that we have and the things that we take for granted.
>
> (Vanessa, ISL participant in 2007 in Brazil)

Worldliness as it is understood here is not antagonistic to the ecumenical foundation of LHU and does not represent a form of secularisation as encapsulated in Martin Luther's doctrine of the two kingdoms of God (Tappert, 1580/1959). This book, as demonstrated in the conceptual discussion in Chapter 1, does not dichotomise material and spiritual worlds. Rather than being interpreted as a departure from God, this idea of worldliness is better understood in relation to the work of theologians such as Dietrich Bonhoeffer, who asked believers to live a worldly life committed to social justice (Bonhoeffer, 1953/1997), Thomas Aquinas who had earlier related Christianity to Aristotle's 'affirmation of the concrete and sensuous reality of the world' (Pieper, 1991: 49), and most recently the field of liberation theology. It is an understanding of worldliness that requires Christians to be in the world, as in both present and engaged, but not of it, through resisting adulation of that which lacks spirit (John 17: 14–15, *The Jerusalem Bible*).

LHU states that it has a role in the formation and flourishing of graduates with the attributes required by the world of work but also to do the 'work of the world' (LHU, 2011). This is consistent with Newman's idea of a university:

> If then a practical end must be assigned to a University ... I say it is that of training good members of society. Its art is the art of the social life, and its end is fitness for the world.
>
> (Newman, 1852/1959: 191)

Through ISL the authentic self is connected to a broader social, cultural and historical context. This pedagogical approach exposes students to complex contemporary global issues such as interdependence, social injustice and environmental degradation through direct personal experience. Communities around the world become important sites for learning.

Authenticity as worldliness is not congruent with the internationalisation of higher education as it has been seen to perpetuate education for global competitiveness, but rather with internationalism emphasising education for global cooperation. At the same time, worldliness is antithetical to paternalistic, charitable relationships which reinforce dependence and unequal power relations. From this view, ISL can usefully draw upon the radical principles of Catholic social teachings in order to be both 'counter-cultural and critical' (Engebretson, 2009).

An understanding of authenticity as worldliness reiterates the social aspects of authenticity. Through their involvement with ISL, students begin to envision and act towards solutions to 'bigger-than-self' problems. They begin to problem-pose in relation to issues that are not yet fully understood. Individuals develop authenticity through these practices and at the same time nurture communities and societies that promote and value authenticity.

Authenticity as worldliness emerges as students are 'disencumbered by other voices' (Barnett, 2007: 46). Through ISL, students must relate not only to particular or significant others but also with their understanding of the general other. Through encountering and engaging with the worldview of others, students not only look at the world differently but can begin to recognise and understand the lens through which they themselves view the world. They more fully appreciate that 'we don't see things as they are, we see things as we are', a quotation attributed to French born writer Anaïs Nin which exposes not only the limitations of one's own worldview but also the rich possibilities for engaging with others.

Conclusion

To conclude this section, I illustrate how selfhood, reciprocity and worldliness are overlapping aspects of authenticity that are central to learning in this context. For higher education to promote authenticity as selfhood and reciprocity, it cannot be primarily concerned with instrumental relationships that subserve personal fulfilment. For example:

> The part of the philanthropist is indeed a dangerous one; and the man who would do his neighbour good must first study how not to do him evil, and must begin by pulling the beam out of his own eye.
> (MacDonald, 1895/2010: 69)

In particular, it is only through others that our own authenticity can be realised. The authentic self is both shaped by and shapes society. Through personal growth, social change is made possible as worldliness emerges. This is intimated within the guiding principle for ISL at LHU, which includes the statement that 'we recognise that service to others is an important dimension in the spiritual dimension of individuals and institutions' (Bamber, 2008: xiii).

As Part III will further testify, selfhood, reciprocity and worldliness are not conceived as separate atomistic aspects of authenticity but constitutive and mutually dependent elements of the whole.

Segue

Part I has provided a conceptual frame for rethinking transformative learning in relation to a particular notion of authenticity. This analysis, it is argued here, points towards an embryonic notion of an 'ethical ecology of transformative learning'. This will be explicated further in Part IV following the detailed analysis of the student experience of ISL in Part III. The term 'ecology' is increasingly being used as a prefix or suffix to denote theories with a systemic or holistic nature, such as in human ecology, political ecology and social ecology. While a limited number of scholars have related learning to ecology (Bronfenbrenner, 1979; Wenger, 1998; Siemens, 2003; Blewitt, 2006), a definition of any ecology of learning has on the whole proven to be elusive.

Etymologically, ecology means study of home. Its origins are in the word 'okologie' which in turn was derived from the Greek 'oikos' meaning 'house, dwelling place, habitation'. The ecology metaphor of learning is illustrative here since in becoming authentic the learning self becomes at home with itself and able to 'dwell'. Relating ecology, or study of home, to transformative pedagogy is not an original idea. The hospices where boys studying at the University of Paris in the thirteenth century learned and lived under a communal rule were known, among other names, as pedagogies. Pedagogy was understood here to be a home that, through attending to the intellectual and spiritual formation of students, nurtured the transformative dimensions of learning as discussed here.

The notion of ecology evinces growth, fragility, evolution, sustainability, continuity and discontinuity as explicated in the foregoing analysis. These ideas are deployed in Chapters 6, 7 and 8 to help understand learning in the context that is the focus of this inquiry. As Part I has demonstrated, as a theory of learning, transformative learning itself has its own ethical ecology: a way of reinventing itself through connecting to other learning theories with a focus on the ethical.

The terminology of 'ecology of transformative learning' is suggestive of the interwoven levels of learning with which the learning self is engaged. This comprises the three dimensions of authenticity introduced here, of worldliness, reciprocity and selfhood, which are isomorphic with three ecological levels or registers of 'the environment, social relations and human subjectivity' (Guattari, 2008: 19–20), as outlined by the social theorist Felix Guattari in his exigent call to rebuild the relationship between the subject and its exteriority.

Central to the idea of an ethical ecology of learning is that the learning self and our understanding of learning develop relationally through interconnectivity. Just as Bateson (1973) noted that the fundamental unit of evolution was not the organism but the organism plus environment, the learning self is understood here as being inseparable from the relations through which it both forms and is formed. Furthermore, in an ethical ecology of transformative learning, the learning self develops a responsibility and value orientation towards these interconnections. In a similar vein to the ideas of 'deep ecology' it 'seeks to expand notions of the self beyond the confines of ego and personal history, and to extend concepts of self-interest to include the welfare of all beings' (Macy, 1991: xvii). Through an ethical ecology of transformative learning, the learning self acts not only in individual but collective interests. It seeks to enhance the well-being of each aspect of the world upon which it may have an effect. This is particularly pertinent to service-learning, where participating educators seek to solve issues relating to poverty and social injustice. Part II sets out to further contextualise this study and begins with analysis of the key concepts and practices in International Service-Learning.

References

Adorno, T. (1973) *The Jargon of Authenticity*. Guernsey: Guernsey Press Co. Ltd.
Appiah, K.A. (2005) *The Ethics of Identity*. Princeton: Princeton University Press.
Bamber, P. (2008) Introduction. In Bamber, P., Clarkson, J. and Bourke, L. (eds) *In Safe Hands: Guiding Principles for International Service-Learning*. Stoke on Trent: Trentham, viii–xxiii.
Barnett, R. (2007) *A Will to Learn*. Maidenhead: Open University Press/SRHE.
Barnett, R. (2011) *Being a University*. Oxon: Routledge.
Bateson, G. (1973) *Steps to an Ecology of Mind*. Chicago: University of Chicago Press.
Blewitt, J. (2006) *The Ecology of Learning: Sustainability, Lifelong Learning and Everyday Life*. London: Earthscan.
Bonhoeffer, D. (1953/1997) *Letters and Papers from Prison*. New York: Touchstone.
Bronfenbrenner, U. (1979) *The Ecology of Human Development: Experiments by Nature and Design*. Cambridge, MA: Harvard University Press.
Brook, A. (2009) The Potentiality of Authenticity in Becoming a Teacher. *Educational Philosophy and Theory* 41 (1): 46–59.
Buber, M. (1953) *I and Thou: The Philosophy of Relationship*. London: Routledge.
Cranton, P. (2001) *Becoming an Authentic Teacher in Higher Education*. Malabar: Kriegar.
Cranton, P. and Carusetta, E. (2004) Developing Authenticity as a Transformative Process. *Journal of Transformative Education* 2 (4): 276–93.
Dewey, J. (1934) *Art as Experience*. New York: Perigee Books.
Engebretson, K. (2009) Called to be Holy: The Transformative Potential of Christian Service Programmes in Catholic Schools. *Journal of Beliefs and Values* 30 (2): 193–204.
Giddens, A. (1991) *Modernity and Self-Identity: Self and Society in the Late Modern Age*. Cambridge: Polity Press.
Guattari, F. (2008) *The Three Ecologies* (2nd Edition). London and New York: Continuum.
Guignon, C. (2004) *On Being Authentic*. Oxon: Routledge.
Heidegger, M. (1927/1962) *Being and Time* (trans. J. Macquarrie and E. Robinson). Oxford: Blackwell.
Heidegger, M. (1930/2005) *The Essence of Human Freedom* (trans. T. Sadler). London: Continuum.
Heidegger, M. (1951/1971) Building, Dwelling, Thinking. In Heidegger, M., *Poetry, Language, Thought* (trans. A Hofstadter). New York: Harper & Row.
Jarvis, P. (1992) *Paradoxes of Learning: On Becoming an Individual in Society*. San Francisco: Jossey-Bass.
Kreber, C. (2010) Courage and Compassion in Striving for Authenticity: States of Complacency, Compliance and Contestation. *Adult Education Quarterly* 60 (2): 177–98.

Kreber, C., Klampfleitner, M., McCune, V., Bayne, S. and Knottenbelt, M. (2007) What Do You Mean by 'Authentic'? A Comparative Review of the Literature on Conceptions of Authenticity. *Adult Education Quarterly* 58 (1): 22–43.

Liverpool Hope University (LHU) (2011) About Liverpool Hope University. Accessed 12 July 2011 at www.hope.ac.uk/about-hope/about-liverpool-hope-university.html.

Liverpool Hope University (LHU) (2015) Liverpool Hope University Mission and Values. Accessed 28 August 2015 at www.hope.ac.uk/lifeathope/welcome/theliverpoolhopestory/missionandvalues/.

MacDonald, G. (1895/2010) *Lilith, a Romance*. Los Angeles: IndoEuropean.

MacIntyre, A.C. (1984) *After Virtue: A Study in Moral Theory* (2nd Edition). London: Duckworth.

Macy, J. (1991) *Mutual Causality in Buddhism and General Systems Theory: The Dharma of Natural Systems*. Albany: State University of New York Press.

Mulhall, S. (2005) *Routledge Philosophy Guidebook to Heidegger and Being and Time*. London: Routledge.

Newman, J.H (1852/1959) *The Idea of a University*. New York: Image Books.

Norton, L. (2009) *The Learning, Teaching and Assessment Strategy for Taught Undergraduate Degree 2009–2012*. Unpublished document. Liverpool Hope University. Accessed 12 October 2014 at www.hope.ac.uk/learningandteaching/lat.php?page=strategy&current=strategy.

Pieper, J. (1991) *A Guide to Thomas Aquinas*. San Francisco: Ignatius Press.

Plumb, D. (2008) Learning as Dwelling. *Studies in the Education of Adults* 40 (1): 62–79.

Ream, T.C. and Ream, T.W. (2005) From Low-Lying Roofs to Towering Spires: Toward a Heideggerian Understanding of Learning Environments. *Education Philosophy and Theory* 37 (4): 585–97.

Robeyns, I. (2005) The Capability Approach: A Theoretical Survey. *Journal of Human Development* 6 (1): 93–114.

Scharmer, C.O. (2009) *Theory U: Leading from the Future as it Emerges*. San Francisco: Berrett Koehler.

Siemens, G. (2003) Learning Ecology, Communities and Networks: Extending the Classroom. Accessed 12 February 2012 at www.elearnspace.org/Articles/learning_communities.htm.

Tappert, T.G. (ed.) (1580/1959) *The Book of Concord: The Confessions of the Evangelical Lutheran Church*. Philadelphia: Fortress Press.

Taylor, C. (1989) *Sources of the Self: The Making of the Modern Identity*. London: Harvard University Press.

Taylor, C. (1991) *The Ethics of Authenticity*. London: Harvard University Press.

Walters, D. (2008) Existential Being as Transformative Learning. *Pastoral Care in Education* 26 (2): 111–18.

Wenger, E. (1998) *Communities of Practice: Learning, Meaning, and Identity*. New York: Cambridge University Press.

Part II
International Service-Learning

4 Key concepts and practices in International Service-Learning

Introduction

Service-Learning (SL) is a pedagogical activity that seeks to blend student learning with community engagement and the development of a more just society. International Service-Learning (ISL) programmes have grown as educational institutions and non-governmental organisations have sought to achieve the goal of developing 'global citizens'. SL and ISL provide policy makers with a practical response to their quest for a 'Big Society' and present alluring pedagogical approaches for universities as they react to reforms in higher education and seek to enhance both the student learning experience and graduate employability. However, SL in general and ISL in particular remain deeply under-theorised.

This chapter commences a detailed exploration, which is progressed in Chapter 5, of the context of this study into transformative learning: ISL at a university with a Christian foundation in the UK. It begins with an outline of the emergent pedagogical practice of SL, in particular where this takes place across countries in ISL. Recognising the problematic nature of this educational endeavour, an original definition of ISL is provided that seeks to ensure the ethical integrity of this work. This will be followed by a discussion of recent policy and practice in higher education as it relates to SL. A particular focus is placed upon developments in the UK and USA. The chapter concludes by considering the role of SL and community engagement within faith-based education, addressing calls for discussion around pedagogical approaches underpinning counter-cultural and critical service programmes aligned with the radical principles of the Catholic social teaching (Engebretson, 2009).

Service-Learning

SL integrates community service with the curriculum: a pedagogical approach that emphasises learning as opposed to teaching and draws on theorists who have proposed that we learn through combinations of thought and action, reflection and practice, theory and application (Aristotle, 1941; Dewey, 1938; Kolb, 1984; Schön, 1983). Crucially, SL allows students to reflect upon their experiences, knowledge and understanding of community issues within a structured framework of learning. This provides the opportunity for educators to draw on real world contexts and develop analytical and problem solving skills related to a student's discipline. Definitions of SL are contested in the USA and internationally. 'Service' itself has multiple connotations including the spiritual and religious alongside consumerist notions of service delivery. For some, 'service to others' such as volunteering is of primary importance while for others this service is secondary to an 'academic strategy' which emphasises student learning.

> SL is a form of experiential education in which students engage in activities that address human and community needs together with structured opportunities intentionally designed to promote student learning and development. Reflection and reciprocity are key concepts of service-learning.
> (Jacoby, 1996: 6)

Kolb's experiential learning cycle, including the four phases of concrete experience, reflective observation, abstract conceptualisation and active experimentation, is grounded in the work of Dewey and has provided a foundation for the development of the SL field. SL is based upon cycles of reflection and action, where learning is distinct from 'knowing': in SL, 'knowing' and 'doing' are deemed to be inextricably linked. SL is therefore an active learning approach informed by social constructivist theories of learning: whereby the components of service and learning reinforce and complement each other.

SL provides students with first-hand exposure to complex contemporary issues and the opportunity to explore solutions to these problems: linking the curriculum directly to the students' experience of service. It is an approach to education underpinned by values of service to others, mutuality, empowerment and community development.

For each distinctive interpretation of the term, a plethora of SL programs exist in practice at all levels of education – most notably in the USA, where there has been a significant movement towards models of SL as an extension of the notion of volunteerism over the last half century. In the 1960s, a group of loosely connected practitioners began to explore the integration of community service and academic learning. The involvement of college students with community action was propelled by the launch of Volunteers to Serve America in 1965 and the Peace Corps in 1961. This reflected a concern among wider civil society for ameliorating poverty, as evidenced by the existence of thousands of community action groups at around this time. In 1971, the Community Action Partnership was established to strengthen and represent this network, advocating for policy that addressed social injustice. A concern for what I have termed 'service apathy' (Bamber and Pike, 2013) among citizens in general, and college students in particular, along with an awareness of the development of an individualistic society less concerned with the common good, led to the development of Campus Compact in 1985 and a subsequent growth in SL activity.

National Campus Compact supports colleges and universities to promote public and community service that develops students' citizenship skills and helps campuses forge effective community partnerships. By 2015 it had over 1,100 campus members, with the organization claiming that students on SL programmes completed 6.6 million service hours during 2014. The growing extensity of this SL activity was buttressed by at least two other concurrent developments in higher education: a new impetus for active-learning strategies in undergraduate education and a renewed acknowledgement of the public roles and responsibilities of American higher education, captured in Boyer's notion of the 'scholarship of engagement' (Boyer, 1996):

> The scholarship of engagement means connecting the rich resources of the university to our most pressing social, civic, and ethical problems, to our children, to our schools, to our teachers, and to our cities.
> (Boyer, 1996: 19–20)

SL has therefore gained prominence in American higher education in a short space of time, where John Dewey's pragmatism, Boyer's engaged scholarship and most recently Robert Putnam's concern for the decline in social capital have provided a firm foundation for theorists and practitioners.

In the UK, the recent National Citizen Service and Step up to Serve initiatives have been promoted as bringing a 'double benefit' of improving non-cognitive skills and employability among young people through building and sustaining the good society. The ambitious target set by the 2015 Conservative government is for over 60 per cent of all young people to take part in high quality social action by 2020. The economic benefits of service programmes in America (Belfield, 2013) have been used to justify this intervention. Furthermore, to promote service within formal education in the UK, a cross-party political think-tank has proposed the introduction of a performance measure for schools titled the 'GiveBacc' that would publicise the number of students who had completed 50 hours of 'good quality social action' (Birdwell *et al.*, 2015). These initiatives have been complemented by investment in International Citizen Service, which by August 2015 had already seen 6,750 young people aged between 18 and 25 complete volunteering internationally, as a form of ISL.

International Service-Learning

In International Service-Learning (ISL), students use their skills and knowledge to make a distinctive contribution to partner communities overseas and have a commitment to learn from their engagement in this activity and immersion in their new context. This is an ambitious endeavour with rich possibilities for personal, interpersonal and social learning. For instance, the experience of the unfamiliar through ISL creates the possibility of rendering the familiar strange. At the same time, T.S. Eliot eloquently alludes to the possibilities of reconnecting with ourselves and sense of time and place following a period of such 'exploration':

> We shall not cease from our exploration
> And the end of all our exploring
> Will be to arrive where we started
> And to know the place for the first time.
> (Eliot, 1944: 48)

Through ISL communities in diverse contexts across the world become sites of learning for students as they participate in programmes that attempt to solve issues relating to poverty and social injustice. This presents a number of putative problems such as the proclivity to exploit through propagating a form of new colonialism that demands further interrogation if educators are to avoid exacerbating the social inequities they seek to address. ISL presents educational opportunities with complex ethical considerations.

The emergent pedagogical approach of ISL has been recently defined as:

> A structured academic experience in another country in which students (a) participate in organized service activity that addresses identified community needs; (b) learn from direct interaction and cross-cultural dialogue with others; and (c) reflect on the experience in such a way as to gain further understanding of course content, a deeper understanding of global and inter-cultural issues, a broader appreciation of the host country and the discipline, and an enhanced sense of their own responsibilities as citizens, locally and globally.
> (Bringle and Hatcher, 2011: 19)

Drawing upon the analysis of transformative learning from Part I, this book offers an original and innovative definition of ISL that recognises its transformative potential and ensures its ethical integrity. It is argued ISL can be better understood as a form of ecological engagement with aesthetic, moral and spiritual dimensions that is enacted through participation in the lives and 'worlds' of those living in different countries, and which enables ethical reflection, enhances personal efficacy, and seeks to engender a more just and sustainable society.

> I have been reading stories to the children. They don't always understand what I'm saying, but they love the time and special attention I give them. They also loved the stickers we gave them – our games made a difference from them working through the textbook.
> (E-mail from the author to his family and friends during his first experience teaching in India)

Indeed, evidence of the unexpected negative outcomes of well-meaning development projects in the South (developing world) has led to the conclusion that such interventions reinforce power imbalances (Chambers, 1997). This occurs through patronising approaches and use of resources which cannot be sourced locally, as illustrated in the above example. On a macro level, aid packages have been provided conditional on developing countries adopting economic and structural adjustment. Locally and more subtly, certain approaches to solving problems have been imposed by organisations from the North (developed world), often unknowingly, without consideration of indigenous solutions:

> Rarely is local people's knowledge taught, or their understanding of their world. The reality and understanding that are imprinted are alien and other, introduced from outside and above. So normal teaching transfers not just knowledge but a structured reality; and that is reality as defined through hierarchies based in the cores of power and wealth.
> (Chambers, 1997: 62)

The allure of the opportunity to travel to remote locations off the tourist trail while making a contribution to disadvantaged communities is demonstrated by the proliferation of organisations offering young people from the North volunteering opportunities in the South. The 'voluntourism' industry includes 'gap year' companies accountable to young people as consumers of a product which offers exposure to other cultures, adventure and a life-changing experience that is rarely defined or evaluated. These organisations have been accused of operating without reflection on their impact and the experience they offer young people and exploiting the communities they seek to serve (*Observer*, 2011). Private companies along with non-government and third sector organisations also operate in this field of work, supporting a multitude of initiatives.

> The Tibetan people are wonderful. To see the children so happy says so much. They Indians are friendly but they do try and rip you off.
> (E-mail from the author to his family and friends during his first experience teaching in India)

My own diary entries and e-mails during my own first experience teaching in India expose an excruciating naivety. They include profound generalisations, as in the extract above, which echo traveller tales of the exotic. With hindsight, I focused on the differences, rather than similarities, between others and myself. Reflection upon my own experience has sensitised me to the dangers of returned volunteers, acting as advocates for international volunteering, perpetuating and reinforcing stereotypes with their friends, family and perhaps even young people they are teaching. A failure to learn from experiences such as ISL was however identified by St Augustine, who lived from 345–430 AD:

> Yet men go out and gaze in astonishment at high mountains, the huge waves of the sea, the broad reach of rivers, the ocean that encircles the world, or the stars in their courses. But they pay no attention to themselves.
>
> (Augustine, 377/1961: 216)

An appreciation that the anticipated outcomes for young people do not automatically result from time spent overseas has driven calls for regulation of the international volunteering sector in the UK. This is reflected in the development of codes of practice for international volunteering organisations (NIDOS, 2009). Nevertheless, the UK government's International Citizen Service (ICS) recruitment campaign in 2015 implored young people to 'Challenge yourself to change the world', propagating the idea that well-meaning but inexperienced youngsters can impact positively on the development of resource-poor communities. To recalibrate such initiatives towards what participants learn, a more appropriate strap-line would perhaps be 'Change yourself to change the world'.

A particular concern is that young people lack the capacity to act upon any new-found understanding of social injustice (Bourn, 2008: 12). This view has underpinned policy and practice such as 'active citizenship' (Crick, 2002) in schools and Oxfam's claim that young people become global citizens when they are 'willing to act to make the world a more equitable and sustainable place' (Oxfam, 2006: 3). While the dominant perspective in development education policy and practice has emphasised increased engagement and discrete actions, it has recently been acknowledged that this 'can mask the importance of the learning processes and the complex relationships between learning and behaviour' (Bourn and Brown, 2011: 5).

A growing number of individuals, particularly from developed countries, have enjoyed the opportunity of an international educational experience. Although traditionally these took place over a semester or a full year, their duration is now often much shorter and they are no longer confined to the most affluent students. For example, a number of teacher education projects in the UK include the opportunity to observe alternative educational systems overseas during brief study trips during their postgraduate training. In the USA, participation in international study programmes tripled from 1985 to 2000 (Parker and Dautoff, 2007). There are clearly differences between study abroad and ISL: the latter emphasises reciprocal learning, contrasting with the view that the students themselves are the principal beneficiaries.

Concepts that have developed as central to SL, such as reflective practice, cultural understanding and exposure through immersion, are all pertinent to enhancing the student experience of study abroad. A growing list of countries exposed to SL concepts and practices has led to calls to combine a period studying abroad with SL in this new context (Parker and Dautoff, 2007). For example, in India many universities have established social involvement programmes (Bamber et al., 2009) that complement disciplinary study. Similarly in Europe, science shops established in the 1960s involve students conducting research on behalf of community organisations.

A growth in SL research (Strait and Lima, 2009; McIlrath and Mac Labhrainn, 2007) is demonstrated by the success of the International Association for Research on Service-Learning and Community Engagement. This group has held an international conference annually since 2001 that is attended by delegates from many countries including Argentina, Nicaragua, India, the Philippines, Australia, UK, Ireland, as well as the USA and Canada. At the same time the *Michigan Journal of Community Service Learning* has included two special issues on Global Service-Learning and the website www.globalsl.org has been established to collate evidence-based tools and peer-reviewed research to advance best practices in ISL. As regards practice, the International Partnership for Service-Learning and Leadership (IPSL) also operates semester-long and summer programmes in over a dozen countries in both the North and South (Tonkin, 2004).

Crabtree (2008) proposes a series of theoretical foundations and empirical traditions through which we can better understand the political and intellectual context for ISL and resultant learning outcomes for students. His article is a reminder that while literature on ISL is relatively recent, it has considerable roots in other conversations such as International Education and Cross-Cultural Communication. To this list should be added Development Education, Postcolonial theory, Community Based Research, Character Education and Education for Citizenship to name but a few. While the literature presents a broadly positive picture of the student experience of ISL, there has been very little research conducted into the role of community partners overseas.

Despite substantial anecdotal evidence of the transformative nature of an overseas experience there remains a paucity of research into the exact nature of this learning. First-hand exposure to other cultures opens up an eclectic range of learning opportunities, such as language learning, cross-cultural awareness, personal transformation and growth and the creation of a worldwide horizon. Pusch, for example, explores the continuum from ethnocentric to ethnorelative attitudes as experienced by ISL participants (2004). Parker and Dautoff conclude with a plea for future research to help us understand how both ISL and study abroad can 'enhance feelings of personal connections to others and promote actions reflective of global citizenship' (2007: 49). Echoing the discussion of relational aspects of knowing in Chapter 2, Crabtree concludes that regardless of whether ISL is 'conceptualised as teaching, development work, or a movement for social justice' (2008: 29), we must become more attuned to the relational aspects of ISL and other community-based learning experiences. The following quote, attributed to Lilla Watson, an Australian aboriginal woman, captures the spirit of reciprocity underpinning this approach to ISL:

> If you have come to help me you are wasting your time. But if you have come because your liberation is bound up with mine, then let us work together.
>
> (Watson, 1985)

This provokes us to consider the predispositions and intentions of those who become engaged in ISL activity. That ISL is an increasingly popular strategy among school and college students before they reach the age of 18 raises questions of young people's readiness for this experience. At the same time scholars have noted a recent phenomenon whereby individuals may bypass a sense of responsibility within their own local and national communities to take action on the global stage:

> It is insufficient, however, to feel and express a sense of solidarity with others elsewhere if we cannot establish a sense of solidarity with others in our own communities, especially those others whom we perceive to be different from ourselves.
> (Osler and Starkey, 2003: 252)

There is a risk of perpetuating the notion of a 'globe-trotting elite' (Bamber, 2011a: 57) for whom education in general, and higher education in particular, provides 'a passport to global citizenship'. Martha Nussbaum, however, famously promoted the idea that people can simultaneously have multiple identities and attachments, describing a 'world citizen' (1996) as someone who confesses an interest in and acts upon concerns for both distant strangers as well as next-door neighbours. That increasingly mobile populations identify with diverse local and national groupings across the world, suggests the ideals of state and world citizenship are in fact compatible.

Cosmopolitanism challenges the notion of a zero-sum equation of loyalty, instead arguing the individual can identify simultaneously with religious, cultural, local, national and international communities. Cosmopolitan citizenship is therefore defined as incorporating local, national, regional and global aspects of citizenship:

> Importantly, it is based on a feeling of belonging and recognition of diversity across a range of communities from the local to the global. It is a practice involving negotiation, equitable resolution of differences and work with others to promote freedom, justice and peace within and between communities.
> (Osler and Starkey, 2005: 78)

This understanding of cosmopolitanism challenges the myth of elitism associated with global citizenship that states it is only those who have travelled widely and interacted with diverse cultures that can claim to be citizens of the world.

Service-Learning and higher education

It is increasingly recognised that higher education not only catalyses critical thinking but contributes towards the personal development of both staff and students. It nurtures important relationships between individuals, groups and the wider community in multiple ways. For example, universities play a role in widening participation to groups previously excluded from such opportunities; students from diverse backgrounds study together; universities assume roles both in their local community and on the world stage that demand building partnerships with diverse stakeholders; universities educate professionals such as teachers and social workers, who play an ethical role as advocates of particular aspects of relationships. Walker, therefore, concludes that university education can now be understood to comprise a 'three dimensional triad contributing to rich personal development and fulfilment, vocational preparation and economic opportunities, and a democratic dimension of educated citizenry' (2009: 3). SL in higher education can enhance these personal, interpersonal and academic outcomes for students. This may include enhanced student employability, greater engagement with an academic discipline, a more thoughtful approach to knowledge, changes in personal efficacy and the development of critical thinking and problem solving (Tonkin, 2004: 17).

SL initiatives are not as extensive or substantial in the UK, although engagement of the university with the local community is not a new development. The original university settlement house, Toynbee Hall in London, was established in 1884 and became the basis of the settlement movement that swept England and the USA, inspiring Dewey through his association with Hull House, a settlement house in Chicago, in the late 1890s. In the last two decades of the nineteenth century, students from Oxford and Cambridge universities came to Toynbee Hall during their vacation to work among the poor of the city. In the words of its founder, Anglican clergyman Samuel Barnett, the teachers came 'to learn as much as to teach; to receive as much to give'. Well over a century later, Barnett's words are echoed by students returning from an ISL experience:

> I think we all went thinking we were doing something fantastic, and we probably did do something fantastic, but not as much as what . . . the effect it had on us.
>
> (Angela, ISL student participant, Sri Lanka, 2005)

In terms of policy, attempts to formalise community engagement in the UK are very recent. The terms of reference for the National Committee of Inquiry into Higher Education acknowledged the broader aims of higher education and its role in educating citizens:

> Higher education continues to have a role in the nation's social, moral and spiritual life; in transmitting citizenship and culture in all its variety; and in enabling personal development for the benefit of individuals and society as a whole.
>
> (NCIHE, 1997: Appendix A)

Although this group claimed higher education was critical to the development of a 'democratic, civilised and inclusive society' (NCIHE, 1997: 72), the subsequent Dearing Report has been criticised for ignoring these moral aspects by concentrating much more on instrumental processes. Dearing argued that the challenge for higher education is to build a framework in which the academic disciplines can flourish but students are able to develop key skills and capabilities to function in our changing global society. It suggested work- and community-based learning in order to improve student chances of gaining employment on graduation. Nevertheless, the UK government's response to Dearing, in the green paper 'The Learning Age', apparently recognised the intrinsic value of holistic education:

> As well as securing our economic future, learning has a wider contribution. It helps make ours a civilised society, develops the spiritual side of our lives and promotes active citizenship. Learning enables people to play a full part in their community. It strengthens the family, the neighbourhood and consequently the nation. It helps us fulfil our potential and opens doors to a love of music, art and literature. That is why we value learning for its own sake, as well as for the equality of opportunity it brings.
> (DfEE, 1998: foreword)

Significantly, the New Labour government from 1997 to 2010 adopted a higher education policy of massification and amongst other initiatives introduced tuition fees, league tables and student satisfaction surveys. During their undergraduate experience students are now more likely to work part-time and be dependent on family and friends for financial support, leaving little time for more traditional student activity: an image of the student far removed from that of social activist. The UK government's white paper of 2003, 'The Future of Higher Education' (DfES, 2003), explored the implications of the globalisation of higher education, and the need for innovation in teaching and learning, but failed to address the issue of the civic role of universities (Annette and McLaughlin, 2005: 85).

The new orthodoxy of functional education policy to buttress the knowledge economy was reaffirmed in the report of the Leitch Review of Skills, 'Prosperity for all in the Global Economy' (Leitch, 2006). The DfES international strategy for education, skills and children's services, titled 'Putting the World into World Class Education' (DfES, 2004), also emphasised the pivotal role higher education has to play in ensuring Britain remains competitive in the global skills and knowledge marketplace. This strategy aimed to maximise economic advantage for the UK in an increasingly globalised world. Arguably, it promotes assumptions of cultural supremacy where its model for development is accepted as universal. The underlying goal of any associated education for global citizenship could only serve to 'empower individuals to act according to what has been defined for them as development or an ideal world' (Andreotti, 2006: 124). These policy developments, when considered alongside other initiatives such as the introduction of tuition fees, have had important consequences for the role of the university in the community in the UK.

At the same time, the Russell Commission (2005) advocated developing an ethos of volunteering, understood as 'planned, non-obligatory, pro-social activities to benefit another person, cause or group' (Penner, 2004: 646) across all phases of formal education in the UK. Participation in community activities is known to confer economic and social benefits to both the individual and society. This was supported, until 2007, through the Higher Education Active Community Fund that promoted community engagement and encouraged staff and student involvement with activities that promoted social inclusion such as volunteering.

The introduction of a consumerist framework to higher education in the UK mirrors the 'modernisation' programme of public services. It has been justified in higher education by the desire to increase numbers and maintain quality of provision. The impact on fundamental aspects of higher education can be envisaged: the nature of the curriculum, equality of opportunity, participation, quality of teaching and learning, the profile of the academic and our understanding of the role and purpose of education itself. For example, while free access to higher education was seen as an entitlement by previous generations, it is now seen by some as a good investment by the individual and central to enhancing employability. Some universities have already announced that they are considering awarding students of any subject extra marks for demonstrating 'corporate skills' or job experience. From this view;

> It is hard to see education as a process by which students seek to understand themselves and the world they inhabit, and easier to see it as a form of learning for self-promotion and trophy hunting.
>
> (Lauder *et al.*, 2006: 50)

Ironically, the implementation of the recommendations of the Browne Review into the future of Higher Education in the UK (Browne, 2010) has increased pressure on institutions to consider the role of pedagogical approaches such as (I)SL that will enhance the student learning experience and improve graduate employment rates. As it stands, higher education's perceived obligation to develop civic agency is not high on the public's agenda (Saltmarsh *et al.*, 2010: 395). Universities are more widely understood as market-driven institutions existing for the private economic benefit and upward mobility of individuals as opposed to being social institutions fostering the public good. Students are increasingly likely to go to university to secure future employment rather than to develop their civic agency.

A small-scale study before the introduction of tuition fees showed that undergraduates did not tend to see themselves as individual customers and investors in self (Ahier *et al.*, 2003: 119). This research is now worthy of repeat and may not present findings as we expect. It is notable that institution-wide volunteering initiatives that have been developed focus primarily on enhancing graduate employability. For example, the University of Bristol recently launched the 'PLuS award' whereby students who gain professional and life skills through involvement in locally based extra-curricular events and activities receive an extra-curricular qualification. This initiative values work experience equally to voluntary community action. Manchester Leadership Programme attempts to combine academic study with local volunteering through offering a series of academic units, although these are run by the Careers & Employability Division as opposed to being discipline-based.

The emphasis on 'active citizenship' in UK education parallels developments in the USA, and is reiterated in David Cameron's calls to mobilise the 'Big Society'. The focus recently has been on political participation (voting) rather than SL. There has, however, been a substantial increase in the number of students in higher education accessing volunteering opportunities within their local community and abroad. The initiatives developed to date by UK HEIs are primarily extra-curricular and concerned with graduate employability as detailed above.

ISL exposes the overlapping nature of the 'internationalisation' and 'internationalism' of higher education (Stromquist, 2007; Jones, 2000). While the latter emphasises ethical notions such as 'international community, international cooperation, international community of interests, and international dimensions of the common good' (Jones, 2000: 31), the former is seen to refer to 'greater international presence by the dominant economic and political powers, usually guided by principles of marketing and competition' (Stromquist, 2007: 82). ISL prepares citizens to function in a multicultural society and a global economy through activity that seeks to support the disadvantaged and is therefore a pedagogical approach whose motives and outcomes serve to blur the distinction between what could be described as education for global cooperation and education for global competiveness. This demands a critical approach when one considers that humanitarian crises have been used to justify the 'internationalisation' of higher education.

Critics of community engagement initiatives are concerned by any perceived moves away from the critical thinking associated with research and teaching to the pragmatics of developing a sense of cohesion within society that is generated through establishing reciprocal relationships which arise through partnerships within the community at home and abroad (Sullivan, 2006). It has been claimed that education for democracy and citizenship has historically been seen as the responsibility of the school system in the UK and an irrelevance to higher education (Annette and McLaughlin, 2005: 76). Byron (2000) suggested that faith-based HE institutions in the UK are more likely to build upon the foundations of compulsory education for citizenship within the secondary school curriculum. Disregarding the role of SL in challenging social injustice, Annette (2010) argues that SL should be instrumental to challenging students to think and act politically in a way that volunteering alone does not necessarily do. To date initiatives to this end within HE have not been investigated in any detail either in the USA or UK.

The limitations of research in two particular areas will be addressed through this study. First, although an increasing number of academics are arguing for higher education to take a more substantive role in promoting civic renewal (Crick, 2002), research activity in this area is minimal (Annette, 2010). Second, it has been argued (Naidoo and Jamieson, 2006) that an enduring limitation in relation to the social theory of higher education is that 'researchers have tended to conceptualise institutions of higher education in an overly homogenous way' (2006: 884). The experience of faith-based institutions in particular is worthy of further investigation in relation to their response to the introduction of consumerism and the commodification of learning. This study has been undertaken at a university with an ecumenical foundation as detailed in Chapter 5.

Service-Learning and faith-based education

There has been a renewal of interest in the integration of faith and learning in schools, colleges and universities (Pike, 2010; Green and Cooling, 2009). While many international volunteering and gap year programmes in the UK would distance themselves from the deliberate inculcation of values, it is a significant oversight to write about SL without considering the virtues that it might foster (Bamber, 2011b). Christianity certainly emphasises the individual being or becoming a certain sort of person (if asked to define virtuous behaviour, Aristotle would say that it is what the virtuous man does):

> the mission of a Christian University recognises that there is an attempt to inculcate certain 'faith-based' values. True education must include training in the virtues. A moral sensitivity requires cultivation.
> (Markham, 2004: 8)

(I)SL has the potential to close the gap between the instrumental/utilitarian and the practical/vocational that is characteristic of the liberal–vocational dichotomy. The combination of a university education and completion of a period of service provides a powerful model for inculcating the virtues, strengthening the relationship between higher education and the public good (Nixon, 2011). Newman, for instance, conceived of university education grounded in the liberal ideal of the pursuit of knowledge for its own sake yet did not deny the role of the universities in preparing graduates to serve society:

> It is the [university] education which gives a man a clear conscious view of his own opinions and judgments, a truth in developing them, an eloquence in expressing them, and a force in urging them. . . . It prepares him to fill any post with credit and to master any subject with facility. It show him how to accommodate himself to others, how to throw himself into their state of mind, how to bring before them his own, how to influence them, how to come to an understanding with them, how to bear with them. He is at home in any society, he has common ground with every class; he knows when to speak and when to remain silent; he is able to converse and able to listen; he can ask a question pertinently, and gain a lesson

> seasonably . . . He has the repose of a mind which lives in itself, while it lives in the world, and which has resources for its happiness at home when it cannot go abroad. . . . He has a gift which serves him in public.
>
> (Newman, 1852/1959: 191–2)

Catholic universities have been particularly influenced by Newman's philosophy. Adrian distinguishes between such institutions in the USA that focus on 'peace and justice education and support for the poor' from those that 'reaffirm traditional Catholic teachings' (Adrian, 2003: 27–8). Indeed, while religious education at its best can be a place of transformative encounter, it can also contribute to unhelpful depictions of an estranged other (Lundie and Conroy, 2015). Sullivan challenges a presumption that Church affiliation necessitates a dogmatic and intransigent mindset intent on evangelisation. Instead he proposes that combining an 'unashamed, indeed confident, Church affiliation with openness and inclusiveness towards others who see things differently, should be an important feature of a Christian University' (Sullivan, 2004: 20). This view is consistent with philosophers who have argued that faith-based schooling is compatible with forms of democratic education if it is characterised by 'openness with roots' (McLaughlin, 1996: 147).

Sullivan goes on to assert that Christian activity includes 'offering service to those in need and thereby facilitating liberation from diverse forms of entrapment' and 'entering into dialogue with fellow Christians, with unbelievers or with people from other faiths' (2004: 27). This is one way the Christian university can become the 'critic and conscience of society' (LHU, 2007: 1) in relation to how these activities are understood and enacted as culture and society change and priorities shift. Sullivan reasserts this outward facing aspect:

> A Christian University should play a part in discerning the signs of the times, in critiquing the surrounding culture, in calling into question the categories of interpretation, its yardsticks for evaluation and the leading metaphors that shape its thinking.
>
> (Sullivan, 2004: 27)

Such understanding led a Jesuit academic writing of service in Catholic schools to conclude that this activity must be 'counter-cultural and critical' (Gerics, 1991: 261), having the capacity to not only lead to personal growth through selfless volunteerism but uncovering a 'further dimension of social analysis and criticism'. Although a guiding principle for SL may echo Jesus' words 'In so far as you did this to the least of my brothers, you did it to me' (Matthew, 25:40, *The Jerusalem Bible*), acts of charity, or noblesse oblige, do not necessarily equate with a commitment to justice (Lavery, 2007; Gerics, 1991). This view is reflected in SL research that distinguishes between the service paradigms of 'charity' and 'social change' (Morton, 1995). ISL providers, in particular those with a faith orientation, must be as aware as those in the South of the history of the North's relationship with the developing world:

> First you came to us as missionaries, then you came to us as colonizers, now you come to us as volunteers.
>
> (Tselha Thakchoe, Principal, Tibetan Homes Foundation,
> Rajpur, India in conversation with a team
> of LHU staff and student volunteers)

Christian service must be understood not as paternalistic and charitable works but as the work of social transformation aligned with the radical principles of Catholic social teaching (Engebretson, 2009: 194). This is congruent with Mitchell's conceptualisation of 'critical' SL (Mitchell, 2008) and Walker's call (2009) for university education to involve an alliance of the capability approach and critical pedagogy detailed in Chapter 2. There is an urgent need to understand pedagogical approaches that catalyse such transformation in practice. It should be recognised that this is likely to demand initiating staff and students into 'modes of critical enquiry that recognise the potential importance of what may appear to fall outside the framework of the authoritative' (Nixon, 2011: 98). This in turn demands opening up the institution itself to potential discord:

> Service programs can be important elements in educating for justice and also in clarifying the mission of the sponsoring institution, but the quest for justice may take institutions along unexpected avenues.
>
> (Gerics, 1991: 264)

Conclusion

As detailed in this chapter, the marketisation of higher education has renewed focus on graduate employability. Rather than being a 'view from nowhere', this represents a particular philosophy of education (Arthur, 2008). Of particular interest to this study is the development within faith-based formal education of market approaches, for example propagating education for global competition, that are dissonant with the values and mission of such institutions. It has been claimed that religiously affiliated HEIs are more likely to promote community involvement and SL as unique features of their mission than more substantive definitions of their religious identity (Arthur, 2008: 198–200). Responding to calls to investigate 'mission integrity' (Grace, 2003: 161) within faith-based education, this book considers both the 'intended' and 'experienced' ethos (McLaughlin, 2005: 313) of a university in the UK. This begins in the following chapter with a portrait of Liverpool Hope University, the institution which is the focus of this study.

References

Adrian, W. (2003) Christian Universities in Historical Perspective. *Christian Higher Education* 2 (1): 15–33.

Ahier, J., Beck, J. and Moore, R. (2003) *Graduate Citizens? Issues of Citizenship and Higher Education*. London: RoutledgeFalmer.

Andreotti, V. (2006) A Postcolonial Reading of Contemporary Discourses Related to the Global Dimension in Education in England. Unpublished doctoral thesis. University of Nottingham.

Annette, J. (2010) The Challenge of Developing Civic Engagement in Higher Education in England. *British Journal of Educational Studies* 58 (4): 451–63.
Annette, J. and McLaughlin, T. (2005) Citizenship and Higher Education in the UK. In Arthur, J. (ed.) *Citizenship and Higher Education: The Role of Universities in Communities and Society*. New York: RoutledgeFalmer, 74–95.
Aristotle (1941) Nicomachean Ethics and Poetics. In McKeon, R. (ed.) *The Basic Works of Aristotle*. New York: Random House, 935–1126.
Arthur, J. (2008) Faith and Secularisation in Religious Colleges and Universities. *Journal of Beliefs and Values* 29 (2): 197–202.
Augustine (377/1961) Book X. In *Saint Augustine: Confessions* (trans. R.S. Pine-Coffin). Middlesex: Penguin, 207–52.
Bamber, P. (2011a) Educating for Global Citizenship. In Gadsby, H. and Bullivant, A. (eds) *Global Learning and Sustainable Development*. London: Routledge, 56–75.
Bamber, P. (2011b) The Transformative Potential of International Service-Learning at a University with a Christian Foundation in the UK. *Journal of Beliefs and Values* 32 (3): 343–59.
Bamber, P. and Pike, M. (2013) Towards an Ethical Ecology of International Service-Learning, *Journal of Curriculum Studies* 45 (4): 535–59.
Bamber, P., Bignold, W. and D'Costa, C. (2009) The Impact of Social Involvement and Community Engagement on Students in Higher Education in India and the UK: A Comparative Study. *Journal of the World Universities Forum* 2 (4): 3–16.
Belfield, C. (2013) *The Economic Value of National Service*. Aspen Institute Franklin Project. Accessed 1 August 2015 at www.voicesforservice.org/resources/Sep19_Econ_Value_National_Service.pdf.
Birdwell, J., Scott, R. and Reynolds, L. (2015) Service Nation 2020. London: DEMOS. Accessed 1 August 2015 at www.demos.co.uk/publications/service-nation-2020.
Bourn, D. (2008) Introduction. In Bourn, D. (ed.) *Development Education: Debates and Dialogues*. London: Institute of Education, 1–17.
Bourn, D. and Brown, K. (2011) Young People and International Development: Engagement and Learning. London: Development Education Research Centre. Accessed 4 August 2015 at www.ioe.ac.uk/EngagementAndLearning.pdf.
Boyer, E. (1996) The Scholarship of Engagement. *Journal of Public Service & Outreach* 1 (1): 11–21.
Bringle, R. and Hatcher, J. (2011) International Service Learning. In Bringle, R., Hatcher, J. and Jones, S. *International Service Learning: Conceptual Frameworks and Research*. Virginia: Stylus, 3–28.
Browne, J. (2010) Securing a Sustainable Future for Higher Education: An Independent Review of Higher Education Funding and Student Finance. Accessed 4 August 2015 at www.bis.gov.uk/assets/biscore/corporate/docs/s/10-1208-securing-sustainable-higher-education-browne-report.pdf.
Byron, W.J. (2000) A Religious-Based College and University Perspective. In Ehrlich, T. (ed.) *Civic Responsibility*. Phoenix: The American Council on Education/The Oryx Press, 279–93.
Chambers, R. (1997) *Whose Reality Counts? Putting the First Last*. London: ITDG.
Crabtree, R. (2008) Theoretical Foundations for International Service-Learning. *Michigan Journal of Community Service Learning* 15 (1): 18–36.
Crick, B. (2002). *A Note on What is and What is Not Active Citizenship*. Accessed 4 August 2015 at http://repository.excellencegateway.org.uk/fedora/objects/import-pdf:15186/datastreams/PDF/content.
Department for Education and Employment (DfEE) (1998) The Learning Age: A Renaissance for a New Britain. Accessed 5 August 2015 at http://dera.ioe.ac.uk/15191/.

Department for Education and Skills (DfES) (2003) *The Future of Higher Education*. Accessed 4 August 2015 at http://image.guardian.co.uk/sys-files/Education/documents/2003/07/09/Finalreport.pdf.

Department for Education and Skills (DfES) (2004) *Putting the World into World Class Education*. London: HMSO.

Dewey, J. (1938) *Experience and Education*. New York: Collier Books.

Eliot, T.S. (1944) Little Gidding. In Eliot, T.S. *Four Quartets*. London: Faber & Faber, 39–48.

Engebretson, K. (2009) Called to be Holy: The Transformative Potential of Christian Service Programmes in Catholic Schools. *Journal of Beliefs and Values* 30 (2): 193–204.

Gerics, J. (1991) From Orthodoxy to Orthopraxis: Community Service as 'Noblesse Oblige' and as Solidarity with the Poor. *Religious Education* 86 (2): 250–65.

Grace, G. (2003) Educational Studies and Faith-Based Schooling: Moving from Prejudice to Evidence-Based Argument. *British Journal of Educational Studies* 51 (2): 149–67.

Green, E. and Cooling, T. (2009) *Mapping the Field: A Review of the Current Research Evidence on the Impact of Schools with a Christian Ethos*. London: Theos.

Jacoby, B. (1996) *Service-Learning and Higher Education: Concepts and Practices*. San Francisco: Jossey-Bass.

Jones, P. (2000) Globalization and Internationalism: Democratic Prospects for World Education. In Stromquist, N. and Monkman, K. (eds) *Globalization and Education: Integration and Contestation across Cultures*. Boulder: Rowmann & Littlefield, 27–42.

Kolb, D. (1984) *Experiential Learning: Experience as the Source of Learning and Development*. Upper Saddle River: Prentice Hall.

Lauder, H., Brown, P., Dillabough, J.A. and Halsey, A.H. (eds) (2006) *Education, Globalization and Social Change*. Oxford: Open University Press.

Lavery, S. (2007) Christian Service Learning. *Journal of Religious Education* 55 (1): 50–3.

Leitch, S. (2006) *Prosperity for All in the Global Economy–World Class Skills*. London: HM.

Lundie, D. and Conroy, J. (2015) 'Respect Study' the Treatment of Religious Difference and Otherness: An Ethnographic Investigation in UK Schools. *Journal of Intercultural Studies* 36 (3): 274–90.

Liverpool Hope University (LHU) (2007) Corporate Plan 2007–2011. Unpublished document.

McIlrath, L. and Mac Labhrainn, I. (2007) *Higher Education and Civic Engagement: International Perspectives*. Hampshire: Aldgate.

McLaughlin, T. (1996) The Distinctiveness of Catholic Education. In McLaughlin, T., O'Keefe, J. and O'Keefe, B. (eds) *The Contemporary Catholic School: Context, Identity and Diversity*. London: Falmer Press, 135–54.

McLaughlin, T. (2005) The Educative Importance of Ethos. *British Journal of Educational Studies* 53 (3): 306–25.

Markham, I.S. (2004) The Idea of a Christian University. In Astley, J., Francis, L., Sullivan, S. and Walker, A. (eds) *The Idea of a Christian University*. Milton Keynes: Paternoster Press, 3–13.

Mitchell, T. (2008) Traditional vs. Critical Service-Learning: Engaging the Literature to Differentiate Two Models. *Michigan Journal of Community Service Learning* 14 (2): 50–65.

Morton, K. (1995) The Irony of Service: Charity, Project Development, and Social Change in Service-Learning. *Michigan Journal of Community Service Learning* 2 (1): 19–32.

Naidoo, R. and Jamieson, I. (2006) Empowering Participants or Corroding Learning? Towards a Research Agenda on the Impact of Student Consumerism in Higher Education. In Lauder, H., Brown, P., Dillabough, J. and Halsey, A.H. (eds) *Education, Globalization and Social Change*. Oxford: Oxford University Press, 875–84.

National Committee of Inquiry into Higher Education (NCIHE) (1997) *The Dearing Report: Higher Education in the Learning Society*. London: Department for Education and Employment.

Network of International Development Organisations in Scotland (NIDOS) (2009) International Volunteering Organisational Code of Practice. Accessed 4 August 2015 at www.nidos.org.uk/sites/default/files/IV_COP_VolCharter.pdf.

Newman, J.H. (1852/1959) *The Idea of a University*. New York: Image Books.

Nixon, J. (2011) *Higher Education and the Public Good*. London: Continuum

Nussbaum, M. (1996) *For Love of Country: Debating the Limits of Patriotism*. Boston: Beacon.

Observer (2011) Students Given Tips to Stop Gap-Year Travel Becoming a 'New Colonialism' for Rich West. 31 July.

Osler, A. and Starkey, H. (2003) Learning for Cosmopolitan Citizenship: Theoretical Debates and Young People's Experiences. *Educational Review* 55 (3): 243–54.

Osler, A. and Starkey, H. (2005) *Changing Citizenship: Democracy and Inclusion in Education*. Maidenhead: Open University Press.

Oxfam (2006) *Education for Global Citizenship: A Guide for Schools*. Oxford: Oxfam.

Parker, B. and Dautoff, D. (2007) Service-Learning and Study Abroad: Synergistic Learning Opportunities. *Michigan Journal of Community Service Learning* 13 (2): 40–53.

Penner, L.A. (2004) Volunteerism and Social Problems: Making Things Better or Worse? *Journal of Social Issues* 60 (3): 645–66.

Pike, M.A. (2010) Christianity and Character Education: Faith in Core Values? *Journal of Beliefs and Values* 31 (3): 311–21.

Pusch, M. (2004) A Cross-Cultural Perspective. In Tonkin, H. (ed.) *Service-Learning across Cultures: Promise and Achievement*. New York: The International Partnership for Service Learning and Leadership, 103–30.

Russell Commission (2005) *A National Framework for Youth Action and Engagement. Executive Summary to the Russell Commission*. Russell I.M.

Saltmarsh, J. (1996) Education for Critical Citizenship: John Dewey's Contribution to the Pedagogy of Community Service-Learning. *Michigan Journal of Community Service Learning* 3 (1): 13–21.

Saltmarsh, J., Hartley, M. and Clayton, P. (2010) Is the Civic Engagement Movement Changing Higher Education? *British Journal of Educational Studies* 58 (4): 391–406.

Schön, D. (1983) *The Reflective Practitioner: How Professionals Think in Action*. New York: Basic Books.

Strait, J. and Lima, M. (eds) (2009) *The Future of Service-Learning*. Virginia: Stylus.

Stromquist, N.P. (2007) Internationalization as a Response to Globalization: Radical Shifts in University Environments. *Higher Education* 53 (1): 61–105.

Sullivan, J. (2004) University, Christian Faith and the Church. In Astley, J., Francis, L., Sullivan, S. and Walker, A. (eds) *The Idea of a Christian University*. Milton Keynes: Paternoster Press, 14–34.

Sullivan, J. (2006) The Idea of a University Revisited. Accessed 5 August 2015 at http://facstaff.elon.edu/sullivan/version.pdf.

Tonkin, H. (ed.) (2004) *Service-Learning Across Cultures: Promise and Achievement*. New York: The International Partnership for Service-Learning and Leadership.

Walker, M. (2009) Critical Capability Pedagogies and University Education. *Educational Philosophy and Theory* 42 (8): 898–917.

Watson, L. (1985) Aboriginal Activists. Speech given to United Nations Decade for Women Conference in Nairobi Kenya, 15–26 July 1985.

5 Investigating the student experience of International Service-Learning

Introduction

This chapter seeks to further contextualise the conceptualisation of transformative learning developed in this book through focus upon the particular university and associated ISL programme that provides the basis for this investigation. Liverpool Hope University (LHU) is a British university which has a rich tradition of ISL and a strong Christian identity, both historically and in the present day. This chapter begins with a portrait of LHU that explores how the mission and ethos of this institution has informed and sustained international service activity over the last three decades. It proceeds to outline the methods underpinning the four phases of this investigation into ISL upon which this book is based, from 2006 to 2011, highlighting a small number of related methodological issues pertinent to transformative learning research. This chapter concludes with the narratives of two ISL participants. These accounts highlight different experiences of ISL, the role of the background and biographies of participating students and the ongoing impact of volunteering overseas on their lives. These two accounts serve to introduce the reader to the data that provides the basis for Chapters 6, 7 and 8, providing an initial insight into the framework for transformative learning that is developed in Part III.

International Service-Learning at Liverpool Hope University

LHU, situated in the north-west of England, is a relatively small British university: the 115th largest Higher Education Institution (HEI) out of 165 when measured by total student numbers. The foundations and driving force of this ecumenical institution lie in a Christian mission to tackle poverty and reduce inequality through education. In 1844, the Church of England established the Warrington Training Institution, which served what was, at that time, the radical vocation of training elementary school mistresses. In 1855 the Sisters of Notre Dame, moved by the plight of a huge number of malnourished and uncared for children arriving in Liverpool because of the Irish Potato Famine, set up a school and orphanage in the city. A year later they established Our Lady's Training College in the city: the only institution in England where Catholic girls could be trained as elementary teachers.

In 1979, under the umbrella of Liverpool Institute of Higher Education (LIHE), the leadership of the Catholic and Anglican Church in Liverpool amalgamated Christ's College and Notre Dame (which were both Catholic colleges) and St. Katharine's (which was formerly Warrington Training Institution). It was only a few years later that Sister Maureen O'Carroll, then Deputy Principal of Christ's and Notre Dame College, secured funding from the College's Academic Board to encourage staff involvement in overseas development projects. She was driven by a belief that we must raise awareness of issues of social injustice by learning from the developing world through a process of 'conscientisation', whereby individuals reflect and act upon issues of justice and peace (Paterson, 2008). The Department of Divinity already had links with a school in Zimbabwe and the first project involved a member of staff from Christ's and Notre Dame College supporting this school with English language skills training.

Since then, over 1,000 staff and students have volunteered to support educational development projects in resource-poor communities overseas as depicted in Figure 5.1. This activity was first supported at LIHE by the 'World Development Studies Centre' and 'Third World Development Group'. The 'Ladakh Project' was awarded the Queen's Anniversary Prize for Higher Education in 1996 for its work teaching and training in India for Tibetans. Having attained university title in 2005, the work has continued at LHU under the auspices of 'Hope One World' and 'Global Hope'. During this time, overseas partners have included Tibetan Children's Villages (TCV) in India; SOS Children Sri Lanka; Department for Education, Kwa Zulu Natal, South Africa; and the Sisters of Notre Dame in Nigeria: each with distinctive missions and

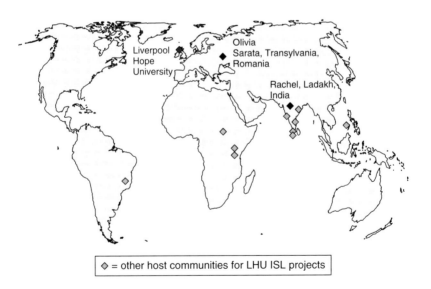

Figure 5.1 Map of ISL projects at LHU

models for working that have provided rich and diverse contexts for staff and student learning. For example, SOS provide an inclusive model for supporting orphaned and dispossessed children and the TCV motto is 'Others Before Self'. As the number of students participating in such projects has increased, the value of such experiences for participants from the UK has been explicitly recognised. A set of guiding principles were developed that highlighted the importance of relationships, reciprocity and mutual learning to this practice at LHU (Bamber et al., 2008).

The theological virtues of faith, hope and love, in addition to the cardinal virtues of prudence, temperance, justice and fortitude, provide an important ethical framework for LHU, as an institution with a Christian foundation seeking to serve wider society (LHU, 2011). These virtues have not only personal but also social and civic dimensions: they are both self- and other-regarding. Certainly 'love' in the senses of 'agape' (often used to describe the love of Christ for humanity), 'storge' (familial love) and 'philia' (brotherly love) between students and partners overseas might become a foundation to which ISL in such a context could subscribe. A degree of congruence is also apparent as the virtues of 'faith', 'love' and 'hope', which appear on the LHU crest and provide the foundations for the university's mission and values (LHU, 2015), also appear to be underpin the development of cardinal virtues which are good for everyone (regardless of faith).

As introduced in the final section of Chapter 4, there has been a renewal of interest in the integration of faith and learning in schools, colleges and universities, and LHU, under its current Vice-Chancellor, has recently reasserted its Christian distinctiveness, for example through targeted recruitment within the faith sector, building on the fact that it is the only HEI with an ecumenical foundation in Europe (LHU, 2007a). Glanzer (2008) concludes that LHU is the only Church-affiliated HEI in the UK which has reached a point of 'critical mass' in relation to its Christian identity and that it rightly boasts of being 'one of the most mission-explicit Christian institutions in British higher education' (2008: 176). He also provides strong evidence to contest Arthur's claim (2008) that community engagement activity, such as ISL, usurps religious identity in the profiles of Christian universities in the UK. For instance, Glanzer's research outlines how LHU leaders identified the support given to co-curricular forms of international service as only one of five ways that LHU exhibits its Christian distinctiveness (Glanzer, 2008: 176).

In 2008, LHU established an extra-curricular Service and Leadership Award (SALA) to recognise student service in local and global contexts. The LHU award is the only such HEI award to date in the UK that includes 'service' in its title. Leaders within LHU identify service-activity as contributing to 'intentional efforts to sustain and strengthen its Christian identity' (Glanzer, 2008: 179). Nevertheless, the SALA documentation does not make explicit connections between the award and formal spiritual or religious education.

Interestingly, the SALA, the umbrella programme for ISL activity at this institution, is facilitated by the university's careers service. The SALA contributes towards meeting the strategic institutional goal of increasing opportunities for all students to have an international experience in order to enhance the student experience and employability rates. The introduction of the SALA raises a series of practical and philosophical questions, such as whether the giving of an 'award' complicates notions of altruism that have traditionally been associated with 'volunteering'. Other issues include acknowledging informal volunteering (such as caring for a family member) and debates around the role of service within the compulsory curriculum.

LHU has sought to balance the promotion of skills that are sought by employers alongside attributes that are important to life in a humane, educated democracy. An aspiration to care for students and create a collegial atmosphere with excellent student services is not necessarily distinctive of a Christian university in a secularised higher education sector. Nevertheless, a desire to be 'market-informed, rather than market-driven' (LHU, 2007a: 4), has been reflected in the university's website section on 'what makes LHU different':

> We do not believe that education is just about equipping people for the world of work; we also educate students for the work of the world. We believe that only students educated within a global context can constructively, fairly and bravely make the changes the world needs.
>
> (LHU, 2011)

The 'work of the world' reveals an aspiration to catalyse personal growth that makes social change possible. This is reflected in the visioning statement of the Faculty of Education, which states: 'the guiding orientation of the Faculty is to develop educational thought and practices which promote education as a humanising influence on each person and on society locally, nationally and internationally' (McGettrick, 2010: 2).

In other corporate documentation however, a desire to secure graduate employability morphs into an aspiration to create global citizens that live out the mission of the institution:

> The experience [of studying at LHU] will equip a Hope graduate to be an informed, confident global citizen with the appropriate skills and attributes sought by employers.
>
> (LHU, 2007a: 6)

> Faculties should consider how they can more effectively serve the needs of students and their future employability by creating better opportunities for student volunteering and experiential learning within the formal academic structures. It is arguable that all students should acquire basic skills in global citizenship.
>
> (LHU, 2007b: 7)

These excerpts from publicity and corporate documents illustrate the overlapping practices of education for global cooperation and global competitiveness, as discussed in the previous chapter.

Establishing the SALA has reinvigorated the focus at LHU on students, rather than community partners, as the primary beneficiaries of volunteering activity. Proponents of this approach to ISL argue they also bring about social change through changing the attitudes of participating students, although this may not be what the students themselves expect to be the outcome of such activity:

> And yet in our world everybody thinks of changing humanity, and nobody thinks of changing himself.
>
> (Tolstoy, 1900: 29)

Of course, educators seeking to 'transform' students must be cognisant of another set of ethical considerations which this study attempts to address: in what ways are they seeking to transform? What are the consequences for students in the short and longer term of adopting this dramatic approach to education? What is the role of partners overseas in this learning process?

The strap-line adopted for ISL by LHU, 'Making a Difference, Changing Lives', is ambivalent as regards the purpose of this work. Like SL programmes elsewhere, this is suggestive of an attempt to balance a broad range of sometimes competing outcomes. While some students are primarily motivated to participate in ISL by a desire to support communities in the developing world, others have been frustrated by sterilised experiences as tourists and see ISL as an opportunity to experience other cultures first-hand and 'live like the locals do' over a period of time. The complexity of these motivational factors, alongside a failure to develop mutuality, has led to SL initiatives being criticised as hypocritical and labelled as 'self-serving'. Certainly, the LHU strap-line for ISL only implicitly acknowledges the importance of reciprocity to this endeavour: the contribution made by those in the North in supporting partners in the South and also the impact of this experience on students from the UK.

This investigation into the student experience of ISL

In order to better understand transformative learning, this research project investigated how LHU students described their ongoing experience of ISL. Through interpreting student descriptions of their experience of ISL, this study sought to analyse features of the transformative learning process in this context and understand the potential for transformative learning outcomes. Given the focus on learning processes and outcomes associated with ISL, this research was concerned with the implications of findings for professional practice (Radnor, 2001), in particular how ISL is constructed in higher education policy and practice.

90 International Service-Learning

Table 5.1 Overview of data collection

Phase	Method	Number of research participants	Date of data collection	Year of ISL experience
1	Semi-structured, intensive interviews	7	March 2007	1993, 1999, 2001, 2003, 2004, 2005
2	Structured grouped interviews	16	March 2008	Summer 2007
3	Semi-structured, biographical interviews	6	May 2009	Summer 2009
4	Focus groups	5	June 2010	Summer 2009

Data was collected across four phases as detailed in Table 5.1. The first phase comprised unstructured interviews with a small purposeful sample (Patton, 2002: 46) of seven returned volunteers in 2007. This drew on the existing database of all 124 students who had completed ISL at LHU between 1990 and 2006 and attempted to include student participants from projects across a range of locations and years. The final sample comprised students who had participated in these projects in 1993, 1999, 2001, 2003, 2004 (2) and 2005. The skew towards recent years was due to over half of the 124 LHU students having had their overseas experience since 2002 and inevitably the contact information held was more accurate for those who participated most recently. The students in the sample had volunteered with LHU in the following project locations: Malawi (2), Tibetan communities in India, Brazil, Sri Lanka, non-Tibetan communities in India, and South Africa. Five of the seven students were now teaching in schools and two were working in other educational settings. Two of the students were mature students when they studied at the university and took part in ISL. The overseas placement for these students ranged from two-and-a-half to seven weeks in length.

The second phase involved structured interviews with all 16 students who undertook projects in 2007. This included all of the above locations and a new project in Nigeria. The final phases included narrative-biographical interviews with six participants prior to departure in 2009, followed by a focus group with the same students one year after re-entry in June 2010. A full mapping of data collection is provided in the Appendix. This approach sought to be iterative in nature in that each phase informed the development of that which followed. The form of data collected and the means for collecting it were adapted to fit emergent themes and ideas as my searchlight on the nature of the ongoing experience of ISL shifted. Phase one and two revealed the extent to which the orientation, disposition and understanding of all research participants was deeply informed by aspects of their own lives. Phases three and four of research therefore explored in greater depth the backgrounds of selected students who choose to apply for places on ISL projects. Collecting data prior to their overseas experience and upon their return provided an opportunity to capture shifts in the way students describe service work, volunteering and community engagement.

Data collection and analysis have been complemented by ongoing observations of ISL in the field. Data analysis has involved phenomenological description (Van Manen, 1990; Groeneweld, 2004) and constant comparative thematic analysis (Cresswell, 2007: 64), followed by a critical, hermeneutical analysis (Allman, 1999). In this book, all quotations are taken from this qualitative data, however, rather than present a detailed systematic presentation of findings, the purpose is to engage in theory-building and work towards an ethical ecology of transformative learning.

Research that began as a case study of ISL at LHU evolved into a conceptual study of transformative learning drawing upon the particular example of ISL. Collecting data relatively early on in this study created a space to attend to a dialectical relationship between text from the interviews, my own experiences, wider reading and data analysis. It provided the time and distance required for me to develop my own understanding of transformative learning as a process of becoming with aesthetic, relational and tacit dimensions. While distinctions have been made between theory coming in *a priori* or *a posteriori*, this research has drawn upon theoretical insights at each stage of the research process.

While theory and empirical data play a pivotal role in this study, they are not its primary drivers. For example, this study does not attempt to elucidate any one particular theory of transformation nor does it seek solely to provide a description of the student experience of ISL in their own words. Being fundamentally hermeneutical, it seeks to understand how the student experience of ISL is embedded in 'larger and often hidden positions, networks, situations and relationships' (Charmaz, 2006: 130). It aims to develop understanding of how the experience of ISL is conceptually grounded and the rich interconnectivity between these concepts. It is the objective of this study to elicit from student transcripts a conceptual framework for understanding transformative learning through ISL that provides an impetus for the formulation of future theory. In this sense, the study on which this book is based has been concept/theory generating rather than being theory-driven.

Recognising the limitations and salience of my own experiences volunteering internationally, from 2001 to 2003 in Papua New Guinea and in shorter placements in India and Malawi in 2000, 2004, 2005, 2007 and 2010, a number of strategies were used to break free of a hermeneutic circle and keep my own habits of mind and being open and responsive. The methodology outlined above incorporated the construction of an autobiographical account that interrogated and made explicit my own positionality in relation to the values and assumptions underpinning this research. Furthermore, data was analysed through a process of contrastive inference to ensure it was not only gathered to validate a preconceived framework. This approach is supported by a propensity to keep an enquiry alive, remain open to new perspectives and resist closure of particular ideas. In addition I completed a structured discussion of interim findings with researchers and practitioners in the fields of education and global learning, that helped inform the model between phases of research.

This iterative and reflective process nurtured the organic development, rather than imposition, of crucial relationships between the emergent concepts.

The methodology guiding this research innovatively combined a number of strategies to create an 'imaginative interpretation' of transformative learning that 'sparks new views and leads other scholars to new vistas' (Charmaz, 2006: 181). For example, this study purposefully scrutinised the interaction between context and the nature of learning itself. The modes of authenticity of selfhood, reciprocity and worldliness were found, as detailed in Chapter 3, to be intrinsic to the institutional scenario and specific arena of practice that provides the context for this study: an established International Service-Learning (ISL) programme at a university in north-west England. Allowing the conceptual framework to emerge from the contextual analysis is an innovative methodological device that may be deployed usefully in diverse research contexts.

Narratives of ISL participants

Part II concludes with the narratives of two ISL participants, who volunteered in Romania and India as depicted in Table 5.1 above. Rachel was married with a family before she embarked on a teaching qualification in 1992. It is now over 20 years since she first visited the Tibetan community in north India. Among the research participants in this study, Olivia volunteered most recently, in rural Romania in 2009. She took her place at university following her study of A levels and a gap year. These particular accounts have been selected because they highlight different experiences of ISL, the role of the background and biographies of participating students and the ongoing impact of volunteering overseas on their lives. The rationale for their selection was not that these accounts are representative of students who undertake ISL at LHU or indeed of those who have participated in this study. Nevertheless, the accounts of other students do resonate with the two stories chosen here. The similarities regarding the structure of their ISL experience ensures these accounts could be described as synoptic. At the same time, the experience of students who participated in ISL in 1993 and 2009 lends further insight into the evolution of ISL practice over the last three decades, as discussed in Chapters 4 and 5.

While Chapters 6, 7 and 8 incorporate an interpretive commentary alongside a thematic analysis, the two narratives which follow have been included to enable the research participants to tell their stories in their own words. These narratives, together with Part III, enable an interpretation of the student experience through both the whole of the data and also in its separated parts. The stories of Rachel and Olivia presented here provide insight into the nature of ISL as a 'unity of experience' (Dewey, 1934: 10) and, through highlighting the multidimensions of the lives and multiple selves of the participating students, are testimony to 'the unity of a human life' (MacIntyre, 1984: 216) that provides the basis for the understanding of transformative learning developed in Part III.

Investigating the student experience of ISL 93

Figure 5.2 SOS Tibetan Children's Village, Choglamsar, Ladakh, India (photograph taken by the author, July 2004)

Rachel, SOS Tibetan Children's Village, Choglamsar, Ladakh, India, 1993

Some of my family had worked on the missions so volunteering overseas was something I had always wanted to do. I was very shy though and had only ever been on holiday to Magaluf before! I was a mature student, doing a teaching degree that I'd contemplated for many years. A friend told me she's seen a flyer up for Hope One World, and I thought 'I'd love to do that!'. I suppose the helping others, the doing something, the service bit was always there but I also liked the idea of an adventure. Being the type of person that I am, I thought, 'I'd never get on it!' but I went home and spoke to my husband, and he said 'Rachel, just go for it!'. I couldn't believe I got an interview! The only question I could think of asking at the end was 'what are the toilets like?' Caroline and Jim, two of the tutors, came up to me a couple of days later and said 'Have you looked in your pigeonhole?' and I was 'There's nothing in my pigeon hole!', and they said to me 'You're going!'. I was just absolutely amazed. From then on it was just talking to the family, my husband and two boys, and preparing them for it as well as me. I know I wanted an adventure, but I began to wonder 'What have I let myself in for?'

We travelled to the SOS Tibetan Children's Village in Choglamsar near Leh in northern India. I travelled out with another student, Gary, and the two tutors. They left us in Delhi to do a viability study for a new project in Dharamsala. We did a couple of tourist things like the Taj Mahal and Jaipura and I phoned home to speak to my mum just crying 'I hate it! I hate it!'. She said, 'when you get to the village you'll be alright'. And I was.

The plane to Leh from Delhi takes you over the Himalayas, the views are just breathtaking. We were there for six weeks in total. The first two weeks without the tutors were really difficult. The whole community were very welcoming, everyone would say hello, but I still felt lonely, very lonely. The school was less welcoming, perhaps as I was a female teacher. I was very ill for the first week, the doctor said it was due to stress and traumatic experience!

The SOS Village provides homes and education for orphaned and dispossessed children, in this case Tibetan refugees who have crossed the Himalayas from Tibet, often leaving their family behind. There were 20 of them living in home number ten where I stayed under the care of their Ami-La ('mother'). The youngest child was five and the eldest was 18. The children do experience the closeness of a family in the SOS village, that's why they call their houses 'homes'. It was very special living in such close contact with those children, seeing them going to school every day.

One night I got really, really upset, I couldn't stop crying. I suppose I was feeling sorry for myself and bored, having nothing to do except read. I was also missing my family. I felt so emotional being with those children, many who had given up their families for their education. They kept me going. Thankfully, an older student who had met tutors from Hope the previous year came to find us and he took us into the city and we met more people, that really broadened our horizons.

In the classroom, the children were more interested in you than preparing for their exams. It was very difficult to get them to settle down. They asked so many questions about my family, how many servants and yaks I had, how I got milk if I didn't have yaks, all those things really. The idea of a milkman who brings milk to the door or a machine that washes and dries clothes was not easy to explain! You started to realise what kind of view they had of the world. It really was only what they'd seen on TV and through Western and Hindi music. It felt important to try and change their view of the Western world, because they had this view that everyone was so wealthy.

One memorable thing was washing at the standpipe at the back of the home. I would wrap this huge towel round me and they would scream laughing because they'd never see anything like it – they didn't realise bath towels could be so big! Their underwear was made of heavier material than school trousers. I thought they must be too hot and they thought I couldn't possibly be warm enough. Nowadays they have pretty bras and things like that which they didn't have before.

Some things were particularly disturbing like seeing the teachers beat the children. It is their culture and who am I to question their culture. Thankfully I don't think they do that anymore. I was definitely out of my comfort zone in the classroom. It's not easy teaching when you are only one step ahead of the class! I had to go into Leh and find books on English Grammar to help me teach a lesson on the past participle. On their desks they'd have ink in a pot, and they were trying to write but they also put their bags on the desk! It used to drive me absolutely mad! I'd say 'First thing . . . put the bags on the floor!' And they'd look at me, 'The bags on the floor?', 'Yes, put the bags on the floor! Don't put the bags on the table! This is how we are working!'. They had never moved the furniture and held a discussion group. They were used to dictation and definitions.

The experience has had a huge impact on me. I always say I learnt more than the children ever did from just being there. I came home in the August and had to go away again in the April, I just couldn't settle, I was crying. My husband said 'Rachel, you're going to have to go back, just go back', and I went back and stayed for three weeks, came back on the Friday and did my finals on the Monday! Two years later my sons came out with us to Leh in our summer holiday. When they were going back to school that September all they asked for were new trousers and a jumper. Usually they had to have everything brand new; jumpers, shirts, shoes, top of the range bag! I just couldn't believe it – my husband was absolutely gob smacked! They went back the next year to asking for everything new though!!!

I have a better idea now of how best to help the school in Choglamsar. The year I went they'd taken lego; when we went back it was in the office in a glass case. They teachers there do enjoy the lecturers being there and they go away inspired, but then a lot of stuff they find it difficult to do in the classroom. I know now that they wouldn't tell you this at the time when you are working with them. They would see negative feedback as being very rude.

I couldn't see the point of going, and just coming home and forgetting about it. They became a second family, and I call them, and they call me, 'My second family'. I've been back to the village eight times since and each time we visit home number ten, and every time I just cry my eyes out! There is a different Ami-la now, and different children but it just evokes such wonderful memories. I keep in touch with most of them and have met some of them in Delhi and Dharamsala. I am always aware of the Tibetan cause, always reading up, keeping in touch. We have joined demonstrations led by the Free Tibet movement.

Since I have been home people have said I am much quieter, much more patient and more reflective. I am very aware of what we've got and how little those children had. At the same time, I have new hopes and dreams. I am no longer truly happy being here and always want to be there. My husband would say the same. I'm always at peace there, when we fly in, as soon as we get over those mountains, it's like I'm home. It's peace and tranquillity. And I can't explain it any better than that really. It's not just about being on holiday, it is living in that community, with the Tibetans, Ladakhis and Kashmiris – we've got some lovely Kashmiri friends there too!

I am less materialistic myself now, I always ask myself 'do I really need it?'. If I spend money, I think that was an awful lot of money to spend, I feel really guilty about it. In school now in the UK when your staff are saying 'Argh! We need this, we haven't got this or that!' And I just think, 'God, just get on with it. Can't you use something else?' I was always resourceful, but even more so now. And I said to some of them, 'you know some children go through school and they don't have a decent sheet of paper to write on!'

I would fundraise for TCV every year in my school in the UK if I could. I know SOS let you sponsor children but I suppose I have sponsored the 20 of them from home number ten in some way or another. I have kept that relationship with them. One of them had a baby so we bought them some things to help keep them warm in the winter. Another was struggling to get into teacher training so we sent him some money over to help him get along. I realise now that tourists and sponsors can have negative consequences. Sponsors travel half way round the world to go to the school and demand the child is brought out for photos to be taken. It can be very unsettling. You can't carry on teaching! All the children are looking out of the window. We were there one year when French tourists came and insisted the children do a cultural show for them. The children were brought out of classes and all the costumes were brought out – just for these French tourists!

Olivia, Sarata, Transylvania, Romania, 2009

I had just completed the first of a four-year course to become a Primary Teacher with a specialism in English Literature when I embarked upon my project in Romania. I grew up in Clayton-Le-Woods in Lancashire around 30 miles from Liverpool. I got an A, two Bs and a C (that's 400 points!) in my A levels in English Literature, Mathematics and Psychology.

College just wasn't a great experience for me. It was so impersonal. Previously, I had been to a Catholic high school where 'everyone would say hello' so I applied to Liverpool Hope because everybody seemed to know who you were. I took two years out after college that included three months travelling with my boyfriend Richard to Hong Kong, Singapore, Australia and New Zealand. I am quite a home girl so I have never done anything like that before. I don't think I could have done it the first time on my own. It made me more independent, but more dependent on Richard because we were doing things together. When we lived in Australia we lived with Richard's Dad who had been over there for 14 years. We didn't do touristy things, we did things that they did like food shopping and going to the park. It's made me want to do less touristy things and see the communities more, and how they live. Before that I was quite happy with just going on a beach holiday every year, and now I would rather go further afield and explore places.

Before I came to Liverpool Hope I volunteered at my local church each Sunday and as part of the charity St Vincent de Paul group at high school that raised money for supporting older members of the local community. We put on 'tea dances' for residents of local residential homes. I was worried at first about what other people would think of me doing these things. But soon I worried less: if you want to do something you should just go and do it! It helped satisfy a need I have to feel needed but overall I think it makes you a bit less selfish. When you are younger everything is about you, but I think doing things like that from that age helped me to be a bit more aware of others.

When I started at Hope, one of the tutors inspired me to volunteer locally teaching maths at Tranmere Football Club with children from quite a run-down area in Birkenhead. When I had worked with children before, it felt like the children couldn't want for anything. This was totally different. It was really good professional development: getting to know children from diverse backgrounds and letting them see a different side to me. I enrolled on the Service and Leadership Award at Hope. I had never really thought about going to Romania, but hearing from students who had been there before encouraged me to apply for the project.

I was nervous but excited. I knew that seeing children in poverty would be an emotional challenge but volunteering felt like a positive action, a way to give something back rather than just giving money. I had grown up in this safe little secure place, and even when we had been travelling I didn't feel unsafe, or far from my comfort zone. I also wanted to see how education works in similar or different settings, for example the 'teacher–student' relationship. I wanted to help others, and to see other people in other cultures and how they live because it's so different to mine.

The aim of our project was to show both the teacher and the children that they can learn through play. I knew we wouldn't be able to change the whole schooling system, but I wanted to show the teacher that it can be quite fun for them as well. I was also really looking forward to working with teenagers. I am fine if you put me in a room full of children, or a room full of babies, or toddlers, but I hoped this would develop my confidence working with different groups of people.

As we pulled out of the airport there was this big advert that said 'Expect the unexpected' – that just summed up the whole experience. Seeing that sign couldn't have been planned any better! Christian, who was the school teacher in Sarata we were working with, had lived there his whole life and now ran the village school on his own. I was really apprehensive when we met him. He is quite a stern looking man but when he smiles he just melts your heart. He made the whole trip. He made us feel so welcome. The first thing he said to us when we arrived was 'how can I make it better, what can you do to help, what am I doing wrong'. He couldn't speak English fluently so we used a translator. We really bonded one evening when he tried to get us to drink this local whisky drink Palinka. We didn't speak the same language but we just managed to know what each other was saying. We laughed that whole night!

There were 12 of us there from LHU including three staff and nine students. We all slept together in a small, dark and dusty disused room. We slept on airbeds and lilos and we just fitted in, eight that way, and four across this way. We had torches, and we would shut the door and lock ourselves in at night. If you had told me before that was the sleeping arrangements I wouldn't have gone. But I loved lying there and you know it was strange because I didn't think I would be like that.

I never was good with dirt and bugs but being in the forest there, the spiders seemed to be magnified. If I had seen a spider like that at home I would go 'Mum, Mum get the spider' and make a fuss, but there you just kind of snap out of it, other things are more significant. I have never felt like that before it was such a strange feeling, and it wasn't me, but it has changed me now here I have stuck like that . . . you see that there are bigger things. I suppose it's out of respect because that is their life.

It was quite an intense experience. You slept together, went to the toilet together, ate together, got dressed together, showered together, washed out of a bowl together. We did everything together but if somebody needed a bit of space you kind of read it, and they just would go and have a sit down somewhere. Keeping the journal really helped. In the evening we would discuss what was going well and how we felt about things. We said things you wouldn't say to other people. We talked about why we went there, what we liked, what we were a bit apprehensive about. It didn't feel strange to have conversations like that. There was one student who hadn't really been that happy and this really helped her. We were just very open with each other.

I remember, early one morning this lady arrived, dressed quite formally, knocking on the door of our sleeping room – which was a real mess.

She wanted to take us on a tour of the high school and make a speech to assembly. We had to rearrange things really quickly as we were supposed to be running an end of week show. In that situation, you can't really plan things, they just happen.

The main issue in the area was that children go out to work rather than go to school. Christian was so eager to change things, and get the children into school. He took them on a day trip to see a war memorial from the Peasant's Revolution. The faces when the children were out! They were so excited! The statue was quite run down but they were careful touching it. It just made me realise how lucky our children are – they take it for granted going out all the time.

There was one particular family we got to know that really made a deep impression on me. The parents would probably be in a mental hospital if they were over here and the lads would probably be in care. One wanted his picture taken with us. He was so embarrassed about the dirty clothes he was wearing and that fact he had lost a finger in his work as a blacksmith that he insisted on standing behind our entire group, with only his head in the picture.

My Dad is a non-practising Catholic and although my mum has not been christened she regularly goes to church. I go most Sundays and have always just enjoyed going to church, and I always have believed in God. It makes me feel safer and that's just a comfort for me I suppose. When we went to church in Sarata we had no idea what this priest was saying! When he stood up, we stood up and when he sat down we sat down, and it went on for so long. But everybody was just so focused and connected in the church, and I have no idea what they were praying for: but church was so important to them and they were very spiritual. It was important that they saw us go to church in Sarata and be a part of their culture and their community, and I think that made a real difference when we were there. For me this was normal, but for others, they weren't like this until they got to Sarata.

If I had heard someone else's stories of what we had seen I think I would have felt a lot of pity. But while we were there I didn't feel sorry for them. The way they live isn't what you are used to so you do get a bit sad. But that's how they live and in some respects they are a lot better off than us, families are a lot more important. I know they don't have a lot of things but they are happy, the children are happy.

We tried to include the Roma children and the teenagers as they didn't have much experience of school. Each day more and more of them would turn up. I did wonder whether they will still go to school once you have left, but we gave them an experience with each other as well as with us. We taught them an English phrase, but we sang it so they would remember it, and they used to walk down the road in the village, and they would sing it to you, and so I hope . . . little things like that I hope that they still have.

I really miss the group I went with, even a year later. I love meeting up with them all, we get on so well. Something will happen that reminds us of our time away and we just say 'oh it's Sarata'. I'm not sure anyone else really understands what we mean though! We didn't really know each other that well before we went away, we were just thrown in together. There was no tutor/student divide or hierarchy though – we were all on a level.

When we left Sarata we booked into this hotel to have a shower and sleep before we got on the plane. Laura and I were sharing a room and we were so surprised to see a toilet that flushes! We were brushing our teeth and we turned the tap on and we got our toothbrushes and we both turned the tap off, and I would have never, ever have done that before. We went out for a meal in this restaurant and it felt like such a strange transition where we had our feet in two very different worlds.

I found it hard coming home, really hard. We all said it was really difficult to talk about it with people who hadn't been. My Mum was really excited to see me, and I just remember saying like 'please don't ask me anything Mum, because I don't want to talk about it'. I knew her reaction would be 'oh isn't it a shame' and I couldn't face that. I was even totally indifferent about seeing my boyfriend! I was on a real downer, I missed everyone. You get into a routine, you get into doing things a certain way. I think that it is such unique personal experience that you experience with the people around you. We all felt like that when we came home.

The experience has really helped me to develop as a teacher. I was quite apprehensive about certain things, but I think now it has given me confidence in a lot of situations. If I can do that, what else is possible? It has made me want to go back and go to similar places like that. I was questioning whether I could become a teacher: but now I know I can do it.

Seeing Christian teach and his passion for teaching, and his passion for the importance of school has reinforced my passion for teaching. When you look at him you just think I want to be like that as a teacher . . . we all cry when we talk about him . . . he did genuinely want to help everybody in the village . . . that is exactly who I want to be . . . I want to care that much how he does . . . he is just so passionate. He didn't do it for pity, he just wanted them to go to school and he wanted them to enjoy school, he wanted them to be children. I am much more relaxed now in the classroom. I am more passionate about teaching and I could even say I love the children now. It has taught me to think more on my feet. I know that I will be okay and I know that I want to do it, so I just relax and get it done.

Conclusion

This chapter has illustrated both the multiple dimensions of the ISL experience and complexity of the lives of student participants for whom ISL is only one part. It has also sought to highlight a number of pertinent methodological issues as detailed earlier. In particular, it has served to contextualise the schematic analysis in Chapters 6, 7 and 8 which pulls apart the holistic nature of the lived experience of transformative learning to develop understanding of the themes that emerged from the data.

References

Allman, P. (1999) *Revolutionary Social Transformation*. Westport: Bergin & Garvey.
Arthur, J. (2008) Faith and Secularisation in Religious Colleges and Universities. *Journal of Beliefs and Values* 29 (2): 197–202.
Bamber, P., Clarkson, J. and Bourke, L. (2008) *In Safe Hands: Guiding Principles for International Service-Learning*. Stoke on Trent: Trentham.
Charmaz, K. (2006) *Constructing Grounded Theory*. London: Sage.
Cresswell, J.W. (2007) *Qualitative Inquiry and Research Design: Choosing Among Five Approaches*. London: Sage.
Dewey, J. (1934) *Art as Experience*. New York: Perigee Books.
Glanzer, P. (2008) Searching for the Soul of English Universities: An Analysis of Christian Higher Education in England. *British Journal of Educational Studies* 56 (2): 163–83.
Groeneweld, T. (2004) A Phenomenological Research Design Illustrated. *The International Journal of Qualitative Methods* 3 (1): 3–26.
Liverpool Hope University (LHU) (2007a) Corporate Plan 2007–2011. Unpublished document. Accessed 4 April 2012 at www.hope.ac.uk/secretarys-office/corporateplanning.html.
Liverpool Hope University (LHU) (2007b) *Hope One World Review: Final Report and Recommendations*. Unpublished document.
Liverpool Hope University (LHU) (2011) About Liverpool Hope University. Accessed 12 July 2011 at www.hope.ac.uk/about-hope/about-liverpool-hope-university.html.
Liverpool Hope University (LHU) (2015) Liverpool Hope University Mission and Values. Accessed 28 August 2015 at www.hope.ac.uk/lifeathope/welcome/theliverpoolhopestory/missionandvalues/.
McGettrick, B. (2010) Faculty of Education, Liverpool Hope University, 2010–12 Strategic Map. Unpublished document.
MacIntyre, A.C. (1984) *After Virtue: A Study in Moral Theory* (2nd Edition). London: Duckworth.
Paterson, K (2008) Prologue. In Bamber, P., Clarkson, J. and Bourke, L. (eds) *In Safe Hands: Guiding Principles for International Service-Learning*. Stoke on Trent: Trentham, vii–xiii.
Patton, M.Q. (2002) *Qualitative Research and Evaluation Methods*. London: Sage.
Radnor, H. (2001) *Researching Your Professional Practice: Doing Interpretive Research*. Buckingham: Open University Press.
Tolstoy, L. (1900) Three Methods of Reform. In Tolstoy, L., *Pamphlets: Translated from the Russian* (trans. Aylmer Maude). London: Free Age Press.
Van Manen, M. (1990) *Researching Lived Experience*. New York: The State University of New York.

Part III

Transformative learning as the process of becoming authentic

Introduction

Part III contains illustrations and analysis of the transformative processes of becoming oneself, becoming persons-in-relation and becoming other-wise through participation in International Service-Learning. Put together this provides an account of what is meant here by transformative learning as the process of becoming authentic. Chapters 6, 7 and 8 will each identify the conditions that are necessary for transformation to take place, the processes that enable this transformative learning and the related resultant dispositions in relation to the different modes of authenticity: selfhood, reciprocity and worldliness respectively. Data is presented alongside a critical discussion of the ways in which this illuminates the conceptual framework for transformative learning that emerged through this study, as depicted in Table PIII.1.

An aim of the research upon which this book is based was to induce a conceptual framework that would be accessible to lay persons, fit closely with the situation from which it had emerged and be sufficiently general to be applicable to diverse substantive areas. There is a tension between the complexity of concepts explored across Parts I and II and the presentation of a framework for transformative learning in such a simplified form. There is an acute need to reconcile the creative process of developing a conceptualisation of transformative learning in this context with how it is objectively represented. It is worth recalling that this conceptual framework evolved through the analysis of data alongside the interrogation of the context of this study and related literature, as detailed in Part II. For instance, the notions of selfhood, reciprocity and worldliness emerged as aspects of authenticity intrinsic to the context of this study, as detailed in Chapter 3. Furthermore, the construction of this framework in a matrix form is suggestive of certainty, finality and implies the concepts it contains have an impermeable nature. However, the table presented here is not a conclusive and definitive framework but a heuristic device to support the reader in understanding my interpretation of the data. While suggesting a tentative relation between categories, the divisions between sections are purposefully depicted as transparent to represent the porous and overlapping nature of these concepts. At the same time, it must be remembered that this

Table PIII.1 The conceptual framework

	AUTHENTICITY AS SELFHOOD: becoming oneself [integrity]	AUTHENTICITY AS RECIPROCITY: becoming persons-in-relation [recognition]	AUTHENTICITY AS WORLDLINESS: becoming other-wise [cosmopolitanism]
CONDITIONS	Openness with self	Openness with others	Openness with the other
	Perseverance, resilience and flexibility	Anticipating reciprocity	Capacity to critically reflect
		Connectivity with others	Connectivity with the other
	Connectivity with self		
PROCESSES	Reflexivity and distance	Felt sense of the worlds of others	Critical reflection alongside immersion
	Encountering challenge	Deliberation and exchange	Participatory problem solving
	Evaluating service	Shared reflection	Reconnecting with the other
	Raising existential questions	Reconnecting with others	
	Reconnecting with self		
DISPOSITIONS	Honesty and humility	Mutual trust	Acknowledging incompleteness
	Being	Recognising others	Questioning hegemony
		Being with others	
	Reconnecting with time	Empathy and compassion	Valuing other ways of knowing
	Personal efficacy		Reconnecting with place
			Tackling injustice

conceptual framework illustrates what is possible to happen in transformative experiences such as ISL rather than what will necessarily happen.

The first section of each of these three empirically based chapters considers the personal conditions, or individual dispositions and orientations, which provide a fertile starting point for becoming. Openness and connectivity are conditions for transformation with respect to becoming oneself, becoming persons-in-relation and becoming other-wise. The personal conditions which encourage and obstruct the development of authenticity are identified. These conditions, or capabilities, interact with broader contextual factors such as the nature of day-to-day life in the host community, the type of service work undertaken, how the ISL experience is constructed and the socio-economic profile of the country being visited.

The second section of each of these chapters focuses on the transformative processes which shape and form the process of becoming. These have a distinctly temporal dimension and are at work in all stages of ISL: before, during and after the actual international experience. This study presents evidence that transformation is not usually cataclysmic or epochal but instead experienced by students over a period of time. These transformative processes flourish when the particular conditions for learning outlined earlier in each chapter are in place. Identifying these processes involved attempting to isolate related incidents and practices of significance. Some of these transformative processes can be controlled by students and tutors. They can be instigated, avoided and exploited. For example, ISL takes place in a context in which students meet people who are initially strangers and often will never see again in their lives. This is an example of the fabric of ISL that can be taken as a given in this context. There are also robust and potent transformative processes embedded within the fabric of ISL that are beyond the control of students and tutors that make a significant contribution to their learning. The transformative processes are overlapping and often mutually interdependent. For example, immersion in a developing country and ongoing self-reflection combine to encourage students to reassess their priorities in life: for example, their focus shifts towards what is present in their life rather than what they lack.

It is the resultant dispositions discussed in the third section of Chapters 6, 7 and 8 that provide a platform for future transformation. For example, reflexivity, resilience and receptiveness, discussed in Chapter 6, are dispositions students acquire through ISL, which are in turn the conditions for future transformative learning. Students develop practical habits of being such as flexibility, adaptability and responsiveness, which are developed overseas and which feature in their life on re-entry. In this way, this study demonstrates the ways in which the conditions for transformation can, and indeed must, be made and remade as discussed further in the final chapter of the book.

While the manifestations of any transformation in action or actual behaviour were more easily identified both in the transcripts and by the students themselves, of greater interest to understanding the development of the authentic self, as it is understood here, are the dispositions that enable these manifestations. This is consistent with understanding dispositions as whatever it is that disposes us towards action. So understood, dispositions can be observed in related behaviour but at the same time are entities divorced from cognition. This term is therefore adequately distinct from 'learning outcomes' and allows for both cognitive and affective components as discussed in Part I.

In each chapter the commentary upon the conditions, processes and dispositions exposes the contradictions and paradoxes inherent in transformative learning and illuminates unexpected and negative outcomes of ISL. These are captured in the final sections of Chapters 6, 7 and 8, which explore the barriers to transformation in relation to each aspect of authenticity.

6 Authenticity as selfhood
Becoming oneself [integrity]

Introduction

Drawing upon data from the student experience of ISL, this chapter elucidates the notion of 'authenticity as selfhood' and suggests students experience transformative learning through ISL as they develop integrity. This is conceptualised as a journey of 'becoming oneself' that is concerned neither solely with the development of an authentic self that is original nor solely with that which is to be created. Through exploring not only 'a' or 'the' self, but selfhood and becoming oneself, this chapter looks beyond the multiple identities or personas that we adopt and present to the world. This understanding of authenticity as selfhood involves reconnecting the self with itself, others and the broader context.

Understanding transformative learning as the development of authenticity as selfhood responds to criticisms of transformative learning research that is limited to exploring the diverse roles we take on in different situations: for example, the way we change our behaviour in particular social situations. This chapter looks beyond learning that simply reworks our identity or 'tinkers with our being' (Newman, 2012: 43). The conception of selfhood developed here is consistent with the understanding that selfhood comprises three interwoven areas (developed from Harré, 1998: 4–5): what I see myself to be (an awareness that we possess a unique set of attributes), what I do and what others see me to be (how we are objectively perceived – the impressions we make on other people). This construction of selfhood balances aspects of individuality and autonomy with the role played by others. It takes account of, but is not defined by, the fact that we adopt different identities and have several voices at our disposal.

Just as Ricoeur concluded that 'there is no self-understanding that is not mediated by signs, symbols, and texts' (1992: 15), authenticity as selfhood is shown here to emerge through relationships and connections with others. ISL participants draw upon and gain insight into their own selves through interaction with others, for example through chance encounters with individuals and formal events such as community celebrations. It is through encountering others and through dialogue with other people's conceptions of who they are that students develop a fuller conception of their own identity. This contributes towards their own understanding of what constitutes the good life and the beings and doings they choose to value, such as '*Reconnecting with time*'. Furthermore, this engagement with others helps students to develop capabilities such as perseverance and resilience to achieve these dispositions.

This chapter will outline significant aspects of a student's journey as they embrace, respond to and learn from their thoughts, feelings and action through participation in ISL. Drawing on biographical detail, it will demonstrate that, through ISL, students connect with their sense of self, lifestyle, personal and professional lives. In ISL students bring their whole selves into this learning environment. Immersion and aesthetic engagement within a different culture demands receptiveness and openness towards, and recognition of, alternative ways of being. Participants in this study were seen to experience a shift from modes of having to modes of being.

The development of authenticity is shown to be an ongoing process of becoming. For some individuals this is a restorative experience as, for example, they 'reconnect' with their moral compass and restore an organic relatedness to time following their overseas experience. This chapter will explore how students experience shifts in their values, beliefs, dispositions and awareness of their own personal efficacy over time. It will illustrate how transformative learning occurs for students as new knowledge 'becomes them'.

This chapter will also highlight destabilising aspects of transformative learning. For some students, reflecting upon their own assumptions is disorientating as they struggle to resolve their new outlook with their ongoing lives. These students live out contradictions as they become aware of the gap between the way of living that they aspire to and those of which they are capable. Integrity emerges as an overarching virtue (with both self-regarding and other-regarding dimensions), which underpins authenticity as selfhood. The conditions for developing integrity are different from the conditions under which we can go on as the same self. For example, through ISL students are seen to repudiate even their deepest impulses. This transformative process of becoming ourselves is shown to include both continuities and discontinuities in our being and takes place over time. Virtues such as honesty, humility, self-knowledge, fortitude, courage and patience will be shown to subserve integrity in this context.

Conditions

Openness with self

> Mr Banda asked us 'what was our culture?' and we couldn't answer him. I felt dreadful. We were asking him lots of questions about his culture without having reflected on ourselves.
>
> (Mary [Phase 3 Group Interview 2])

Mary, who volunteered in Malawi in 2007, demonstrates openness with self that comprises both openness *to* self and openness *of* self. This is a condition for learning with both self and other-regarding components. Openness *to* self involves self-reflection upon one's own orientation, worldview and understanding of self, for example, one's motivation for undertaking ISL. On the other hand, openness *of* self involves receptivity to other orientations, worldviews and ways in which the self is perceived by others. These other-regarding conditions for becoming oneself could be described as intellectual and bodily aspects of hospitality that demand openness of self to diverse voices, ways of being and possibilities for living. The twin aspects of 'openness with self' recall the sensing and presencing of Theory U that includes both letting go and letting come (Scharmer, 2009), as outlined in Chapter 2.

Some students spoke directly about the importance of self-reflection whilst overseas; for example, Olivia's account illustrates the intensity of the experience and the role of reflection:

> you slept together, you ate together, you went to the toilet together, you did everything together, we got dressed, we showered together, we washed like out of a bowl together, so things like that, but if somebody needed a bit of space they would just go and sit . . . I would just sit and write in my diary, and that was my bit of space, a lot of us kept a diary.
>
> (Olivia [P4 FG2])

Students acknowledge the importance of not having fixed expectations of what they will be able to contribute or personally gain from the project. ISL participants, they argue, can be constrained by the rigidity of their own expectations of the experience. This demands what could be described as a state of 'receptivity' to aspects of the experience:

> I think that you go out there thinking that . . . expecting, but the experience out there brings the unexpected completely, and so just go for it, don't go out there thinking I am going there for that reason and that purpose.
>
> (Coleen [P2 GI2])

Some ISL participants, like Coleen, could be described as being highly driven. Some describe participation in ISL as the culmination of a lifelong ambition. They report being 'excited' (Becca) and 'honoured' (Lucy) to be selected to participate. Furthermore, the opportunity to complete ISL had motivated their choice of LHU to complete their study. This suggests a number of students engage with ISL with heightened awareness and receptivity to what they are experiencing:

> I guess because you are going into a different situation you are going in with far more interest and enthusiasm than if it was your everyday job.
>
> (Andrea [P2 GI6])

A longing to complete ISL and determination to make the most of the experience may accentuate or compromise students' receptivity or heightened state of awareness. For example, students may become constrained by a fixed and narrow understanding of what their ISL experience will involve and what they will gain from the experience. This represents a failure of openness *of* self.

Perseverance, resilience and flexibility

Encountering unfamiliar and unexpected challenging circumstances is an important process in becoming oneself. This highlights the conditions of perseverance, resilience and flexibility to becoming oneself. The importance of 'flexibility' exposes the role of discontinuity within authenticity as selfhood: the conditions for becoming oneself are not always the conditions under which one can carry on as the same self. For instance, students experience transformation when aspects of ISL contrast dramatically with their own personal biography and previous life experiences. Characteristics of ISL that were unfamiliar for a number of students included living alongside staff and students from the UK, travelling in developing countries and for some travelling outside of the UK. Rather than being overwhelmed by these experiences, the student accounts demonstrate that they successfully drew upon personal attributes of resolve, tenacity and perseverance. Ann, who volunteered in India in 1999, said:

> . . . the fact is I'm very much at home person . . . I've just been away for three weeks. I always thought I'd never be able to really leave home or go away . . . although you're with a team of people, you are alone in certain sense I think. You've got people around you, but to me it was quite lonely as well being there. And the first few days to week being there I really struggled, especially at night. I'd get in bed and just want to cry! And then once that was over with it was such a good feeling!
>
> (Ann [P1 I2])

Ann's description suggests the ability to be self-contained and self-sufficient can help students to accommodate new experiences that contrast with their previous habits of being or worldview. Similarly, on her return, Olivia describes how perseverance and resilience can be both a precondition and outcome of authenticity as selfhood:

> I think what it teaches you about yourself is about pushing your own boundaries and you find yourself in some situations that are completely different from anything you have ever experienced before, and you learn to kind of realise what your own strengths and weaknesses are, and it's sometimes the hardest things . . . at the time you really think I really cannot do this, but if you succeed and get it right or do well, it's so rewarding.
>
> (Olivia [P4 FG2])

The capacity of students to push their own boundaries and overcome the physical and practical as well as emotional and psychological challenges inherent in ISL, for instance through encountering poverty, is an important aspect of becoming oneself in this context.

Students find that the unpredictability of their experience overseas contrasts with their more clearly structured day-to-day lives in the UK. It appears that comfortableness with being in a state of uncertainty or not knowing what to expect is a precondition for becoming oneself in this context. Readiness for transformation in this context demands an openness and flexibility that has physical and practical dimensions:

> ... so you have to like re-arrange things really quickly, but that is just what happens ... you can't plan things ... things just happen ... we didn't really know where we were sleeping ... we also really didn't know each other ...
>
> (Gwennan [P3 I5])

However, it should be noted that students who had previously enjoyed and relied upon set routines and structure in their lives were also predisposed to transformation through ISL as detailed in the discussion of *reconnecting with time* later in this chapter.

Connectivity with self

> I think because of my personal upbringing and stuff like that was already a part of me, I was not a big materialistic person, but it just kind of brings it home to you and makes you realise even more ...
>
> (Vanessa [P2 GI4])

The importance of connectivity between students' experience of ISL and their ongoing personal and professional lives demonstrates the importance of continuity to transformative learning. The individual personal biographies of participating students play a significant role in developing authenticity as selfhood. For example, significant life incidents, such as the death of a close family member, influence students' approach to and experience of ISL. Personal upbringing with relevance to ISL, such as engagement with charitable activity, exposure to different religious traditions and aspirations to live ethically, are seen to provide rich starting points from which to learn. ISL can therefore be seen to play a role in nurturing and amplifying related beliefs, values and dispositions.

This highlights restorative aspects of transformative learning: ISL can reaffirm that which is already in the student's consciousness, as opposed to bringing this to light for the first time. Of course, the negative consequence of restorative learning is that false assumptions can be reinforced. For example, poor self-image may be reaffirmed or damaging prejudices and stereotypes can be propagated, as will be explored further in Chapter 8.

Making connections between their participation in ISL and their ongoing life in the UK could be described as a process of personalising that desensitises the learning experience and is an important condition for authenticity as selfhood. For these students their ISL experience integrated and reflected aspects of their personal, social and professional lives. For example, Becca's account demonstrates how a personal interest in the growth of Christianity and her own practice of her Christian faith prior to her departure underpinned her search for similarities and differences between life in the UK and in Africa:

> . . . but Christianity was huge, and I know why it's huge . . . I learnt a lot out there about religion . . . Why are people turning away from religion in Britain? There's that story you always hear . . . God and Satan are having chat, and God says, I'll keep this world. Satan says, no . . . I'll wait thousands of years . . . but they will turn to me eventually . . . and God says 'How can you do that?' . . . And Satan says . . . 'I'll give them everything they want'. In Britain . . . we have it all, TVs . . . this idea of looking in towards one's self . . . if somebody gets kicked on the train, sitting watching them as opposed to helping them for fear of retribution, whether it be legal retribution or physical retribution there and then. But in Africa . . . There are no TVs . . . there is no individualistic tendencies as such, it's all community. Community, community, community. And that's why religion is huge, and they are unashamedly Christian out there.
> (Becca [P1 I3])

Recent, and anticipation of future, relevant professional experience, usually in the field of education, also provided a useful reference point from which students began to make sense of their service work overseas. It impacted upon students' career choice: for example, Ann concluded that 'it made me make more of a decision of what I want to teach in the future' as she decided to train as a secondary rather than primary school teacher. The integration of personal, professional and social aspects of their lives evokes the etymological meaning of integrity, unification of parts into whole, and is central to authenticity as selfhood:

> that I discern what is integral to my selfhood and what does not . . . It means becoming more real by acknowledging the whole of who I am.
> (Palmer, 1998: 14)

Processes

Reflexivity and distance

Ongoing self-reflection is an important transformative process underpinning authenticity as selfhood. For most students, introspection and analysis of self occurs alongside action. The capacity and willingness, or capability, to self-reflect underpins the condition 'openness with self' outlined earlier, but it is also a disposition that is cultivated through ISL for some students. For example, Andrea reveals how ISL encourages reflective learning processes that are sustained beyond the structured learning experience:

> It has changed my life. I find myself taking a step back every now and again, and actually looking at the world and my life, and my place in the world, and thinking does this thing really matter in the grand scheme of things, do all the little things matter . . . I learnt that I am very analytical and I spent a lot of time thinking about my time there and how my life was different when I was there and how my life is different now I am back.
> (Andrea [P2 GI6])

Students, like Andrea, develop reflexivity as a result of their overseas experience and, furthermore, become engaged in meta-cognition, reflecting upon this process of reflection. This process, once established, has implications for other aspects of their lives: students find they continue to reflect upon their way of life in light of their experience overseas. This demonstrates one way in which ISL nurtures habits of mind and ways of being, labelled here as dispositions, that provide the conditions for future transformation. This highlights the porosity of the framework for analysis developed in this book.

Self-reflection is a process of externalisation that involves the tacit becoming explicit: what is 'ready-to-hand' becomes 'present-at-hand'. While some students may reassess their self-image and lifestyle through purposeful self-reflection, they can also find that they experience a shift in their priorities and habits of being that evolves tacitly, beyond consciousness, through a form of assimilation. For example, it was only following time spent with family on her return to the UK that Rachel became more aware of how her experience transformed her ways of being, as she became more reflective and patient:

> When I got home people thought I was much quieter . . . much more patient . . . more reflective . . . more aware of just what we've got, aware of how little those children had.
> (Rachel [P1 I1])

A significant characteristic of the ISL experience is that students spend a sustained period of time living in an unfamiliar environment that contrasts with their own experiences of everyday life. Students re-evaluate their priorities as they comprehend that what is important to them in the UK, such as a career or material possessions, may have less significance in other contexts. As important as exposure to an alternative cultural context, ISL also distances students from the complexity of their lives in the UK. Lucy, for instance, describes how immersion in an unfamiliar context involves disconnecting for a short time from friends and family in the UK:

> But as far as home, I think I only wrote about two emails. It's something that I do now when I'm going away; I kind of cut off and get in to where I'm going.
>
> (Lucy [P1 I5])

The distance that ISL affords from everyday life in the UK creates both opportunities and barriers for student learning. It introduces the danger that the experience is divisive as it amplifies any differences such as between 'here' and 'there' and also 'us' and 'them'.

At the same time, distance from particular aspects of their knowing encourages students to act in the ready-to-hand. Rather than attending to the particular or, as Polanyi would describe it, the subsidiary, students learn to draw upon and trust their tacit knowledge:

> In that environment I was no longer defined by all the things and people that define me at home. I initially felt like I was stripped bare of the things that make me who I am. It was extremely formative.
>
> (Sue [P1 I7])

As students rely on the particulars and attend to the focal, they begin to 'live in the moment' and demonstrate tacit knowledge. Through this indwelling, discussed in Chapter 2, students experience as a whole through focal awareness. This suggests that it is through indwelling that a process of externalisation is catalysed as students confront themselves with the truth about themselves. In this example, Sue becomes aware of what defines her in the UK. Through ongoing reflection, students experience raising what is 'ready-to-hand' to the 'present-at-hand' as they begin to define themselves by their own rather than others' expectations. This process of externalisation occurs as students begin to question not only what they value in their ongoing everyday life but also the origins of these values.

Encountering challenge

Authenticity as selfhood emerges as students are immersed in aesthetic rather than anaesthetic experiences. Encountering unfamiliar settings overseas, students are challenged to cope with unfamiliar and unexpected circumstances that are often quite personal, physical and emotional in nature. In doing so, students develop hospitality, receptiveness and resilience that is both bodily and emotional. For example, it is through dealing with unpredictable and unexpected challenges that students reconnect with an organic concept of time, as they learn to both be more patient and to live in the moment. In this context students can rely less on familiar routines. For example, during an ISL experience overseas a programme of activity will often be adapted or abandoned at short notice, and students have to learn to think quickly on their feet:

You've always got to be prepared for the unexpected, and just have to improvise.

(Katie [P1 I4])

Students have no option but to encounter challenges that arise in ISL. These include overcoming fears of flying, living away from family and loved ones, encountering poverty, spending time with people they have not met before, dealing with the presence of various insects and unfamiliar animals, changes in diet and language barriers. They often portray ISL as being 'outside of their comfort zone' as they undertake physical and emotional activities overseas that they would perhaps otherwise seek to avoid. For example Rita, who volunteered in 2007 and took part in phase two of this project, found it easier to challenge her inhibitions in front of strangers:

> Every time we went to a new school to visit they would put on a cultural display for us of dancing and they would come around with a feather stick, and give it to us and we would have to come and dance with the group, and the first time that they did it, it was really nerve wracking in front of all these people watching us, and they would laugh, and we danced a little bit stupidly, I just was thankful I would never see these people again, but towards the end I just loved it, and towards the end it was just great to get up, and the last cultural display was in the school that we spent most of our time in, and so we got up for ages and danced with everyone, and it was really quite a joyful celebration of what we had been doing there.
>
> (Rita [P2 GI1])

A particular feature of ISL is that students get to know strangers that they are unlikely ever to see again. This is an aspect of the fabric of ISL in this context. This can provoke learning, as demonstrated by Rita, but also presents a danger to ISL providers in that it accentuates the separation of the overseas experience from the everyday life of students in the UK. Rita's account also highlights the role of aesthetic engagement and 'embodied knowing' in transformative experiences. In particular, she reveals how she immersed herself in the situation until she became 'totally present'. The corollary to this finding is that educators must be cognisant of ways in which potentially aesthetic experiences are anaesthetised, as will be discussed in Chapter 9.

As students reflect upon how they deal with these challenges, they re-evaluate their priorities and their own pre-suppositions. Lisa spent the first three days of her project without her own luggage, which included cosmetics and beauty products she had previously depended upon. She had no option but to try out a different way of being:

> I also realised that I am very very materialistic . . . a few incidents happened, and I made a bigger deal out of them than I think I should have . . . but

you know it wasn't the end of the world, and you know those things are all material things that can be replaced, and I managed perfectly well without them, and I enjoyed it.

(Lisa [P2 GI5])

Habits of being developed overseas as a result of facing particular challenges can be surprisingly resistant to change upon return to the UK. Sometimes these have been assimilated by students during their ISL experience. Olivia, who participated in the final phases of this study and whose narrative was presented in Chapter 5, had no choice but to conserve a limited water supply. Habits she developed during her short immersion overseas have subsequently become part of her way of being. Her comments suggest that practising this different habit of being, combined with a rational justification for her changed actions, have helped to sustain this change in her actions:

> I used to leave it running but now I turn the tap off . . . when you fill the basin full of water you think 'I don't really need all that water I will just fill it to there' you know little things like that.
>
> (Olivia [P4 FG2])

Overwhelmingly, student accounts emphasise the physical, practical and emotional aspects of these challenges rather than challenges to their worldview. However, some students advise future participants to be prepared for challenges to their worldview that result in cognitive conflict. For example, being out of your comfort zone in ISL also involves having to confront controversial issues, such as apartheid, HIV/Aids and the plight of dispossessed children, important aspects of becoming other-wise as will be explored in Chapter 8.

For many students, it is the prospect of the multiple and diverse challenges inherent in this activity that attracts them to ISL in the first instance. Having enjoyed overcoming the challenges of ISL, some students report that they would like to pursue further challenges in the future. None of the students seek to overturn the assumption that ISL is a challenging activity, for example, by downplaying the difficulties they encountered in completing their project. This discourse serves to propagate a narrative that accentuates the differences between life in the UK and overseas.

Evaluating service

For Taylor (1989, 1991) any description of the self must acknowledge the extent to which human identity is deeply interconnected with our understanding of the good. In undertaking ISL, participants are often acutely concerned that their project has a positive impact on the lives of others in the developing world. 'Giving something back' and 'making a difference' to the lives of others provide a horizon of significance which frames the student experience of ISL. Taylor's notion of 'horizons of significance' has been described elsewhere as 'the authoritative principles, rules, values, and norms that are expressive of the socially prevalent conception of the good life' (Bonnett, 2003: 233). They provide an 'essential reference' (Bonnett, 2003: 233) for our sense of ourselves as they develop dialogically with others, and will be discussed further in Chapter 7.

Horizons of significance are contested in the public sphere (Taylor, 1991) and may lead to changes in what could be described as a 'shared background of things that matter to us in society' (Kreber, 2010: 184). In the context of ISL, this demands deliberation or evaluation regarding how others can be put before self or how difference can be made to the lives of others. Through this process, students move from an orientation of 'doing for others' to valuing 'being with others' as will be explicated in Chapter 7. The latter is a new horizon which takes on significance for students as part of this transformative experience.

The process of 'evaluating service' can be particularly constructive for students but demands consideration of negative and unexpected consequences of their intervention. At the outset, students tend to have polarised views as regards their contribution: some are of the opinion that they have the capacity to change the world through their project, and others question deeply what, if anything, they can contribute. Student reflection upon the 'good' of ISL, or the difference that is made through ISL to the lives of others, does not always take place and is not always critical in nature. Coleen concluded that it was enough that she had 'put a smile on their faces, even for just that one moment'. A dialogue with accompanying staff and host community members would perhaps lead to a more critical assessment.

Rachel was encouraged to consider a more nuanced evaluation of what difference can be made through discussion with accompanying tutors and informal conversations with the local teachers she was working with. Reflecting upon what she could do to make a difference, she identified the importance of congruence between her own values and actions.

> It makes you much more aware . . . It's so easy to go in and say, I think you could do this and I think you could do that . . . but if you're not doing those things yourself, then you're not a good teacher . . . it makes me think about the things I want to talk to other teachers about . . . it's making me look for new ideas that will obviously benefit the pupils who I teach in our school.
>
> (Rachel [P1 I1])

This account recognises that any consideration of what can be done to make a difference implicates the self: for example, through congruence between values and actions and connections made with ongoing lived experience. This process of evaluating how to make a difference to the lives of others in relation to one's own life demonstrates *phronesis*, or practical reason, defined by Nussbaum as being able to form a conception of the good and to engage in reflection about the planning of one's life (2000: 78). This presents a view of ethical reflection that moves beyond traditional understanding of reflexivity.

Raising existential questions

ISL provides a rich context for raising questions of ontological significance, such as questions about things that really matter, existence and the ultimate meaning and purpose of life. This occurs as students immerse themselves in this different context and try to make sense of the lives of their partners overseas. This illustrates the process of becoming authentic as understood by Martin Heidegger and discussed in Chapter 3. This involves confronting ourselves with our own finitude as we take care of our own existence and that of others. For Heidegger, authenticity is concerned with 'there-being' (*Dasein*), whose own being is an issue for it. In this study, as students encounter poverty, social injustice and issues of life and death, such as the plight of Tibetan refugees or orphans of HIV/Aids, they reflect back upon their own lives and reassess their priorities:

> I learnt that the things that were important to me before I went weren't necessarily the things that I thought about out there were actually important to me.
>
> (Alice [P2 GI1])

These existential questions, provoked by encountering the other, provide some of the horizons which take on significance to students regarding their vision of the good life. Becca describes how lasting images of the fragility of life overseas continue to give her a sense of urgency and purpose:

> I realise things like . . . life . . . life is a gift. People squander life . . . we are all guilty of it at times, we don't make the most of the day, we don't make the most of the week. I used to say at work . . . can't wait 'til Friday.
>
> (Becca [P1 I3])

Becca's emergent understanding of the value of life may occur irrespective of having a particular faith. Some students describe their experience overseas as being spiritual, for example through witnessing the faith of community members:

> Sue and Laura are not like religious here, but they do feel very spiritual in Sarata, which is quite spiritual. We had quite a lot of conversations about it because I went to the church with them . . . just the three of us, and we talked about why I believe and why they don't believe and we had a really nice conversation exactly, and we did talk about what is different here . . . and Sue said she just feels you know that she gets that from everybody and it is important to them and it is important to her when she is there.
>
> (Olivia [P4 FG2])

Olivia's account illustrates that exposure to diverse aspects of the lives of others, as will be conceptualised in '*Openness with others*' and '*Felt sense of the worlds of others*', informs the full development of the self of the student, which includes personal, social, professional and spiritual dimensions. Olivia claims other members of her group, who would not usually attend church, did so while on the project. Sue was the only other student who identified religion and a renewal of faith as being a significant part of their ongoing ISL experience. For her, witnessing the commitment to faith by partners overseas had a particular impact:

> When you are encountering people for whom faith is such a strong part of their lives you can't help but re-evaluate your own commitment. Going to Mass with teachers from the school and talking with the taxi driver who had 'God is Great' stickers all over his car were really important parts of my experience. I had not been to church for a number of years before I went away but I go regularly now.
>
> (Sue [P1 I7])

Reconnecting with self

On their return to the UK, students report reconnecting with self as they recollect conversations or particular incidents from their time overseas. Some keep photographs on display at home to provide a continual reminder of an aspect of their experience. Students make connections between what they experienced overseas and their ongoing everyday lives. ISL is only one aspect or stage in a larger process of becoming themselves. It is not seen as an isolated event in students' lives but connects past, present and future experiences. For example, Rita and Rachel below reiterate how ISL is a restorative process:

> I have become slightly less materialistic, not that I was really very materialistic before, but even less so now.
>
> (Rita [P1 GI1])

> I think I was always resourceful, even before I went . . . at the interview or on the application I wrote that . . . but more so now . . . in school, when your staff are saying 'Argh We need this, we haven't got this!' And I just think . . . God, just get on with it!
>
> (Rachel [P1 I1])

Dialogue with others regarding their experience of ISL is pivotal for students as they continue to reassess their own assumptions. Students also make connections between conversations with individuals they meet in their everyday lives in the UK and their time overseas. For example, Becca recalled an encounter in a Liverpool supermarket that triggered her to reassess her way of being:

the wee old lady on the till said to me the other week 'You're wishing your life away!' And when you're in Africa, and you see how precious life is, you sort of realise . . . this kid's going to die of AIDS . . . and there are people doing this to their bodies, or whatever . . . life's a gift whether you believe or not you've got to make the most of it, you've got a huge potential.

(Becca [P1 I3])

The students consistently value the opportunity to put their learning into action within both their personal and professional lives on return to the UK. The final section of this chapter on '*Barriers to integrity*' includes a discussion of the difficulties students face in aligning their values and actions.

Dispositions

Honesty and humility

Through ISL students gain a deeper sense of self that includes an enhanced awareness of their strengths and weaknesses. This occurs as students encounter unfamiliar and unexpected challenging circumstances and also as students reflect upon their own lives with the benefit of the distance that ISL provides. As ISL exposes students to their own personal weaknesses, inadequacies and vulnerabilities, they develop a deeper sense of honesty with self and humility. For example, Chapter 7 will explore how, during ISL, students move away from a disposition of independence and self-reliance to one which recognises their fragility and allows others to support them. Similarly, Chapter 8 will explore how students realise through ISL that their view of the world is distinct from others and may also have flaws. In relation to authenticity as selfhood, ISL places students in situations that challenge students to rethink their self-image. Rita refers to being 'not as worldly wise' in relation to her own lack of confidence to engage with the emotional and physical challenges of everyday life in Delhi:

I am not as independent as I thought I was, not as worldly wise as I thought I was, there were a few things that shocked me . . . to the point where you know especially in Delhi I found it quite difficult to go out of the hotel.

(Rita [P2 GI1])

Gwennan demonstrates a disposition towards honesty and humility as she acknowledges the implications of acting upon her view of the world:

I always thought I was an open minded person I thought I would never judge anyone, I would never look at anyone and think 'oh no look at them' but it made me realise that I did judge people, but not judge them in a way which is a nasty way I judged them in the way I have been brought up and the things I know.

(Gwennan [P3 I5])

This sense of humility resonates with the notion of 'democratic humility' (Button, 2005) and is also illustrated in Chapter 8 as '*Acknowledging incompleteness*', as ISL participants begin to realise they don't have all the right answers to solving issues of poverty through development.

Being

Through distance from life in the UK and exposure to alternative ways of living, students report gaining a new perspective on life in the UK in relation to value placed on material goods, relationships with family and friends, routines and aspects of spirituality. Vanessa for example recalled:

> you realise how materialistic this country is, not just our country the culture, everyone has got to have the latest phone, MP3 player, or car, anything, it's all about stuff, and when you are taken away from all that, and you are put into a situation where they don't have as much stuff, it is more based on people and relationships with people, and the way people act with each other, and kindness and it makes you realise that that is what is the most important and all that stuff does not matter at all and what you have in terms of things of monetary value it means nothing you're never any richer for any of that stuff it's all about what is inside you.
>
> (Vanessa [P2 GI4])

As students reassess their priorities in life through a process of '*Raising existential questions*' as explored earlier, they have a tendency to shift their focus towards what is present in their life as opposed to what might be missing:

> my life isn't or wasn't as fantastic as I thought it would be because I have a house and a car, and it made me realise it's actually what's within that makes the bigger difference, and I came back much less materialistic and more driven to helping others.
>
> (Sue [P1 I7])

Sue's account demonstrates what could be described as her shift from a mode of having to a mode of being. Similarly, Lin transformed her attitude towards her belongings as a result of her experience in Brazil. Recounting her attachment to her belongings before her trip she said:

> I have always wanted things and wanted to keep and have things for myself only because I have always had loads of siblings and never had privacy and never had anything that was just mine we always had to share anyway.
>
> (Lin [P3 I1])

Following the trip she reported:

> I got rid of a lot of my things as well . . . started selling things . . . because I feel like I have got . . . it's overbearing . . . you don't realise how much stuff weighs you down you know just having things, and so I have got rid . . . Even . . . I had birthday cards from when I was 11 like every single birthday card up until now and even last week . . . I mean it's took me a long time to get rid of them.
>
> (Lin [P4 FG1])

Students move beyond attaching significance to material objects that have existence not being. As students experience a shift from valuing having to valuing being they become more receptive to the beings and doings that other people choose to value. This theme will be explored further in '*Valuing other ways of knowing*' in Chapter 8.

Students describe this shift in their worldview as putting their life 'into perspective'. For instance, students report regaining a people-centred approach as they reconnect with family and friends on re-entry. While some students report becoming more restless and develop a concern for tackling injustices through political action, others become more appreciative of their material possessions and opportunities. They report feeling less guilty for the life they lead in the privileged West:

> your viewpoint changes you enjoy your life I know I enjoy my life a little bit more, I enjoy my family more, my friends, everything I do, I don't take things for granted I think, but then I am not guilty for the way I live either, because you realise that people live very differently and that's not to say that they're not enjoying the way they live in a different culture, but I just appreciate the life that we have, and especially the life our children have which to me I probably did not do before. I have fun more.
>
> (Alexia [P2 GI6])

Students also exhibit characteristics of temperance, as demonstrated earlier by Olivia, who conserved water on return to the UK. Mary and others report resisting purchasing celebrity magazines and beauty products; she concluded, 'I realise now that you just need basic things to survive, and as long as you have got your family and friends around you that's all that really matters'.

A subsequent rejection of materialism reveals a possible paradox inherent in ISL. Resource-rich students from the UK value material goods less through ISL as they themselves expose resource-poor communities around the world to the latest technology such as digital cameras during their time overseas. This may, for example, reinforce conceptions within these communities of what they lack as opposed to possess. These observations reiterate that ISL practitioners must be acutely aware of the unexpected consequences of their intervention.

Reconnecting with time

While having is something that can be possessed and retained, being occurs in and through time. For example, it is recalled through our memory. Becoming oneself in this sense is less concerned with a particular end product and more the process of being. As such, it involves a reconnection with time. Students often report being more content with their life on return to the UK and that their life has shifted in pace, for instance as they become more patient and reflective. For some this emerges through a conscious process, as they rationally reassess their priorities. For others it occurs subconsciously: having lived alongside others in resource-poor communities where life is relatively less complex and chaotic, they find that they assimilate different habits of being. Furthermore, exposure to unexpected challenging circumstances, as described earlier, encourages students to live in the moment:

> I am just more relaxed and the pace of life has slowed down a lot more and a lot happier in that I have seen you don't have to be rushing around all the time to enjoy life, and to just make the most of it.
>
> (Rita [P2 GI1])

A reconnection with time on re-entry has implications for both the personal and professional lives of students. Vanessa, who subsequently became a teacher, describes a disposition to 'go with the flow' as she adopted a less rigid or prescriptive approach to the curriculum:

> I am a bit more relaxed . . . you have to go with the children . . . you cannot do it in a rigid . . . you know there is not a set pattern for everything, whereas I was quite like that as I like structure, but it has helped me break down a bit . . . just because it's not done in that way it will get done in this way, and I think you need to be like that in school. I think it is more that you go with the flow.
>
> (Vanessa [P2 GI4])

Students often report a more positive outlook on life: being happier, enjoying life more, having more fun and being determined to make the most of life. The ISL experience leads some students to lose their inhibitions. They report being more carefree and less conscious of self. For some this is understood as overcoming bodily inhibitions. This is experienced as dwelling defined as homeliness, or being oneself in our environment (Heidegger, 1930/2005).

> It definitely helped me to lose all my inhibitions, and to be silly and be more creative and imaginative with the children and ideas . . . really it learnt me to have more fun and not be worried and conscious about myself so much.
>
> (Liz [P2 GI6])

Personal efficacy

Overcoming the challenges encountered through ISL enhances the self-esteem and confidence of students. Alice explained how the 'little trials and tribulations you go through on the way are just worth it' and that 'at the end of it the sense of achievement that you have is that great'. Students also report gaining confidence in their intercultural competence, such as their ability to communicate across cultures. Some report using skills that they had not used before. Many students report being apprehensive prior to the trip yet subsequently feel that they would like to do something similar again and have developed the courage to 'explore' the world more:

> it's helped me to be a bit more adventurous to know that there is a big huge world out there to go and explore and to go an experience other cultures, and I think that trip gave me the skills, it helped me to be a better communicator.
>
> (Liz [P2 GI6])

As students become aware of their strengths and weaknesses, they articulate an increased confidence in their ability to learn:

> I think I've learnt about myself basically: I can go and do that, I can go abroad, I can meet people, I can make friends. Certain things . . . I suppose coping and preparing . . . the whole experience I wasn't sure whether I could do it, and I've learnt that I can.
>
> (Lucy [P1 I5])

Through ISL students develop perseverance and resilience. They develop practical habits of being, such as flexibility, adaptability and responsiveness, which feature in their life on re-entry. This is demonstrated in Vanessa's flexible approach to curriculum as outlined in the previous section. Many students could be described as unflappable/imperturbable on return to the UK. Students develop a new determination to overcome similar challenges both at home and overseas and have the confidence to grasp future opportunities as they arise.

> it's made me want to do something similar in the future, but perhaps stretch myself a little bit further, and see how much more I can adapt into new situations.
>
> (Lisa [P2 GI5])

Increases in self-confidence are often linked directly to ongoing work in the UK. For instance, Ann reflected upon the 'confidence it gave me, that self-belief that I was a good teacher'. For some returned volunteers their professional roles become explicitly linked to their experience of ISL, for example as they take responsibility for international links within their schools. Olivia articulates the interaction between reconnecting with time and increased confidence as a teacher:

> In Romania we made crafts and then you do time fillers, so I learnt that instead of standing there thinking seven children have finished what am I going to do I can think quicker now I think . . . it has taught me to think more on my feet . . . I think I have relaxed a bit more . . . I think I have relaxed because I am a bit more passionate about it as well, so I know that I will be OK and I know that I want to do it, so relax and you will get it done.
>
> (Olivia [P4 FG2])

Perseverance and resilience are related to self-esteem and confidence, which are important for learning to take place. Barnett suggests the fundamental principle of higher education should be that the student is involved in a process of becoming, whereby 'the student has to be right within herself, has to believe in herself, have faith in herself, and have a measure of confidence in herself before anything of worth can happen in her learning' (Barnett, 2007: 58). For some students, perseverance and self-confidence are important conditions for learning that develop more fully through ISL.

ISL serves to clarify and re-orientate student thinking regarding their hopes for the future and career direction as they report being more focused on what they want to do. Vanessa said 'I just knew what I wanted more when I came back'. Katie 'completely shifted the job what I wanted to do, so now I work in the third sector I work for a charity'. Student aspirations for the future often include further international activity that ranges from volunteering and travel to formal professional employment overseas. '*Reconnecting with self*' and '*Personal efficacy*' clearly overlap. Chapter 8 will explore how through '*Reconnecting with the other*', ISL participants recognise the nature of problems facing the world and acknowledge that they do have a role they can play, recognising the simple actions they can take which are both local and global in orientation. This is important to enhancing personal efficacy.

Nevertheless, some students struggle to identify any ways in which they were able to make a difference or would be able to do so in the future as it relates to their conception of the good life:

> When I came back I had . . . because of the amount of emotions you went through when you were there, when I came back there was a very surreal emotion. One week I was this important person, and I was doing something important, and when I came back I was very sad and very down, because it was as though I wasn't getting up every day to do something to help these people and that, but for myself personally it was like I didn't have anything to do in life . . . it was so strange, very, very emotional.
>
> (Gwennan [P3 I5])

This destabilising experience for students becomes manifested in their own limited expectations for their personal and social efficacy as will be explored in Chapter 8 in '*Tackling injustice*'. This is something ISL facilitators can support, through managing expectations for what students are able to contribute to the project and establishing support networks on re-entry that provide opportunities for students to put their learning into practice.

Barriers to integrity

The dispositions identified as central to becoming oneself in this context, such as reconnecting with time and shifts from a mode of having to being, are evocative of contentment with life that is not shared by all students, particularly upon re-entry. The student accounts illustrate the obstacles to realising integrity as a social virtue: social circumstances can prevent or obstruct us from speaking and acting upon our best judgement. This exemplifies the notion of adaptive preferences within the capability approach as outlined in Chapter 2.

While some students in this study reported an enhanced sense of agency or personal efficacy, others feel disempowered: despite a desire to act further to alleviate poverty they feel paralysed and unable to do so. Following their ISL experience they become cognisant of ways in which they are complicit in sustaining inequalities and injustices. Some experience feelings of guilt for living in the privileged West. Some students articulate a pressure they now feel to 'practice what they preach' on return to the UK as regards issues such as fair trade. For example, students find their attempts to resist the culture of individualism that they become acutely aware of on re-entry are constrained:

> There are things you can't change . . . it's such a rush-rush lifestyle over here, it's all about work, work, work . . . better yourself . . . how good can you get your life . . . In this society you couldn't snap out of it, unless you wanted to lower your quality of living . . . there is a push in this society to have a 'quality of living'.
>
> (Becca [P1 I3])

Lucy's account also intimates a struggle to cope with the contradictions between her transformed worldview and reality of life on return to the UK. Rather than a journey of becoming oneself that integrates these different perspectives, Lucy alludes to the obduracy of her way of being in the world, indicating that the endgame of this struggle in the longer term is to return to where one started:

> The month or so that follows a project will be rather depressing . . . you've left some friends behind, you've left the situation behind . . . that without too much inconvenience you could probably help endlessly . . . you're not as active when you get back . . . there are a lot of things missing when you return back. But you do get back to normal . . . you do . . . it only takes two years!
>
> (Lucy [P1 I5])

Self-deception and weakness of will are obstacles to becoming authentic as argued in Chapter 3. Developing integrity and becoming oneself involves first overcoming self-deception, for example as students discover what it is they value, and second overcoming weakness of will, for example as they begin to live in accordance with these values.

While students develop consciousness of what they believe to be the right thing to do, in some cases a lack of congruence between values and actions reveals the contradictions in their everyday lives and the ways in which they compromise their integrity. This is evident in the student descriptions of both their experiences overseas and re-entry. For example, the ethical dilemma of choosing where to shop whilst overseas exposed a mismatch between values and actions. Lucy describes a desire to live in solidarity with partners overseas whilst in Malawi, but she and her team opted not to do their shopping in the local market and instead shopped in the city centre at the expatriate supermarket at night:

> Yeah, the supermarket thing . . . Obviously, there are four people coming back with bags of stuff . . . and yeah, you've spent more than the wages maybe for a month of the teachers. What we did, when we went to the supermarket, we used to come back late at night and sneak all the stuff in, so it wasn't done deliberately during the day in front of everybody. Inevitably you will get one or two people come out who want to help you move some stuff . . . but it was better when we did that at night time.
> (Lucy [P1 I5])

The decision to do this was taken by the group of two staff and two students and is suggestive of a lack of fortitude or courage: doing what is right in the face of difficulty. Vicky's account below providers a further illustration of the difficulties students face in reconciling their new frames of reference with their actions on return to the UK. This indicates that the capability of courage to act in the world is potentially an important aspect of the process of becoming for students:

> It's a bit rubbish really because you come home on the plane and you are like yes I am never going to eat meat and I am going to be really healthy, and I am going to exercise all the time and you just don't because you come back and you get into your routine of life, and everything falls into place, so like I totally hold up my hands and say no nothing has really changed for me but at the same time I think your attitude to everything changes, and there is a bit more of a will to make things change you know, and definitely getting involved in things again and definitely willing to make a bit of a difference in any different thing, but I still want to do the things I set out for me to do but it's just more difficult, well it's no excuse, but it's more difficult when you come back and get into your daily routine, and also were in third year so everything just comes back and everything is on top of you

at once so it's very difficult to keep all the things and all the ideals that you had and try and change them. Hopefully I will be able to do all those things after I finish my dissertation.

(Vicky [P2 GI4])

Some students, like Vicky, feel disempowered: despite a desire to act further to alleviate poverty they feel unable to do so. Both Vicky and Lucy also demonstrate an apparent failure of lack of functioning of practical reason as discussed in '*Evaluating service*'. Nevertheless, through this process students demonstrate a renewed relationship with justice. For example, becoming critically self-reflective involves becoming aware that we are making a premature judgement or being inconsistent in acting out our values. This is manifested on their return to the UK as students attempt socially responsible action and to practise virtues and dispositions in their day-to-day personal and professional lives. In doing so, students revive their commitment to what they say and do:

> In being committed, a student is expressing her own thoughts or actions; the personhood of the student is put into the thought or action. The student has not merely integrity, but even has courage in projecting her thoughts or actions, and she has determination to press herself so as to yield that expression of herself.
>
> (Barnett, 2007: 49)

Of course, acting upon one's own reasons is a necessary but insufficient condition for integrity: doing so can be incompatible with integrity. In particular, what we do should not be at the expense of our judgement about what it is that is worth doing. What is required is courage, a self-regarding component of the disposition towards authenticity that has strong emotional and moral components:

> Courage would be unthinkable in a world within which people did not act; but, equally, it would be unthinkable in a world within which actions were devoid of ends and purposes. It necessarily involves an element of moral agency – and of understanding.
>
> (Nixon, 2008: 87)

Participants in this study perpetuate a narrative that celebrates their perseverance in overcoming the challenges of ISL as explored earlier in this chapter. Educators must begin to highlight the courage required to live committed lives aligned with our conceptions of the good. This highlights that integrity is both a self- and other-regarding virtue.

> To have integrity is to understand that one's own judgement matters because it is only within individual persons' deliberative viewpoints, including one's own, that what is worth doing can be decided. Thus one's

own judgement serves a common interest of co-deliberators. Persons of integrity treat their own endorsements as ones that matter, or ought to matter, to fellow deliberators.

(Calhoun, 1995: 258)

Integrity therefore involves acting, following deliberation with others, in a way that is congruent with our shared conception of the good life. It involves a mutual concern for nurturing a shared understanding of what is worth doing. Integrity is also a social virtue in that our decisions of how to act in relation to our own conception of the good life influences others regarding their understanding of what is worth doing or a life that is worth living.

While Calhoun equates integrity with 'standing for something' (1995), this does not preclude the necessity of students being alert to the negative and unexpected outcomes of their actions. Students must instead become more confident in the uncertain and ambiguous nature of this activity and accept the fragility associated with it:

> when what is worth doing is under dispute, concerns to act with integrity must pull us both ways. Integrity calls us to simultaneously stand behind our convictions and to take seriously others doubts about them.
>
> (Calhoun, 1995: 259)

This exposes the overlapping nature of the conditions for transformation and the resultant dispositions in this context. For example, from this view, the resultant disposition of enhanced personal efficacy is best developed and balanced alongside honesty, humility and openness with self. This also highlights the important role of significant others in the becoming of the authentic self as will be explored further in the following chapter.

References

Barnett, R. (2007) *A Will to Learn*. Maidenhead: Open University Press/SRHE.
Bonnett, M. (2003) Education as a Form of the Poetic: A Heideggerian Approach to Learning and the Teacher-Pupil Relationship. In Peters, M.A. (ed.) *Heidegger, Education and Modernity*. Lanham: Rowman & Littlefield, 229–44.
Button, M. (2005) 'A Monkish Kind of Virtue'? For and Against Humility. *Political Theory* 33 (6): 840–68.
Calhoun, C. (1995) Standing for Something. *The Journal of Philosophy* 92 (5): 235–60.
Harré, R. (1998) *The Singular Self*. London: Sage.
Heidegger, M. (1930/2005) *The Essence of Human Freedom* (trans. T. Sadler). London: Continuum.
Kreber, C. (2010) Courage and Compassion in Striving for Authenticity: States of Complacency, Compliance and Contestation. *Adult Education Quarterly* 60 (2): 177–98.
Newman, M. (2012) Calling Transformative Learning Into Question: Some Mutinous Thoughts. *Adult Education Quarterly* 62 (1): 36–55.
Nixon, J. (2008) *Towards the Virtuous University: The Moral Bases of Academic Practice*. London: Routledge.

Nussbaum, M. (2000) *Women and Human Development*. Cambridge: Cambridge University Press.
Palmer, P. (1998) *The Courage to Teach: Exploring the Inner Landscape of a Teacher's Life*. San Francisco: Jossey-Bass.
Ricoeur, P. (1992) *Oneself as Another* (trans. Kathleen Blamey). Chicago: University of Chicago Press.
Scharmer, C.O. (2009) *Theory U: Leading from the Future as it Emerges*. San Francisco: Berrett Koehler.
Taylor, C. (1989) *Sources of the Self: The Making of the Modern Identity*. London: Harvard.
Taylor, C. (1991) *The Ethics of Authenticity*. London: Harvard University Press.

7 Authenticity as reciprocity

Becoming persons-in-relation [recognition]

Introduction

This chapter investigates how students experience transformative learning as they discover their own authenticity and connect with the authenticity of others. It will outline the conditions students start with and the processes they go through as they develop authenticity as reciprocity. This chapter will reiterate that transformative learning, understood as a process of becoming authentic, has important social and relational aspects. It will emphasise that being true to oneself involves connecting with particular others. Deliberation and ongoing relationships play a central role in the student becoming authentic. This idea will be extended in Chapter 8 through exploring the relationship between the student and the general other.

The focus shifts here to authenticity as reciprocity and how students participating in ISL experience transformative learning through recognition. This brings into view the various relationships at the core of the ISL experience: students and their accompanying teams from the UK comprising both staff and students, children and adults in the communities overseas where the service work is taking place and also significant individuals and groups that students meet during their time travelling beyond the project location.

This chapter illustrates the experience of transformative learning as individuals become engaged in both their own whole-person knowing and the whole person knowing of their fellow learners. This is redolent of Rebecca Nye's concept of 'relational consciousness', which is characterised by an 'unusual level of perceptiveness' in the way learners 'felt related to things, especially people, including themselves and God' (1998: 5). This provides the basis for learning within relationship and underpins what is described here as 'authentic relationships'. Authenticity is seen to emerge through the mutuality of a community where 'each cares for all the others and no one for himself' (Macmurray, 1961/1999: 159). This extends the suggestion that 'no human being comes to knowledge of himself except through others' (Jackson, 1995: 118). The requirement to take care of the other is cogently argued by Polish journalist Ryszard Kapuscinski in his reflection upon the philosophical writing of Emmanuel Levinas: 'the Self not only has to relate to the Other, but must assume responsibility for him' (Kapuscinski, 2008: 70). This is pertinent to this ISL programme, where one overseas partner, the Tibetan Children's Villages, bears the motto 'Others Before Self'.

In this chapter, gaining a felt sense of the worlds of others is contrasted with dismantling the other's ideas from a distance, as theorised in the notion of separated knowing. A form of connected knowing emerges, as introduced in the discussion of relational aspects of knowing in Chapter 2, that recognises the role of engagement in the narratives and lived experience of others. This involves the development of authentic relationships with accompanying staff and students as well as with community partners overseas. Relationships and dialogue are shown to be the catalyst for students to question their own assumptions and also provide the basis of ongoing moral affiliation. For example, as students connect with partners overseas they build empathy and ultimately learn to live in solidarity as they begin to show compassion and genuine care for others.

Through ISL students become acutely concerned with nurturing the growth and development of others. It has been claimed that the only universal moral good is care/concern for 'the other' and that this in turn can only be demonstrated in human relationships (Jarvis, 1992: 49). Students are seen to shift from a mode of 'doing for' to 'being with' community partners overseas. Through these relationships with particular others, learners' assessments of what they can 'do for others' and the role that they can play are transformed, grounded in an emergent understanding of the importance of reciprocity.

The student accounts here illustrate that caring for something authentically means to let it manifest itself in its own way. It is suggested that this is manifested in relationships characterised by 'power with' as students 'leap ahead' rather than 'leap in' as they work alongside partners overseas. Students begin to demonstrate empathy and compassion rather than pity for those they are working with. This evokes Buber's description of the I–Thou relationship that is characterised by openness, directness, mutuality and presence and contrasts with the I–It or subject–object relationship in which 'one knows and uses other persons or things without allowing them to exist for oneself in their uniqueness' (Friedman, 2002: xii).

Becoming persons-in-relations and developing authentic relationships are processes which depend upon recognition. Recognition, understood in the active sense of identification of objects distinct from myself, has been equated with recognition as colonisation (Lingard et al., 2008) and exposes the exploitative potential of pedagogical approaches that seek to transform. Authenticity as reciprocity is manifested in I–Thou rather than I–It relationships (Buber, 1961). Of central concern here is to understand how we can learn to live together with a shared commitment to the recognition of difference. For Ricoeur 'the course of recognition' leads to recognising oneself as both subject and object and culminates with 'mutual recognition' (2005). It is recognition of oneself as another, or self-recognition, that enables a reversal from recognition as colonisation to recognition as reciprocity that is particularly relevant to this context.

Conditions

Openness with others

Students demonstrate openness with others as they willingly immerse themselves in the lives of others. ISL can be seen to involve a mutual receptivity or reaching out to each other that involves an openness to others and is dependent upon the openness of others:

> If you were living there, you spoke to locals, and they were so interested in the UK . . . the UK was their old colonial side of things . . . it was a two-way thing . . . people were very interested in us, people began to know us.
>
> (Becca [P1 I3])

The openness of others is also reflected in the warmth of the welcome students receive from host community partners, for example Lucy commented that she had 'never felt so safe on first arriving somewhere, you know when they come to meet us and pick us up in the bus . . . it was just like an instant connection there with them'. This mutually reinforcing spirit of friendship provides a fertile ground for authenticity as reciprocity. It illustrates ways in which 'my capability for justice and friendship towards others is . . . dependent upon the capability of others for justice and friendship towards me' (Nixon, 2008: 124).

A consistent feature of the student accounts is that they took time to build relationships with children and adults overseas. Olivia describes how her willingness to immerse herself overseas and connect with community members in their everyday lives was valued and helped forge relationships:

> we stepped outside the door of church, and a lot of them had all congregated to see us . . . we got our hands shook, people were giving us kisses, they gave us their flowers that they had been given from the priest. One Romanian man started to speak to us and you just speak back you don't really know what they were speaking about . . . something . . . [laughter] but they made such an effort and I think it was really important that they had seen us go to church and be a part of their culture and their community, and I think that made a real difference when we were there.
>
> (Olivia [P4 FG2])

In demonstrating awareness of how her actions are perceived by community members overseas, Olivia's account illustrates the development of self-recognition as she begins to realise that she is herself someone else's other.

Alice demonstrates how an interest in and openness towards the lives of others in the classroom enabled her to begin to understand the experiences of a Tibetan refugee she had met. Her 'hospitality' combined with her capacity to self-reflect catalysed her own personal transformation:

> We just asked the children did they have any questions . . . but one boy in particular sort of just called me to one side, and he explained what it had been like in Tibet, he was an only child . . . he only had his mum in Tibet, and he was only 15, and he felt responsible, his major worry in life was feeling responsible for his mum, and trying hard in school because he wanted to make this big achievement so you know he could look after his mum in the future . . . and that to me it just made me want to grasp all the opportunities that I have got.
>
> (Alice [P2 GI1])

This account also illustrates how Alice began to hold in tension the differences and similarities between her life and that of a 15-year-old Tibetan refugee:

> I felt like he was asking it as a question, 'what can I do about it', and I felt like there wasn't a definite answer I could give him. It just brought it home to me you know the different struggles that different people face.
>
> (Alice [P2 GI1])

Students also outline the importance of being prepared to place themselves in the care of others: the 'safe hands' of both community partners and the accompanying team from the UK. Vanessa, for example, argues that students should be ready and able to both support others and be supported by others. She began to realise 'where you can help the team' and also 'where you might need a little help yourself and just to learn to accept that and to learn to help each other'.

This illustration of mutuality and reciprocity evokes Nussbaum's twin components of the capability of affiliation. This involves not only being able to recognise and show concern for other human beings but also 'being able to be treated as a dignified being whose worth is equal to that of others' (Nussbaum, 2000: 79). Supporting others and allowing oneself to be supported requires trust, respect, humility and a sense of justice and equality. It provides the foundation for reciprocity, whereby all are able to learn from and teach each other as will be explored further in this chapter.

Anticipating reciprocity

Service-learning provides a vehicle for volunteers to fulfil a desire to do something worthwhile for others. Reflecting upon volunteering experiences prior to ISL encourages students to conceptualise volunteering as different from a charitable act of doing things for others. Vanessa described how she had volunteered as a teenager, taking children from disadvantaged families on trips to the countryside. She articulated how this enabled her to develop skills of empathy, as she became 'more aware of others'. Students with such experiences were able to envision and anticipate reciprocity through ISL. For example, Olivia reflected upon her personal motivation for previous voluntary activity:

> I just really like helping people and not helping in a patronising way, but putting yourself out there, like offering to do things and . . . like all these Tea Dances that we used to do . . . they enjoy you serving them.
> (Olivia [P3 I3])

A desire to avoid 'helping in a patronising way' demonstrates an ability to begin to see things from the perspective of others. It demonstrates an emergent understanding of how such charitable acts are experienced by others. At the same time Olivia honestly recognised that her previous experience of volunteering had given her a 'feel-good factor' that she sought to replicate through ISL. This may be related to attempts to increase 'self-worth' and boost low self-esteem. This suggests that students who are lacking in confidence or who are more personally vulnerable may be attracted to undertake ISL. Friedrich Nietzsche, the nineteenth-century German philosopher, saw acts of pity as being anything but selfless, altruistic acts (1878/1994). Instead, those who pity are seen to be subconsciously thinking of their own self, and act not out of pure selflessness but rather to eliminate some sort of internal pain. Reflecting upon whether everything we do is in our self-interest, the Jesuit priest and author Anthony de Mello concluded that the worst kind of charity is 'when you're doing something so you don't get a bad feeling' (1990: 25). A number of the students openly suggested here that they volunteer because it alleviates their guilt for not doing anything to support those in developing countries. This highlights the importance that students are open to and develop self-awareness of their motivations for undertaking experiences that seek to transform.

Students must be able to move beyond dichotomous thinking about the benefits of ISL, for example, that it serves either themselves or the overseas partners. This happens for some students prior to departure and in some cases prior to application, as they begin to question whether they have the knowledge, skills and attributes to support or make a difference to communities overseas. For instance, Lucy kept asking herself prior to departure 'Have I got anything to offer?' Revisiting this question over time relates to the development of the dispositions towards '*Honesty and humility*' in Chapter 6 and '*Acknowledging incompleteness*' in Chapter 8.

Connectivity with others

Connectivity with others is demonstrated by the development of personal and professional relationships with accompanying students and tutors, partners overseas and family and friends on re-entry. This demands receptivity or openness to others as outlined earlier in this chapter. For instance, Katie and

Ann described how they learnt from working in a community of practice and assumed the role of apprentices to accompanying staff:

> I could soon see that I was imitating the way they talked to the other teachers and senior managers in the village. They were very effective in getting their message across and making things happen.
>
> (Ann [P1 I2])

The modelling of conduct through the examples of others is a central component of education as understood by virtue ethicists and character educators. However, there are negative consequences of idolising particular individuals, most obviously if students become subservient or begin to avoid taking responsibility for their own actions. This occurs in this context as students find themselves immersed in unfamiliar situations beyond their comfort zone. For example, Andrea described how she began to trust her lead project tutor to the extent that he was relied upon to make decisions throughout their project experience:

> he is organising the whole thing, his whole heart is behind it, he was like a teacher, he was a friend, he was like a father and just everything and the amount of preparation he had thought of everything, every eventuality that we came across he thought of, and was prepared for and I was so in awe of him by the time we came back.
>
> (Andrea [P2 GI6])

There is a danger that students become over-dependent on accompanying staff. This can sanitise the experience for students as they avoid engaging with some of the challenges of ISL such as communicating with others in a different culture.

Groups that did not place the tutors from Liverpool Hope in an elevated role were apparently more able to foster transformative learning as it is understood here. These students saw themselves on 'the same level' as the tutors and described this relationship as being brotherly/sisterly rather than paternal/maternal. Close relationships develop over a short period of time, with some team members reporting travelling overseas together having only met each once or twice prior to departure. While overseas, accompanying staff and students would usually shop together, cook for each other, and help each other with tasks related to their service work:

> and there was no tutor/student divide. There was no hierarchy it was just we are all here together and this is what we do . . . if I said well I really need to go and do that then you just go and do that please . . . it was like yes that's fine, and if she said to me just go and do that will you please, yeah, yeah, that's fine we were all on the same level nobody . . . we all had such a good relationship.
>
> (Olivia [P4 FG2])

Collapsing the distinction between tutors and students in this way created opportunities for developing authentic relationships where all are able to learn from and teach each other. It also models the relationships that should be forged with host community partners.

It is important that students undertaking ISL feel comfortable living closely alongside their team from the UK. Strong relationships with accompanying staff and students provide invaluable support for numerous students. At the same time, students must navigate a range of physical and emotional challenges from living closely alongside their team from the UK a challenge, as described by Lin:

> I had never spent that much time with one person like constantly and there's nowhere where you can go to just get away, you just can't like pop off to town, or you know go to another room. When I was there I was like . . . I can't handle this I can't live with someone in this way.
>
> (Lin [P4 FG1])

For Alexia, living closely with others in this way forced her to reflect on how she develops relationships in the future and will be considered further in the processes of becoming persons-in-relation. For some the intensity and strain of living alongside accompanying staff and students compromised the team's ability to make a meaningful contribution to those they were supposedly serving:

> it takes time to build relationships, and in a two week period, you have got all your group issues, you have got your issues with feeling comfortable, and just as you start to feel comfortable and just as you feel that you are actually doing something positive it's time to come back.
>
> (Rahima [P4 FG1])

Recognising that transformative experiences cannot be understood separately from other aspects of students' lives, '*Connectivity with others*' incorporates the ways students include family and friends in their experience of ISL. Rachel, for example, described how it was her husband who encouraged her to participate in the first instance. Through ISL students recognise new ways in which their worldview is influenced by their interaction with their family and friends. For instance, Rachel also revealed in discussing her motivation for completing ISL that 'I had family who'd worked on the missions, and it was something I always wanted to do'.

Processes

Felt sense of the worlds of others

> I think getting to know them it's the only way to do it . . . getting to know them how they live, and it's more of a deeper understanding because I

think at first you just have a surface level understanding, and then you realise why they do these things and you get to know them better.

(Gwennan [P3 I5])

As students live alongside host community partners they gain a felt sense of the worlds of others. This occurs through socialising, eating together, sharing resources such as food, water and electricity, playing games and travelling together on local transport. This evinces connected rather than separated knowing: through this process, ISL students are encouraged to embrace personal experiences and feelings and engage in the narratives of others, rather than pursuing an overtly rational analysis. For example, Sue spent a day shadowing one of the SOS Children's Villages' mothers who care for a group of orphaned and dispossessed children:

> We came across a woman called Eunice, and she lived in one of the houses and she looked after 14 children and five of her own biological children had died to AIDS, and she was the happiest person that I had ever met. She was looking after these children, and she had suffered so much heartache yet she was one of the strongest women I had ever met and it just kind of put everything into perspective for me because I used to really get down about small minor things, and I thought this woman is the strongest person I have ever met and it just kind of brought me back down to earth.
>
> (Sue [P1 I7])

It is through gaining a felt sense of the worlds of significant others such as Eunice that students can begin to move beyond generalised representations, such as partners overseas being 'poor but happy' and 'fantastic' people, as will be discussed further in barriers to cosmopolitanism in Chapter 8.

The connections forged between the students and the individuals they meet through ISL often emerge around aspects of overlapping identity, such as shared aspirations, hopes and fears. For some this occurs as they immerse themselves in life beyond the site of service. For Lin, a single mother with a young daughter, encountering a beggar on the street who had a small child was particularly formative. Similarly, Olivia's relationship with Christian, a teacher in Romania, made a deep impression

> he just understood the whole village, and he tried with everybody, he was lovely, and he did genuinely want to help everybody in the village, and try to make a difference, and it does make you think like I really want to . . . I want to be like that as a teacher I think.
>
> (Olivia [P4 FG2])

Christian continues to inspire Olivia as a role model long after the completion of her overseas project. Olivia's connection with him was forged through time spent socialising together and observing his work in school. Although they needed a translator to converse together, it is clear from her account that their shared time together was as important as any particular conversation they had:

> we didn't speak the same language we had such a laugh I think we laughed the whole night, but we just managed to know what each other was saying.
> (Olivia [P4 FG2])

Her account goes onto describe the bodily connection she had made with him:

> He is so eager to change things, because children don't go to the school parents think it is more important for them to go out to work, so he just wants them to go to school and his face with the children he is quite a stern looking man, but he is so lovely and he has got the biggest heart, and he was just . . . when he is with the children his face lights . . . and when he smiles because he is quite stern looking . . . when he smiles he just melts your heart he is absolutely lovely.
> (Olivia [P4 FG2])

The others whose worlds the students gain a felt sense of include the accompanying staff and students from the UK. Ann described the way in which an accompanying tutor made a lasting impression on her way of being in the world. The 'laid back' and 'calm' personal qualities she experienced in both an accompanying tutor from Liverpool and community members overseas made a particular impact:

> Steve is such a laid back person . . . he doesn't panic and he just takes things in his stride . . . it's helped me be more like that. I think I'm more like that in the classroom now, lots of people have said it to me . . . when I came back . . . that I had changed in that respect, I was more easy going . . . take things as they come, rather than . . . I like to have everything planned out, I need, or I did need, to know what I'm doing . . . but once you're there . . . it's just not like that . . . that's very much their attitude . . . it was just very calm.
> (Ann [P1 I2])

Emotions and feelings play a crucial role in gaining a felt sense of the lived experience of others. They help to surface and expose what students care about and also convey this to others. For example, students may experience shock and anger as they witness material poverty, joy at the response of children to a particular activity; they may feel frustrated at the late arrival of teachers to a workshop they are facilitating or anger at the behaviour of an accompanying team member. This reiterates that emotions are not blind or irrational but 'involve judgements about important things, judgements in which, appraising an external object as salient for our own well-being, we acknowledge our own neediness and incompleteness before parts of the world that we do not fully control' (Nussbaum, 2001: 19). Emotions provide insight into our own judgement of what matters for our own flourishing. The role of emotions and feelings will be explored further in this chapter with regards to the process of '*Deliberation and exchange*' and students' dispositions towards '*Mutual trust*'.

The particular context 'of the worlds of others' with which students are engaged is critical. The overwhelming impression students report is that the resource-poor communities in which they have served place greater value upon people, relationships and community:

> There's more of a community feel, well, in all the villages, that we've been to, than there is here . . . people are more tolerant!
>
> (Angela [P1 I6])

Overcoming the challenges of ISL often involves 'trying on' the affective and rational ways of being of members of these communities as students gain a felt sense of their experience. Encountering the tolerance, determination and resilience of those that students had perceived to be less fortunate makes a particular impression on students:

> Because you know you see people that don't have anything and don't make a fuss and you just have to get on don't you . . . things just become insignificant that would be significant here.
>
> (Melanie [P4 FG2])

While ISL participants can 'try on' the points of view or ways of being of community members overseas, their circumstances remain fundamentally different in that students will return to the UK following their ISL experience. Arguably these students can never fully 'try on' the habits of mind or being of overseas partners.

Experiencing a '*Felt sense of the worlds of others*' embeds and sustains ongoing transformation of habits of mind and being and provides the foundations for *phronesis*, understood as practical wisdom in action. For instance, Andrea concluded her ISL experience continued to 'put my life in perspective and the things that I do'. Katie also illustrates how transformation, anchored in shared experiences and immersion in this different context, can be sustained in the student's being and actions over time:

> And sometimes, when things aren't exactly going right . . . I just think back to the challenges they are facing in their lives . . . and think . . . is it worth getting upset over a flat tyre, or things like that. Nothing seems to bother you as much as it did before.
>
> (Katie [P1 I4])

Deliberation and exchange

Students often find that individuals they meet while they are overseas have an impact on their worldview that endures. Openness with others becomes manifested in honest and open dialogue between ISL participants and host community members in which they challenge assumptions that they hold about each other's lives. This is described by Becca as a form of a 'cultural exchange' and is exemplified well by Alice's discussion with a 15-year-old Tibetan outlined earlier.

Deliberation and exchange describes ways in which the perspective and worldview of partners overseas support students to look beyond their own superficial observations. For some, this involved open dialogue with young people and adults overseas regarding cultural similarities and differences. Shared experiences such as births, deaths and celebrations provide useful starting points for exchange. For instance, through discussing with children what they did in their spare time, Megan reflected upon her own experience of children's hobbies in the UK.

Exchanges with community members can be provocative and force students to both reflect upon their own assumptions and begin to understand the perspective of those they are living alongside. For example, it was a brief encounter with a local man which challenged Jenny to think beyond her work overseas in terms of what she was doing for others, a theme developed further later in this chapter in '*Being with others*':

> as we walked into the slum on the way to the school we met a man who asked us what he was going to gain from us being here. I realised at that point that this whole thing, the whole project was all about us – and of course he was right. How had I been so stupid, tricking myself into thinking this was something that I was doing for others?
>
> (Jenny [P2 GI3])

Students recall significant moments of self-recognition: when they came to recognise their own self as someone else's other. This helped them to confront the truth about themselves and their own lives in the UK. This recalls Mr Banda's request that Mary describe her own culture in Chapter 6. Initially Mary had been determined to find out more about those she was living alongside overseas. This interaction challenged her to consider the two-way nature of exchanges between herself and community partners. Through their descriptions of 'feeling dreadful' and 'being stupid', Mary and Jenny capture the role of emotions and feelings underpinning the deliberative process:

> Recognition and deliberation require, and are conditional upon, an acknowledgement of emotional and affective attachments. We do not become reasonable by divorcing ourselves from these attachments: our reason, rather, depends, upon these attachments for its commitment and focus. What is at stake is our presence as mindful and sentient beings within the deliberative process.
>
> (Lingard *et al.*, 2008: 20)

Mr Banda's provocation forced Mary to reconsider both her own assumptions about culture and those of the host community members. This process led her to acknowledge both similarities between the two cultures, such as community celebrations where families come together, and differences.

ISL represents a form of public deliberation: through contestation students find that they are themselves challenged as they challenge others. This reiterates Taylor's claim (1991) that we are dialogically constituted, and that it is in dialogue with other people's understandings of who we are that we develop a conception of our own identity, as explored in Chapter 6. Moreover, Taylor concludes that our identities are defined 'always in dialogue with, sometimes in struggle against, the identities our significant others want to recognise in us' (Taylor, 1991: 33). Students experience transformative learning through deliberation and exchange as they become defined by their own expectations rather than others.

This understanding of deliberation and exchange is consistent with the epistemology of pragmatism, where concepts and conclusions are always provisional, and open to revision and rejection. This moves beyond a relativist account of transformative learning, assuming that through intersubjective communication we can come to a more integrated perspective. This includes, for example, dialogue around how best to support the lives of others through service, as will be explored further in '*Being with others*'.

Shared reflection

Some project teams from the UK incorporated group reflection within their daily programme. Olivia describes how this process was initiated by tutors and subsequently undertaken separately by students:

> We all had lunch together, and we would all talk . . . we were all quite open with each other, and then at the end of every day, or before our activities and things we would all make an effort to sit down . . . all of the group sit down and just talk about the day . . . everybody talked about how you are feeling and everybody was really open, and then on the last night Sue said 'right we are all going to write down three things that were our best things and three things that were the worst', and if she had suddenly come out with that we would all be like 'My God I don't want to say that, I can't say that in front of . . .' But because we were all 'Oh yeah, yeah' and nobody had an issue with it, and everybody was really open and it wasn't strange for us to do that, and then we would all go back down when we went to bed just the students we would go back down and we would usually sit around the table and just have a drink and chat, and we were all really open with each other, it was really nice.
>
> (Olivia [P4 FG2])

Accompanying tutors play a significant role in nurturing the self-esteem of students, enhancing their personal efficacy and supporting them to align their values and actions, as discussed in Chapter 6. Lucy describes how reflecting with tutors supported her as she gained personal and professional confidence:

> It was just helpful . . . not even so much giving you the ideas, but basically just giving you some encouragement, you know, once you come back and you say . . . 'Well, I did this today' . . . and you know, you have your doubts when you come back: Did I let them down? Did I just make an idiot of myself? And they can provide the reassurance and say, 'No, you did this, if you look at what you did, you taught them this, you did that' . . . and with that reflective process, you'd come home feeling depressed, or you'd let yourself down, or you'd let them down . . . the Malawians . . . Did I really teach them anything? Did they find that productive? . . . and then on reflection, once speaking to the tutors and the student, you work out, yeah, you do contribute something.
> (Lucy [P1 I5])

Students describe numerous dilemmas they face whilst they are overseas such as whether to eat food they are offered, where to shop for food, which resources to leave with host community partners or whether to not to give money to beggars. This can provoke powerful visceral reactions as students respond emotionally to these experiences, demonstrating one way in which students gain a felt experience of the worlds of others. Lin illustrates how tutors have a role in supporting students to respond and process these experiences:

> I came across a few people begging and stuff and it just made me feel really bad, but people said to me don't because they will just follow you, and they will keep on asking every time they see you, and there will be more . . . I was nearly crying because one woman . . . we were by the beaches and she had her child with her, and she was asking me to buy food, so I did because it was food for her child, so I just couldn't . . . I was dead upset thinking about it, it really upset me . . . we spent ages afterwards talking about why I felt so bad and what I might have done.
> (Lin [P4 FG1])

Shared reflection upon dilemmas overseas in this way can help students respond with integrity and practise practical wisdom, as explored further in '*Participatory problem solving*' and '*Barriers to integrity*'.

Reconnecting with others

The connections nurtured with significant others whilst overseas are often sustained for some time on return to the UK. Many students maintain relationships with the staff and students they travelled with. For instance Olivia, who volunteered in Sarata, Romania, reflects:

> we all still talk . . . like I still speak to everybody . . . we were talking about something happening . . . I can't remember what it was now, but we were talking about something happening and you just go 'Oh it's Sarata'.
> (Olivia [P4 FG2])

On re-entry, some students maintained contact with children and sometimes with teachers they had worked with overseas. Through an ongoing dialogue with staff at TCV Choglamsar, Rachel realised that the teachers' initial evaluation of the project could not be taken at face value. In letters following the project, TCV teachers explained how they had been frustrated to be taken away from their normal teaching role to attend the workshop and for cultural reasons would not provide negative feedback face to face. Through a process of '*Reconnecting with others*' she was able to see beyond the superficial.

Families and friends that engage with students on their return to the UK with respect to their overseas experience can help ensure that ISL has an ongoing significance in the lives of students. Lucy, for example, said:

> I've spoke about that a lot . . . but I think they share that as well, they'll shout me, you know . . . 'Malawi's on the Telly!' . . . And I'll be there explaining all the things . . . maybe Malawi isn't too different from other parts of Africa as well, so you can relate to all that.
> (Lucy [P1 I5])

In fact it was through time spent with family on her return to the UK that Lucy became cognisant of a shift in her habits of being:

> I am much more relaxed now and comfortable in myself. My family noticed that in me and they are right.
> (Lucy [P1 I5])

Often students become frustrated as they feel their families and friends are unable to support them in this way. For these students the period of re-entry can be disorientating as they feel unable to share their experiences. Olivia's account of her arrival home portrays these feelings and emotions vividly:

> I found it hard coming home, really hard coming home . . . my Mum was really excited to see me, and I just remembering saying like 'please don't ask me anything Mum, because I don't want to talk about it. When I want to talk about it I will talk about it with you', and her face was just like . . . fell . . . she tried to be really happy, but it was like 'OK' because I know she really wanted to know about it but I couldn't face talking about it, and getting the reaction I knew she . . . she is so enthusiastic about

things, and I know that she would always listen to me and always even if I just said 'I painted a wall today' she would be like 'that's brilliant, well done', and she would she would be really enthusiastic and think I am great for doing it, but I didn't want the 'oh isn't it a shame' like that . . . I didn't want any of that and I couldn't face that . . .

It was so hard and [I] remember my boyfriend coming after he had finished work, and I remember him pulling up, and I just opened the door really casual and he was like 'Hi, hi Babe', and I am sure he expected me to run and like 'Oh I have missed you' and he said 'what shall we do tonight' it was like 'I don't care I am not bothered' . . . and I just wasn't unhappy to see him, I wasn't sad to see him I was just completely indifferent, and I stayed like that for a good week . . . I was on a real downer when I came home.

(Olivia [P4 FG2])

A resistance to sharing personal reflections of their overseas experience, demonstrated by Olivia and other students in this study, contrasts starkly with the openness and hospitality to others they demonstrate while overseas.

Of particular relevance to '*Reconnecting with others*' is the possibility of what could be described as 'transformation by proxy'. Becca revealed the impact of ISL beyond participating students:

The event had such an impact on me: I talk about it in such a way that people are there with me. I think my mother and father were really taken by the whole thing for me. They shared my stories with others in their emails.

(Becca [P1 I3])

Similarly, Rachel describes how her children were transformed. They had been able to revisit the Tibetan refugee community in India as a family two years after Rachel completed her original project:

It made me much less materialistic, and it had that effect on my sons I must admit . . . although they never said anything . . . They went in 1995 . . . when they were going back to school they had to have everything brand new; jumpers, shirts, shoes, top of the range bag . . . and when we got home I said to them, come on, what do you need to go back to school? And one of them said, I need trousers, and the other said, I need trousers and a jumper . . . and I just couldn't believe . . . although they'd not said it, it had had an effect on them. My husband was absolutely gob smacked!

(Rachel [P1 I1])

Alexia also reports the impact of her ISL experience upon her own children who have built a relationship with the children they sponsor in Africa and also participate in awareness-raising events in school. While 'transformation by proxy' reveals the potential impact of ISL beyond participating students, the discussion in Chapter 8 of the tendency for ISL to reinforce stereotypes highlights the potentially negative impact of ISL on the authenticity of others to which this may lead.

Dispositions

Mutual trust

Chapter 6 introduced the idea that through ISL students accept their own personal vulnerabilities and develop humility. This theme re-emerges in relation to becoming persons-in-relation as students move away from independence and self-reliance to an orientation where they are able to let others support them. Students accustomed to leading relatively independent and autonomous lives find that they become dependent upon others in an unfamiliar environment they find harder to control. The practical, physical and emotional challenges students encounter demand reliance upon and commitment to others in a way that students contrast with their previous experiences. For example, Ann explained how she began to trust members of her team from the UK:

> I'm very much 'if you want something doing then just do it yourself'. I like to be in control. And I think going there that you can't be in control, and you've got to let other people do something for you sometimes . . . you can depend on other people.
>
> (Ann [P1 I2])

Many students also express relief and surprise that they were able to develop rapport with community partners quite quickly on arrival at their overseas destination, as described in '*Openness with others*'. This reflects the acute apprehension students feel when encountering unfamiliar others in an unfamiliar environment. For instance, Lucy described the 'instant connection' she felt when her team were met at the airport on arrival in Malawi by members of the teaching staff. Her account suggests a trusting relationship developed in a short space of time as she came to feel that she was in safe hands. The journey in the bus she refers to involved little direct communication due to the lack of a shared language. It can be concluded that the 'instant connection' felt by Lucy emerged from simply being together. Recognising that the emotions experienced through ISL are in effect 'acknowledgements of neediness and lack of self-sufficiency' (Nussbaum, 2001: 22) further exposes our dependence upon others that underpins this transformative experience.

Students often embark on ISL with a primary concern for what they can do for others yet find the experience involves learning how to let others do things for them. Ann's account above demonstrates the development of mutuality and an emergent understanding of reciprocity whilst overseas. This is reflected in the interactions that take place concurrently with host community members.

We soon realised that the approach 'this is how you should do it' was totally inappropriate. When we were marking the books we sat in the staff room with the class teachers and had a look at the work and discussed it . . . we tried to involve them as much as we could and we all learnt a great deal.

(Coleen [P2 GI2])

Coleen's approach evokes characteristics of I–Thou relationships (Buber, 1953): a genuine intent to affirm and foster each other's being through bringing oneself into the relationship. This theme will be elaborated in '*Being with others*'. An understanding of mutuality is reinforced as students gain a felt sense of the worlds of others and engage in deliberation and exchange, transformative processes outlined earlier in this chapter.

Being with others

A number of students outline a transformed orientation to their service from 'doing for' to 'being with' children and community partners overseas. For instance Coleen realised that adopting a 'this is how you should do it' approach to working with partners overseas was 'totally inappropriate'. Similarly, Angela came to realise that rather being there on the project to 'deliver something for them' she was instead 'part of their team'. Having initially perceived their role to include teaching community members overseas, students began to understand more fully the way in which they were learners.

Having been unsure of what they could contribute without formal teaching experience, Cath began to recognise the value of informal learning in this context:

When I was out there I felt that my contribution towards the whole planning and teaching I couldn't really contribute much considering I don't come from a background of teaching skills. I brought my guitar out, and every lunch time I was playing in a band, and brought like a musical aspect to it, and the children out there had never seen a guitar, and I remember one child calling it a violin, and all that kind of stuff, so I think I kind of may be brightened their day I would like to think.

(Cath [P2 GI3])

The disposition towards 'being with' rather than 'doing for' others mirrors and builds upon the shift from a mode of having to being as discussed in Chapter 6. The shift from 'doing for' to 'being with' is also demonstrated by Coleen's account as she reflects upon how she was 'available 24 hours a day, seven days a week' during the project, and local community members soon felt they could 'just knock at the door' and 'speak to me anytime'.

Having experienced 'being with' particular others overseas, ISL participants find that they reconnect with their family and friends on return to the UK.

This happens as they consciously value community, relationships and the time they spend with each other:

> I think the things that have changed for me are the things that I enjoy, spending time with friends and family is really important, being part of a community is really important.
>
> (Alice [P2 GI1])

A number of students become aware of the forces that prevent people spending time with each other on their return to the UK, as highlighted in '*Barriers to integrity*' in Chapter 6. For example, Becca articulated her frustration with returning to a 'rush-rush lifestyle' she perceived to be all about 'work, work, work'. Melanie echoes Becca's distress:

> you know I went to my shops at home and I passed about 20 people and no-one looked at me, whereas overseas I would have talked to every single person, it just made me feel very sad for a long time.
>
> (Melanie [P4 FG2])

A disposition towards 'being with others' recognises that fundamental to any attempts to make a difference to the lives of others is 'who the ISL participant is'. Rita illustrated this orientation when she was asked about the contribution she made to the host community. She chose not to highlight any specific action or intervention but the character and dispositions of the team of staff and students from the UK:

> it's the qualities as well of you as a person that . . . you can have your QTS, you can be a teacher, you can have the degree, but it's the person that you are you can bring so many qualities, and just chat with someone on your project as it's more important than anything else.
>
> (Rita [P2 GI1])

Some students themselves come to the view that if ISL makes them better people, irrespective of how their project brought about any broader social change, then that is of value in itself. Angela's account reflects how students come to a balanced perspective as regards their contribution:

> I think we all went thinking we were doing something fantastic, and we probably did do something fantastic, but not as much as what . . . the effect it had on us.
>
> (Angela [P1 I6])

Horizons of significance are subject to deliberation in the public sphere. The student accounts demonstrate how reflection and discourse around how we 'make a difference' lead to changes in shared understanding of what does matter to us and what we ought to desire. In this way horizons 'do provide needed standards' that can 'themselves be deliberated and contested, and thereby, over time, change' (Kreber, 2010: 188). 'Being with others', as it is conceptualised here, emerges from the student accounts as an alternative horizon of significance to 'making a difference' and is congruent with the ethical approach to ISL, grounded in reciprocity, advocated here.

Recognising others

The process of '*Recognising others*' is central to a transformed orientation to doing for others. Sue, for example, suggests future ISL participants should 'go out there with an open heart, and open mind and do what's best for the situation you are in, and not for yourself'. This illustrates a shift away from transformative learning characterised by instrumental relationships that subserve personal fulfilment, as criticised by Taylor (1991) in his discussion of contemporary understandings of authenticity. In fact, this study presents evidence that concern for others has ongoing implications for the authentic self:

> Significantly, in seeking to achieve another's development, individuals are themselves engaged in the highest forms of reflexive learning, and they themselves grow and develop. Paradoxically, in not seeking to be themselves, they continue to learn to be and to become. In authentic action, human essence always emerges from existence, and individuals grow and develop as persons.
>
> (Jarvis, 1992: 115)

Becca articulates how the rational process of '*Evaluating service*' encouraged her to begin to think 'outside of self':

> One little act can help that . . . you see on the ground what can be done. I think it's an appreciation of life . . . it makes you think outside the box . . . not just opening your mind, but spiritually. You see in yourself how your spirituality can be detracted from . . . you spend your life with TV, or temptations, or whatever . . . Africa, and the Hope One World project encourages you to think outside yourself. Spiritually . . . the whole point of the project . . . it encourages you to think . . . to think, for a change.
>
> (Becca [P1 I3])

As students become able to think 'outside of self' they recognise others and develop their capacity to support others. Through '*Being with others*', as explicated in the previous section, students become mindful of developing themselves as agents in relation to the development of others as agents, who they begin to recognise as having an equal capacity for authenticity. They come to understand what it means to put the interests of others before their own. This occurs as their relationships become characterised less by *power over* or *power to* but instead begin to cultivate *power with*. *Power to* represents an imbalance of power whereby one person assumes themselves to be in a position of authority to develop the other. It is exemplified by 'doing for others'. The previous section highlights that this power relation can be internalised as an apparently natural state of affairs. *Power over* and *power to* evoke Heidegger's notion of inauthenticity in that 'to care for something *in*authentically would mean to manipulate it for selfish purposes' (Zimmerman, 1986: 44).

Power with is underpinned by shared agency and is mutually transforming. It is realised through joint action with others and thus is a feature of authenticity as reciprocity as it is understood here. It has been described as 'the ability to take one's place in whatever discourse is essential to action and the right to have one's part matter' (Heilbrun, 1988: 44). Generating *power with* requires all partners to be willing to 'hand over the stick' (Chambers, 1997: 156–7), as discussed in Chapter 4, which is likely to be resisted when there exists the fear of losing privileges or economic status. This evokes Heidegger's notion of authenticity in that 'To care for something authentically means to let it manifest itself in its own way' (Zimmerman, 1986: 44).

Furthermore, differentiating between *power to* and *power with* recalls Heidegger's distinction between 'leaping in' and 'leaping ahead'. Practising *power to* is equivalent to 'leaping in' as we assume responsibility for the other and in doing so diminish their authenticity. *Power with* is more like 'leaping ahead' as we authentically care for and foster the authenticity of the other. *Power with* demonstrates formal recognition of each other through fostering the growth, development and authenticity of each other's being. As students come to recognise the beings and doings that others value, they begin to 'leap ahead' rather than 'leap in' for the other.

This study presents evidence that students move towards relationships with host community members and their team from the UK that are characterised by *power with*. For instance, during the project Olivia and a fellow student had become concerned about another member of their team. They encouraged her to make the most of the experience by reflecting upon her motivations and aspirations for the project:

> it was a little bit planned between a few of us, but because we wanted to try and make a certain person more involved, she was very withdrawn . . . So we started the conversation . . . but it wasn't an unusual conversation because we had already had it, 'so why did you come to Romania, what made you want to come?' so we went around everybody and we all talked and it was really nice, . . . there are a lot of things that a lot of us had said that you wouldn't say to other people, and we talked about why we went there, our motivations for going, what we liked, what we were a bit apprehensive about, and we all just had those conversations . . . it wasn't strange to have them . . . we were very open with each other . . . it was nice it was good.
>
> (Olivia [P4 FG2])

This chapter suggest that to be authentic, interactions must be grounded in I–Thou rather than exploitative I–It relationships (Buber, 1953). Furthermore, I–Thou relationships are the source of future transformation since 'through every I-Thou encounter, the I is transformed and this affects the I's outlook of the I-It relation and of future I-Thou encounters' (Guilherme and Morgan, 2009: 567). Indeed, students demonstrate a new orientation towards developing the authenticity of others upon return to the UK. Becca, for example, realised the importance of individuals becoming educated by finding things out for themselves rather than being told what to think, an example of students becoming disposed to 'leaping ahead' rather than 'leaping in':

> It does go from thoughts to actions . . . on a micro-macro level . . . spreading the word about the lessons you've learnt in life. Actions in that sense, but not indoctrinating.
>
> (Becca [P1 I3])

Empathy and compassion

While pity is an orientation towards another's suffering that implies a degree of distance or aloofness from the one suffering, the etymological meaning of compassion is 'suffer together' and demands empathy and subsequent action. A felt sense of the lived experience of host community members is significant in enabling students to develop empathy. Yet, empathy may be self-centred and doesn't necessarily involve any regard for the other person's good. The capacity to both imagine the plight of the other and believe your own possibilities are the same underpins compassion. Indeed, it is through compassion that we assert the right of others to recognition, by 'responding sympathetically to the plight of other persons by holding in emotional tension the difference between my situation and theirs' (Nixon, 2008: 89).

Students learn to see things from the perspective of host community partners as they face and negotiate dilemmas they experience while overseas, such as deciding where to buy food. Students find that they move from an orientation of pity or sympathy to empathy and developing compassion. Students move beyond feelings of pity as they explore alternative approaches to a paternalistic and charitable response. For example, Olivia, inspired by a community member who devoted his energy to encouraging young people in the community to go to school, reflected that 'he didn't do it for pity . . . it was nothing like that, he just wanted them to go to school and he wanted them to enjoy school'.

In order to envisage the unintended consequences of their behaviour and decisions they take overseas, students must be able to empathise and see from the other's perspective. Rachel, for example, realised that the resources she had taken out from the UK had perhaps reinforced a sense of inadequacy amongst partners:

> The year I went we'd taken Lego; when we went back it was in the office in a glass case. I feel as though it's 'Look what we've got', and you can put it on show and that will surely only make people feel inadequate.
>
> (Rachel [P1 I1])

Partners overseas clearly placed great value on these resources and Rachel felt uncomfortable reinforcing this within a resource-poor community. Moreover, witnessing the resourcefulness of the teachers she was working alongside led her to question her own 'resource-full' approach to classroom practice. This demonstrates how students develop compassion as they connect with the situation, and indeed with the joys, suffering and authenticity of others. Students begin to relate the lives of others to their own actual and potential vulnerabilities and begin to sympathetically position themselves in relation to this. It is suggested here that through compassion we can successfully assert the right of others to recognition.

Barriers to recognition

The relationships described in this chapter involve students, tutors and their families from the UK as well as community partners in the host ISL countries. There is a danger that unequal relationships, that promote *power over* between students and tutors from the UK may be reproduced in relationships that students have with community partners. The interview transcripts expose assumptions held by students that potentially perpetuate power imbalances through elevating the status of the visitor from the UK (e.g. giving them things and doing for others). For example, Megan said 'they will always remember that they had a white person teaching in their school, and that they were able to interact with us'.

Power imbalances between those from the UK and overseas partners are reinforced when students without any teaching experience assume this role while overseas, with the consequence of de-professionalising practitioners in the ISL host country. At the same time, through working solely with children, some ISL participants relinquished opportunities to develop mutually beneficial relationships with adults and other professionals. Angela's account suggests a lack of confidence is a barrier to students building relationships with adult community members. She reflected: 'I always want to stay with the children, and . . . work with the children, because that's what I'm good at'. This demonstrates how authenticity as selfhood, in particular enhanced '*Personal efficacy*' as detailed in Chapter 6, can potentially interact with the development of authenticity as reciprocity.

A number of students reflected on the value of cultural exchanges. None of the students reflected on the fact this cultural exchange is orchestrated primarily by the partner in the North, nor the fact that attempting to enter into understanding the world of the other paradoxically reinforces privilege. The ISL programme that is the focus of this study remains locally defined and does not provide opportunities for reciprocal visits to Liverpool. Students do not reflect on the fact that they get to know their partners overseas through first-hand experience in a way that is denied to overseas partners. None of the students interviewed in this study put forward suggestions that overseas partners should visit the UK as part of a genuine exchange grounded in reciprocity. This illustrates ways in which the voices of community partners can be marginalised in ISL practice and must be reclaimed. In failing to nurture each other's authenticity, there is the associated danger that authenticity, like global citizenship, remains a privilege of a cultivated minority.

Although students were seen to articulate a more realistic assessment of any changes brought about by their project, this was not always framed in terms of mutuality. Alice, for example, said:

> I don't necessarily think that we did inspire the teachers to suddenly start changing their way that they taught straight after we left, but we perhaps gave them a few ideas to change a few things if they wanted to, and perhaps may be they took out a few things from what we were doing rather than the whole picture.
>
> (Alice [P2 GI1])

Students must be supported to confront their own assumptions and encouraged to reflect upon any lack of congruence between their values and actions, as explored in '*Barriers to integrity*'. Students allude to living as locals without reflecting on the fundamental difference in their positions in that they, with a return plane ticket to the UK, are able to leave the project at any time of their choosing. For example, Lucy valued gaining an 'authentic' experience of life in Malawi but also talks about the need to spend weekends in tourist locations to have a break from the intensity of the experience.

References

Buber, M. (1953) *I and Thou: The Philosophy of Relationship*. London: Routledge.
Buber, M. (1961) *Between Man and Man*. London: Collins.
Chambers, R. (1997) *Whose Reality Counts? Putting the First Last*, London: ITDG
De Mello, A. (1990) *Awareness*. Grand Rapids: Zondervan.
Friedman, M. (2002) Introduction. In Buber, M. *Between Man and Man*. Oxon: Routledge, xi xx.
Guilherme, A. and Morgan, W.J. (2009) Martin Buber's Philosophy of Education and its Implications for Adult Non-Formal Education. *International Journal of Lifelong Education* 28 (5): 565–81.
Heilbrun, C. G. (1988) *Writing a Woman's Life*. New York: W.W. Norton and Company.
Jackson, M. (1995) *At Home in the World*. Durham, NC: Duke University Press.
Jarvis, P. (1992) *Paradoxes of Learning: On Becoming an Individual in Society*. San Francisco: Jossey-Bass.
Kapuscinski, R. (2008) *The Other*. London: Verso.
Kreber, C. (2010) Courage and Compassion in Striving for Authenticity: States of Complacency, Compliance and Contestation. *Adult Education Quarterly* 60 (2): 177–98.

Lingard, B., Nixon, J. and Ranson, S. (2008) Remaking Education for a Globalized World: Policy and Pedagogic Possibilities. In Lingard, B., Nixon, J. and Ranson, S. (eds) *Transforming Learning in Schools and Communities: The Remaking of Education for a Cosmopolitan Society*. London: Continuum, 3–36.

Macmurray, J. (1961/1999) *Persons in Relation*. New York: Humanity Books.

Nietzsche, F. (1878/1994) *Human, All Too Human*. London: Penguin.

Nixon, J. (2008) Relationships of Virtue: Justice as Practice. In Lingard, B., Nixon, J. and Ranson, S. (eds) *Transforming Learning in Schools and Communities: The Remaking of Education for a Cosmopolitan Society*. London: Continuum, 117–33.

Nussbaum, M. (2000) *Women and Human Development*. Cambridge: Cambridge University Press.

Nussbaum, M. (2001) *Upheavals of Thought: The Intelligence of the Emotions*. Cambridge: Cambridge University Press.

Nye, R. (1998) Relational Consciousness: A Key to Unlocking Psychological Facets of Children's Spirituality. Paper presented at the International Seminar on Religious Education and Values, 13–16 July.

Ricoeur, P. (2005) *The Course of Recognition* (trans. D. Pellaur). London: Harvard University Press.

Taylor, C. (1991) *The Ethics of Authenticity*. London: Harvard University Press.

Zimmerman, M.E. (1986) *Eclipse of the Self*. Athens: Ohio University Press.

8 Authenticity as worldliness

Becoming other-wise [cosmopolitanism]

Introduction

This chapter will seek to understand not only how persons relate to each other but how the authentic self can reconnect with the broader social, cultural and historical context. Bringing context to the fore demands understanding where the learner is situated both physically and socio-culturally: this includes, that is to say, the surroundings of the immediate learning event and the background context shaping society. Interrogating the ways that the authentic self both shapes and is shaped by society provides a response to Adorno's critique of the inadequacy of authenticity directed inwardly (Adorno, 1973) and his implicit call to educators to consider a deeper understanding of the social context and the ways ourselves and cultures evolve over time. Furthermore, in recognising that authenticity is only made possible by our social world, becoming otherwise, like becoming ourselves and becoming persons-in-relation, has a crucial role to play in nurturing and sustaining the conditions for a society where authenticity as an ideal can be realised.

The external contextual factors relevant to this study include socio-economic disparity and historical social injustices. This chapter will therefore explore how ISL participants experience shifts in their worldview as they rethink cultural values, norms and rituals over time. Evidence is presented that ISL both challenges and reinforces assumptions and stereotypes students hold regarding volunteering, poverty, aid, approaches to development and the role of education. For instance, following ISL students propagate generalisations regarding the 'poor but happy' and 'fantastic' people they have been living alongside overseas. At the same time some students experience transformation in their social efficacy as they move beyond a charitable perspective on volunteering towards an action orientation focused on systemic change that challenges structural aspects of social injustice.

The transformation of travel, technology and communications that has accompanied globalisation has ensured that our lives have become interrelated with countless others. Chapter 7 outlined the ways in which students develop deep affection for particular individuals overseas and accompanying team members as if they were close family, friends or even lovers. A particular disposition of this care for others is elucidated by Aristotle in his *Nicomachean Ethics* (1925: 1166a 30–1): 'The decent person . . . is related to his friend as he is to himself, since the friend is another himself'. This chapter will explore the ways in which people become other-wise as they demonstrate this same care for people they know only vaguely and often not at all. For instance, ISL participants begin to live in solidarity not just with particular or significant others but also with the general other, for example through conserving resources and relinquishing material goods.

The overlapping notions of individual and society are foregrounded in this chapter, and transformative learning is seen to involve both personal and potentially social transformation. This is used to illustrate the overarching concept of cosmopolitanism and how students develop 'authenticity as worldliness'. For Ulrich Beck, in a world of global crises and dangers produced by civilisation, the human condition has already itself become cosmopolitan (2006: 2). From this cosmopolitan perspective, 'the old differentiations between internal and external, national and international, us and them, lose their validity and a new cosmopolitan realism becomes essential to survival' (2006: 14). This chapter will demonstrate how ISL participants experience ongoing shifts in their identity between the local and the global. Students are seen to develop a sense of social responsibility that is both local and global. It is argued that cosmopolitanism demands engaging authentically with our commonalities and differences as discussed here in relation to 'connectivity with the other'. From this view, cultural differences are not absolute and can only be fully understood relationally. We must learn from other cultural trajectories and their inter-relationship with our own, and this necessarily demands confronting issues of power imbalance and social inequality.

Authenticity as worldliness, as it is understood here, is consistent with Rizvi's definition of cosmopolitan learning as an attempt to 'develop in students a set of epistemic virtues with which to both understand current discourses and practices of global interconnectivity and to develop alternatives to them' (2008: 30). This occurs through ISL in what is described here as '*Participatory problem solving*'. Rizvi uses the term 'epistemic virtues' to highlight 'habitual practices of learning that regard knowing as always tentative, involving critical exploration and imagination, an open-ended exercise in cross-cultural deliberation designed to understand relationalities and imagine alternatives, but always from a position that is reflexive of its epistemic assumptions' (2008: 30). The epistemic virtues of cosmopolitanism illustrated in this chapter include the disposition towards '*Acknowledging incompleteness*', '*Questioning hegemony*' and '*Valuing other ways of knowing*'.

Conditions

Openness with the other

The condition for becoming other-wise of 'openness with the other' includes receptivity to other cultures and approaches to educational policy and practice. Students demonstrated this receptivity when outlining their motivations for undertaking ISL, which included to 'learn about other cultures', 'see what education is like in another country' and 'give something back to places that I have never seen before, but only heard on the news'. Similarly, Katie recommended that ISL future participants 'get to grips with the customs of the country before you go there'. These students illustrate aspects of what could be described as 'hospitality' towards different cultural traditions and practices. They recognised, often prior to departure, the limitations of their understanding and the ways in which they may be constrained by their past experiences.

Students also demonstrate openness to the other as they begin to engage with unfamiliar concepts and issues such as poverty and infant mortality whilst overseas. Those prepared to immerse themselves in this different context broadened their ISL experience as they interacted with indigenous people beyond the formal site of service:

> We thought, we can't experience this country stuck in the confines of a nice little SOS village, you know? We need to experience it. We had a lot to learn about Africa. In the confines of the village, you can't learn about local issues.
>
> (Becca [P1 I3])

Critical understanding of the way the world works and the forces of globalisation often develop from and through overseas experience, as will be explored in the resultant dispositions of '*Acknowledging incompleteness*' and '*Valuing other ways of knowing*' later in this chapter. Indeed some ISL participants only became motivated to find out about other countries and issues following their overseas experience. Some students expressed regret they had not researched the location they were visiting prior to departure. This raises questions around the role and limitations of programmes that prepare for students for ISL.

The intensity of the everyday experience of ISL can prevent students from engaging with issues related to culture, poverty, development and the role of education. Transcripts suggest students must navigate the practical challenges of the overseas project before they can open themselves to the complexity of the socio-cultural context in which they find themselves. This reiterates the importance of the capabilities of perseverance, tenacity and resilience in encountering physical and emotional challenges, as discussed in Chapter 6:

> There were a couple of days that we just stayed in the house all day on our own. The tutors went off to the swearing in of a village head man, you know a cultural celebration. It wasn't like we were traumatised by the whole experience but just found it difficult putting ourselves out there.
>
> (Coleen [P2 GI2])

In such cases, the support from team members focused instead on overcoming more practical challenges related to language barriers, hygiene and diet. Angela relayed how the group didn't reflect upon their cultural experiences 'coz it was quite intense throughout the day . . . so when we got together at the end of the day it was just about [getting] to know each other . . . we kept everything light and fun'.

Capacity to critically reflect

The experience of a contrasting socio-economic and cultural context has the potential to significantly disrupt the worldview of ISL participants. However, this is also dependent upon the capacity of students to reflect both critically and ethically upon their experiences, their own assumptions and those of others. More than one student concluded that 'you cannot help but learn from the experience', yet on further investigation these students were referring to personal development and self-understanding as opposed to a more critical understanding of the way the world works. For example, the personal challenges students encounter detailed in Chapter 6 rarely related to cognitive conflict or overcoming assumptions in relation to power and hegemony.

Exposing and overturning student generalisations relating to 'the other' is particularly problematic. This study includes evidence that students are inclined to validate their experiences by drawing on assumptions which they already hold. This highlights the danger that through ISL students confirm, rather than challenge, their underlying assumptions. For example, teachers overseas presented glowing evaluations of the UK students' work, yet were in fact, for cultural reasons, reluctant to present an honest critique. Looking beyond the superficial takes place through what Mezirow called objective reframing (1991): requiring students to critically reflect upon the concepts, beliefs, feelings or actions that are communicated to them, for example, through what they observe, hear or experience. This is similar to literary or art criticism and demands becoming cognisant of the assumptions that others hold or communicate.

Generalising about those they have spent time with overseas, as illustrated by Lucy's description of the 'fantastic' people in Malawi, indicates that ISL participants have been unable to think critically upon their experiences and observations. Participants in this study often refer to community members overseas as being 'poor but happy'. This suggests they are unable to see beyond their interactions as being with a homogenous group of people who accept their lot as being poor or at least are unable to articulate anything other than this. In a further example, Rahima perpetuates stereotypes regarding the other as she romanticises life in Malawi, describing it as 'like going back in time'. This illustrates the potential for students, through ISL, to replace one stereotype with another, for instance from perceiving the 'West to be best' to 'idealising living simply':

Authenticity as worldliness 159

and that's what these people in these third world countries have got they have got nothing else, so they actually rely on that one wonderful thing that we have all got and that is each other, the moment and what is around us.

(Rahima [P4 FG2])

Rather than painting a picture that idealises subsistence living and 'picturesque' rural life, Lucy's account portrays more sinister aspects of poverty drawing upon imagery from an iconic American film:

We went to Area 22 and visited a home there. That was a really deprived area . . . we went to the area of the market which was like something out of *Indiana Jones* actually . . . it was all under cover, very dark, I suppose quite intimidating in a way . . . we'd had warnings initially before we went . . . you know, it's a dodgy area, watch your pockets with the pick pocketing.

(Lucy [P1 I5])

These accounts do not portray the range of lived experiences of poverty both within and between countries. Similarly, Vicky's description of her arrival in Brazil includes a series of broad generalisations:

be prepared to be more shocked than you think that you will be because one of the biggest things for us was when we got off the plane in Rio . . . you go from a plane that's massive and completely materialistic and full of money to a place which is like ultimate poverty and really shocking and really horrible, and really dangerous.

(Vicky [P2 GI4])

In equating a lack of material possessions with ultimate poverty, Vicky demonstrates a failure to recognise alternative conceptions of poverty that focus on well-being, the security of livelihoods and associated capabilities.

The 'poor, but happy' observation reflects an emergent understanding of diverse aspects of poverty beyond material wealth. It represents an initial shift beyond a deficiency view of those living in material poverty. Lucy's account explains how she came to think beyond the stereotype of 'poor but happy' as she recognised things that partners overseas did have, such as a 'family network':

I've never heard such infectious laughter coming from the children around the village . . . apparently, looking at them, they don't seem to have very much in terms of material things . . . but they've a great family network, although the situation might be desperate at times, I don't know . . . but really happy, full of life . . . that was something, I was surprised . . . I was expecting to be kind of shocked . . . you know, poor people, miserable . . . but it wasn't.

(Lucy [P1 I5])

The presupposition of 'poor but happy' is reaffirmed as many of the students interact primarily with children overseas. It could be expected that children will have an instant emotional response and be excited by the presence of new individuals, often bearing material gifts, and usually taking photographs with sophisticated technology that creates interest and excitement.

To avoid perpetuating stereotypes and generalisations, students must begin to balance differences and similarities between themselves and the other as explored further in the next section. Students use various strategies to look beyond their initial observations and what is communicated to them. Lucy used her imagination and ability to empathise to see beyond the 'poor, but happy' generalisation:

> It is likely there is something in the background, a lot of unpleasant things in their background . . . maybe it's just seeing strangers, it makes them happy or whatever . . . they were able to put on that kind of front.
>
> (Lucy [P1 I5])

The visceral nature of the ISL experience is demonstrated in that a number of students, like Vicky above, refer to being 'shocked' by their experience of poverty. The strong emotions and feelings that students experience provides a window into their consciousness and is a rich starting point for critical self-reflection. Interrogating why students find such images particularly shocking has the potential to expose deeply held assumptions. This reiterates the value of gaining a '*Felt sense of the worlds of others*', as detailed in Chapter 7, and of '*Critical reflection alongside immersion*' as discussed later in this chapter.

While the majority of students undertake ISL to develop personally and professionally, the examples of reinforcing stereotypes provided here demonstrate non-learning (Jarvis, 2006). Students must be able to critically reflect upon and understand the structural and historical aspects of their own assumptions, for example as they relate to inequalities. Mezirow, for example, refers to systemic critical self-reflection on assumptions pertaining to the economic, educational, linguistic, political and taken-for-granted cultural systems, and is of particular interest here. This involves individuals exposing and challenging their own assumptions about the wider world. Examples of systemic critical self-reflection on assumptions in this study relate to overturning the hegemony of Western thinking regarding, for example, the role of education and the value placed upon resources and material goods.

Connectivity with the other

Through exploring common experiences such as birth, death and hobbies, ISL students are able to focus on aspects of their lives that are both similar to, and different from, overseas partners'. An openness to these alternatives and capacity to relate them to their own life enables students to think beyond generalisations regarding the other. Students found that they were regularly asked questions about their family and friends and to describe life in the UK. Vicky described this as a form of cultural exchange, concluding 'learning stuff about us really was the thing that they seemed to be most interested in'. For Megan this involved discussing aspects of everyday life with children overseas:

> My thing that I remember most is when we were talking to kids, and you know when they were getting to know you and introducing themselves and their families, but also what they did in their pastimes, and so we were expecting them to say things like football, and playing games, and stuff like that, but they were saying in my spare time I like to fetch water for my parents, or in my spare time I like to brush the floor, or wash my father's car, things like that . . . and I just wasn't expecting them to say anything like that.
> (Megan [P2 GI3])

This illustrates how ISL involves students learning about the other in the other's own terms: an example of 'self-recognition', as introduced in Chapter 7. Through connecting with the other, students develop a more balanced and integrated perspective, for example regarding the nature of their own life at home. Exposure to the unfamiliar is seen to render the familiar strange. At the same time, ISL involves overseas partners learning about others, the students from the UK, both in their own terms as well as in ours. This process supports the development of a shared understanding that both our representations are socially constituted.

The attention paid by overseas partners to the ISL students' portrayal of life in the UK highlights the importance of students being able to critically reflect on issues in their own country and relate to issues pertinent to the country they were visiting. Some students developed an understanding of the contextual similarities between where they were visiting and their home country prior to departure. For example, Ann, through discussion of the need to experience different cultures, articulates how she was able collapse the distinction between 'here' and 'there':

> I wasn't going to experience the culture . . . that happened as part of it . . . to me, there are different cultures everywhere; you don't need to travel all the way there.
> (Ann [P1 I2])

Similarly, in anticipation of encountering begging in Malawi, Rahima was able to relate this to the issue of homelessness in the UK:

> We have got that in this country . . . we have got homeless people in doorways . . . and people do exploit whatever their problem is to beg for money, and you know it's just a different degree a different level, a different . . . you know the people on the streets can't get benefits in this country, so you know they are kind of begging for their money, and beg, borrow, and steal . . . the same as over there.
> (Rahima [P4 FG1])

The student accounts often reflect a broader narrative that reifies 'authentic' experience of the other. For example, some students emphasise that ISL provides exposure to pristine indigenous cultures which they contrast with the 'man made' world. Similarly, students contrast being a tourist with their 'authentic' experience of travelling, and in doing so propagate a false distinction between the 'real world' and the 'made world':

> I have done America and things like that but I have always got like . . . I have always had a bug to go and step outside the tourist area, and the tourist industry and go see the real world really more so than the made one.
>
> (Gwennan [P3 I5])

'*Connectivity with the other*' as described here is required to challenge a narrative that accentuates the differences between life in the UK and overseas. The view here is that other cultures are not completely separable from our own. Indeed, 'cultural formations can only be understood in relation to each other, politically forged, historically constituted and globally interconnected through processes of mobility, exchange and hybridisation' (Rizvi, 2008: 33).

This section makes clear that the conditions for authenticity as worldliness are inter-related: '*Connectivity with the other*' demands '*Openness with the other*'. Similarly, the capacity to reflect critically upon assumptions is inter-related with the student's ability to connect the experience of ISL to their own life. For example, critical reflection is provoked for some students as they keep in mind what is familiar to them as they experience what is unfamiliar during their time overseas. Rita, reflecting upon living alongside those with fewer material possessions, illustrated this process, saying 'it was like we were there and we knew we had been here'.

Processes

Critical reflection alongside immersion

A number of ISL participants contrast their experience of immersion in a different context with that of being a tourist. Katie argues that this approach cultivates a more integrated perspective on culture and poverty as students 'live how they live':

> Before when I travelled in India I was just travelling, and I was moving around a lot, so you don't get the insight really as I've had now living in Ladakh for two weeks. You pass through, and you think . . . 'Oh, it's terrible' . . . But to actually experience it is something different . . . it was a good experience to live how they live.
>
> (Katie [P1 I4])

Through immersion students become able not only to reason from the point of view of others but also to relate to and feel with their sentient ways of being, as outlined in Chapter 7, in the process of gaining a '*Felt sense of the worlds of others*'. This process involves cognitive, emotional and aesthetic engagement, enabling ISL students to more fully understand the 'background' of those they are living alongside:

> in terms of seeing things on the news and its 'Oh, it's Africa' . . . before I went . . . you know you'd watch things on TV, and you sort of imagine it and you feel it; but having been there and met people who looked similar to the people on the TV you can relate to it a hell of a lot more . . . so you can relate, not only to the people there, but the environment they are living in, you can see outside of the TV, you can see what's left and right of it, even though it's not there, you can imagine, and the background to the people, and it has a bigger impact.
>
> (Lucy [P1 I5])

Experiences beyond the project location helped students to contextualise their experience of service. For example, Becca contrasted the relative security and peacefulness of the SOS Children's Village with life in the 'outside world', 'beyond the confines of the village'. This broader perspective is gained through a range of activities, including visiting tourist destinations, building relationships with expatriates, travellers and indigenous people.

The students engage in systemic critical self-reflection on their assumptions, for example regarding what it means to be poor, through active engagement and building relationships with particular individuals. Through immersion in the local context, Lucy began to judge wealth not only by personal possessions but also by capabilities such as security in work and access to fertile land:

> Then we had an opportunity to visit another house, which I imagine by local standards to be rather wealthy . . . a woman who worked for the government; she had a secure job . . . They had VCRs, television . . . obviously food was not a problem, water . . . they had a nice garden, I think they grew their own vegetables as well, which would mean they wouldn't have to go down to market and do that trek.
>
> (Lucy [P1 I5])

Students who stand back and analyse their experience from a distance whilst overseas struggle to move beyond a 'surface level of understanding' and can become trapped within their existing worldview and reaffirm their presuppositions. For example, Andrea recalls her initial observations of poverty in India:

> We left the airport and soon were seeing men lying on the floors sleeping by the road – it was just like I imagined, they had nothing.
>
> (Andrea [P2 GI6])

164   The process of becoming authentic

In fact it is common for relatively wealthy street sellers to sleep next to their roadside stalls in Delhi. It is through both dialogue and gaining a felt sense of the lives of children and adults overseas that students are able to challenge their assumptions about the similarities and differences between life in the UK.

The research participants articulate how they broaden their view of the world as they connect with the lived experience of people in the countries they travel. For example, Lucy spent time with children reading and writing in their diaries and through this process came to understand more fully the background to their lives. She found that their lives were not as comfortable or happy as her initial observations had led her to believe, presenting a challenge to her stereotype of 'poor but happy' children. Gwennan eloquently articulated how she came to understand stereotypes could be overturned: 'as soon as you saw things you made a judgement on what you saw but then . . . you delve deeper'. Like Lucy, Olivia also found participation in extra-curricular activities to be particularly formative. She reflected upon the behaviour of the Romanian children during a field trip to a local war memorial:

> The statue was quite run down but they were careful touching it, and . . . you just think how lucky . . . you don't realise you take for granted going out all the time, and seeing things but they just relished the whole day.
>
> (Olivia [P4 FG2])

This experience led her to reflect upon how the experiences our education system affords young people can be taken for granted. What is crucial is the way in which Olivia positions herself in relation to the differences between her own experience of education and that witnessed in Romania. In recognising that educational practices are locally defined, Olivia was able to move beyond a parochial assumption that one particular way is better than another. Chapter 7 outlined the ways in which we become persons-in-relation as we reflect back on ourselves in relation to particular others. Here, this reflection has implications for how students orientate themselves to systems and structures.

Critical reflection in this context involves students becoming aware of their own perspective and how it is transformed through engagement with the other. This is the process by which students become defined by their own rather than others' expectations, such as family, friends and society. Students are no longer constrained by other voices and are in fact 'disencumbered by other voices and messages' (Barnett, 2007: 51). In this way, authenticity as worldliness is achieved not in isolation from other voices but in their company. This is redolent of Heidegger's conception of coming at things in their own way – not through personal detachment but in a modification of those voices. It is through interaction and engagement with others that students can come into their own space. This reveals a virtuous circle which the transformative pedagogue is challenged to break into, since 'a student is able to take hold of that which she encounters owing to her being disencumbered; and taking hold, she enhances her state of being disencumbered' (Barnett, 2007: 46).

Critical reflection alongside immersion echoes the view that becoming cosmopolitan depends upon a dialectic of participation and distanciation (Hill, 2010: 12). The latter 'provides a critical space for us to stand back and question, examine, criticise and also discover the multiplicity of forces that constitute our background world and situatedness' (Hill, 2010: 13), yet, without the former, the authentic self denies itself the opportunity to learn from connectivity with others and the exploration of competing value systems and similarities and differences. Distanciation without participation leads to separate rather than connected knowing.

Participatory problem solving

Tackling problems such as what resources to take on a project and what clothes to wear alongside an active consideration of actual unexpected and negative consequences of their actions led students to raise their presuppositions to consciousness. Ethical dilemmas, such as whether or not to give money to beggars, provided a rich context to debate aspects of poverty and issues of dependency. ISL students are seen to construct their understanding of strategies to tackle injustice through dialogue with each other. This is demonstrated by Rahima and Isabelle in a focus group:

Rahima: it is all too easy for people to ask for money if you keep giving money at a problem then people expect that you will keep giving money to that problem, but if you actually give help to that problem . . .
Isabelle: For people to help themselves?
Rahima: Exactly and you know that donation of you know worker's time and skills I think is far more beneficial in the long term than throwing money at a problem.

Regarding the problem of choosing where to shop, as introduced in '*Barriers to integrity*' in Chapter 6, Becca and her team decided to shop at the local market rather than in the supermarket, having found out the wages of the local teachers:

> On the very first night we were there we shopped in the local store, because we had our own kitchen, and it was a South African chain, no different to Tesco or anything like that. And we went and we [inaudible word], to get a few things, food and rice and all the rest. And we came back . . . not thinking . . . with bag-loads of stuff to the village. The groceries cost us 60 quid. And Mrs Leffi the headmistress, wouldn't earn that in a year. So what we did from then on, we asked the locals where they went to shop. We didn't know where to go. We couldn't morally come in with 60 quid's worth of groceries every week: that was wrong. So we went to the local market.
>
> (Becca [P1 I3])

The students can be seen here to practice practical reason, understood as 'being able to form a conception of the good and to engage in critical reflection upon the planning of one's own life' (Nussbaum, 2000: 78) as they attempt, collectively, to solve this problem. This involves making a moral decision drawing upon skills of critical thinking, such as finding out more about the salaries of local people and their shopping habits.

Without being involved in meaningful dialogue around the challenges of development initiatives and how difference can be made to the lives of others, such as through discussion with local teachers, the impact of the experience is minimised for participants. This was the case for Rahima who described her contribution overseas as 'baby-sitting' with large classes of children while the LHU tutors worked on professional development initiatives with the class teachers. In working solely with children, some ISL participants relinquished opportunities to develop mutually beneficial relationships with other professionals as outlined in '*Barriers to recognition*' in Chapter 7.

The role of LHU staff can be seen to enhance and also inhibit the development of authenticity as worldliness. For example, ISL participants experience first-hand approaches to eradicate poverty, including those that involve interventions from the west such as sponsorship of children. Some groups concluded that if managed inappropriately, different sponsored children in the same location may receive different levels of support. Rahima, however, did not recognise that it may be inappropriate to send gifts such as laptops to sponsored children:

> there was a disabled lad there and [his sponsor] bought him laptops and computers and all sorts and he hadn't been given access to it . . . I found that quite sad.
>
> (Rahima [P4 FG1])

Problem-posing and imagining alternative solutions are key features of cosmopolitan learning. In the example above, input from an experienced tutor would perhaps have enabled Rahima to make a more considered response. Similarly, the voice of local community members can enable a critical dialogue to support ISL participants to envision an alternative approach. While ISL teams of staff and students from the UK begin working closely together prior to departure and upon re-entry, it is the staff from the UK who communicate with the overseas community partners prior to departure. In doing so, tutors demonstrate 'leaping in' rather than 'leaping ahead' of their accompanying students who would benefit from being involved in this process.

Reconnecting with the other

> when I did get out there wasn't that much of a culture shock until I arrived back in this country, and that's when it all dawned on me the things that we have and the things that we take for granted.
>
> (Vanessa [P2 GI4])

An important aspect of becoming authentic involves revisiting past experiences in the light of new experience overseas. Vanessa's transcript above reiterates the importance of re-entry in the process of becoming. In a further example, Isabelle reflected upon her experience at home with asylum seekers:

> Asylum seekers come to stay because Dad worked with them, but I still feel like I didn't really understand them . . . I remember we had this one guy from Uganda come and stay, and he made some silly decisions about when to apply for asylum and Dad was trying to give him some legal advice and he wouldn't listen to it, and basically got himself deported because he didn't go through the process properly and stuff . . . and I was like 'he is so silly why would he do that . . . ' . . . I think it was because I was still in my setting I feel like it influenced me, but the fact that I actually went away [on ISL] and actually got over myself and I felt like that helped me understand a bit . . . because I think I was a bit narrow minded.
>
> (Isabelle [P4 FG1])

Students begin to connect what they are experiencing in a different context with their own everyday lives: a characteristic of a rooted cosmopolitan identity (Appiah, 2006). Through this process, as illustrated by Isabelle and Cath above, students begin to understand ways in which the global is implicit within the local and vice versa.

Students come to understand that their actions, choices and decisions taken at home can impact positively or negatively on the quality of life of people in other countries. For instance, Cath reflected on how conserving energy at home could reduce the effects of climate change in the developing world:

> it has changed me in quite a few different ways . . . the way I look at the world, and how much electricity we use, I try and turn off televisions and lights that aren't being used, and keeping the fridge door closed, and all the kind of small things that do add up in a sense.
>
> (Cath [P2 GI3])

Recognising the gravity of problems facing the world, students acknowledge the role they can play as they begin to imagine alternative ways of thinking and being:

> it made me think twice about a lot of things especially your lifestyle. I haven't bought a celebrity magazine since I came back. I am boycotting that, there is so much more issues in the world that we should be concerned about, and it's just a shame that not everybody is, but I felt I came back a lot more, may be not much stronger as a person, but a lot more socially aware of things that happen.
>
> (Rita [P2 GI1])

It is the felt experience of the worlds of others that sustains the impact of ISL. It is important for returning students to have something they can do at home to tackle social injustice elsewhere, such as through buying fair trade products. Students also demonstrate a determination to live in solidarity with others around the world regardless of any direct consequence overseas. For example, a number of students report living less materialistic lifestyles and watching TV less. They are often, like Rita above, also motivated by the belief that this will enhance their own well-being. Similarly, Rahima reports giving away her TV:

> Well I don't have a TV anymore. I am slightly more aware, and do you know what life is so much better without these things and it really is you know I am not watching depressing bloody episodes of *Eastenders* and *Coronation Street*.
> (Rahima [P4 FG2])

Students describe seizing opportunities to put their learning into practice upon re-entry. For Megan, this involved raising awareness of what could be described as 'bigger than self' problems facing society through her role as a teacher and her belief that 'it's a unique opportunity we've got being teachers that we can share that with children'. Similarly, Alexia was able to draw upon her transformed worldview in her paid employment:

> I work within mental health so again that's part of my job is challenging the preconceptions people have of people with severe mental health problems, and that all came about really because of the experience [of ISL].
> (Alexia [P2 GI6])

Service activity, which is often closely related to the students' ongoing personal and professional interests, can have unexpected consequences. For example, following her experience teaching in Malawi, Lucy no longer wanted to pursue a career as a primary teacher since 'being back here and having to work with the National Curriculum I have found that to be an entirely different experience . . . it seems a bit complicated . . . it doesn't suit my teaching style, which is more "hands on"'.

Furthermore, ISL can involve experiences, emotions and feelings that students feel are too far removed from the realities of their day to day life on re-entry. This is problematic when the overseas experience has been particularly profound. For example, Becca concluded: 'What I have to say about Africa feels very important.' Similarly, a number of students reported that only those they were away with overseas could fully understand their experience and they therefore cherish ongoing communication with their ISL team.

Dispositions

Acknowledging incompleteness

ISL encourages students to recognise the fallibility of their worldview, including the boundaries and limitations of their knowledge regarding, for example, current affairs, cultural understanding and educational practices. Sue describes how she came to realise that poverty and inequality are usually avoided in our 'safe little bubble in England':

> I was shocked at the poverty of the black people over there, and that's kept away from the news, and it made me realise that there is so much more going on out there that people don't know about, or choose to be ignorant about, because at the end of the day it's easy to put yourself in a little bubble here safe in England isn't it.
>
> (Sue [P1 I7])

For some students these limitations are defined by facts, knowledge and understanding. For instance Alice concluded that the experience 'has taught me to go out there and find that information really. It just makes you want to learn more about those issues'.

As ISL participants critically reflect on issues with which they are familiar in an unfamiliar context, they recognise their view of the world is partial. The ISL experience transforms through making the familiar strange. For instance Becca, working in a secondary school in Malawi, was led to reconsider her understanding of the contribution of education to society and how this can be achieved in her own practice:

> For the first time I actually questioned what education was for. How would completing their Grade 12 exams help these young people function in society? I can honestly say I'd never thought about that before. It has fundamentally shaped my approach in school and in the classroom.
>
> (Becca [P1 I3])

Students involved in educational projects also reassess their pedagogical assumptions, such as their understanding of the nature and implementation of the curriculum, and gain a broader perspective on the role of the teacher. They come to realise that educational policy and practices are locally defined. These ideas are reinforced through opportunities to put their thinking into practice on return to the UK through 'reconnecting with the other' as outlined above.

For some students, their ISL experience not only broadens their understanding but leads them to explicitly question the fallibility of their worldview:

> it's that clash of cultures and it was like the first time I was like 'wow' people think differently to me and I am not always . . . not that I am not always right, but like my view of the world isn't necessarily the whole complete view.
>
> (Carol [P2 GI5])

ISL students begin to question whether their partial worldview and way of being in the world is necessarily the best. For example, a number of students, like Mary, present a negative view of life in the UK, reflecting 'I have realised how actually over developed we actually are in the UK and how much we take things for granted'. Realising that they can no longer rely on what they previously thought to be true can be unsettling for some students. Confronting the limitations of their knowledge can in this sense be destabilising rather than liberating, as illustrated by Olivia's account of re-entry detailed in the previous chapter.

Questioning hegemony

Students experience a shift in their Western-centric worldview regarding poverty and development as they reframe their assumptions regarding poverty and wealth. For example, they began to reflect on how their own well-being was impaired by following a materialistic lifestyle in the UK. Some students began to critically reflect upon how their worldview is formed. This led Rahima to question the hegemony of consumerism:

> We are led to think we need stuff by advertisements about what people have got . . . it is constantly a competition from a very early age as kids . . . the adverts come on at Christmas and you have got to have the latest toy . . . kids pestering their Mum for the latest toy because everyone has got it, so it's constantly been programmed into us from a very early age that we need stuff . . . it's consumerism isn't it.
>
> (Rahima [P4 FG1])

Recognition of a partial worldview and hegemonic thinking leads students to rethink their orientation to their service. For example, Rachel came to recognise the cultural barriers to partners completing an honest appraisal of her work. She concluded that evaluation procedures are indeed context and culturally sensitive.

As students accept that they can be constrained by their incomplete outlook and recognise that there can be negative consequences of holding a partial worldview, they begin to expose unintended and negative consequences of their service project. This is an important part of recognising that ISL takes place within asymmetrical configurations of power. Lucy, for example, perceives that the partnership between LHU and her project location has become defined by what resources are given by those in the UK. She shows an emergent understanding of the pitfalls of defining your contribution in this way:

> The village children kept coming round to the house and asking for things. I knew this was because the students before had come and given all the children presents and stickers . . . I think that's something that's probably established now . . . when the project people arrive there's balloons, there's toys and that on offer . . . we had pupils coming round for balloons

and things like that; it's no problem for us, but then you've got to look at the wider aspect of it, and the implications of that.

(Lucy [P1 I5])

Although she does not articulate it explicitly, Lucy alludes to the ways this resource-full approach can reinforce a culture of dependency and the value of material possessions. Some students came to question the use of resources not sourced locally. Rachel articulated how she developed an understanding of the unintended and negative consequence of her dependence on inappropriate resources, as will be detailed in *'Reconnecting with place'* later in this chapter.

> You had to take yourself away from your Western view.
>
> (Gwennan [P3 I5])

Gwennan, like other participants, reflected upon the prevalence of 'Western' ways of thinking and knowing yet did not reflect on the historic causes of injustices and the culpability of the West. This indicates a failure to recognise that participation in this initiative enhances the prospect of reproducing social inequalities. For example, power imbalances are reinforced when students without any teaching experience assume this role while overseas. The previous section illustrated how students move beyond parochial boundaries as they recognise that educational practices evolve dynamically through time and in relation to a broader context. In relation to questioning hegemony, students must also recognise that their own involvement in ISL plays a part in this evolution, for example as they influence the expectations and aspirations of teachers and students they encounter.

Valuing other ways of knowing

Living and working alongside host community partners, students become receptive to alternative ways of knowing, thinking and acting in the world.

> But the local tour guides were amazing . . . they just spotted wildlife miles off. When we were on the river the guide spotted elephants miles and miles off   and I had my glasses on and my camera with a zoom, and I could not see these elephants . . . and he was like 'They're over there, next to the palm trees' . . . I couldn't see them! Anyway, it took us about 40 minutes to get there chugging along, and when we got there, sure enough, two elephants lying down, and he spotted them miles away . . . he didn't have binoculars or anything . . . he just knew!
>
> (Lucy [P1 I5])

Some students experience a shift from a tendency to judge from one's own cultural perspective to appreciating local approaches as viable solutions. For example, Gwennan came to understand that curriculum and pedagogy must be defined locally:

> I would look at it and I would think well they are not learning at the school and things and that was a little bit judgemental to be honest ... obviously they need the basics the reading and the writing and things and that, and the maths, but they know more in terms of like the seasons ... as soon as you saw things you made a judgement on what you saw, or ... but then as you delve deeper you realise their education was structured around the seasons and they learnt about the farming and things it was like kind of tailor-made to the community.
>
> (Gwennan [P3 I5])

Megan also recognised that consideration of the local context demanded a shift in her pedagogical approach and she began to adapt her planning 'to their own local experience'. Similarly, rather than seeing teachers as recipients of aid that privileged Western ways of knowing, Coleen began to appreciate the reciprocal nature of interactions as illustrated in her shift from 'doing for' to 'being with', detailed in Chapter 7. That students were reluctant to make claims regarding their contribution to the project is perhaps an implicit acknowledgement that their knowledge base was not necessarily transferable to this different context.

Students do not find recognising local knowledge and ways of being straightforward. There is evidence that students were unable to embrace or even accommodate local knowledge. For example, Lucy's intolerance for poor punctuality during her workshop sessions suggests she struggled to account for alternative approaches to time-keeping that reflected a different relationship with time:

> it's the clash of cultures, between 'African Time', when they turn up whenever, and it's a case of ... in order for their sessions to work properly, I think they needed a bit of extra timekeeping.
>
> (Lucy [P1 I5])

Alexia, who had just completed her formal teacher training in the UK, reflected on her two weeks working alongside Tibetan teachers:

> you can only show them so much ... and whether that's continued when you leave by the teachers that are there, is questionable. We all know that while we're there its great and everything ... but when we go away ... is it kept up?
>
> (Alexia [P2 GI6])

Emphasising the importance of involving the local teachers in 'seeing' what were, from her perspective, better ways of working suggests a failure to value local ways of knowing and, ultimately, to question the hegemony of Western thinking. This failure to de-parochialise pedagogical boundaries is criticised widely in the literature on educational borrowing within the field of comparative education (Phillips and Schweisfurth, 2008).

Some students demonstrate a more ethnorelativist approach that recognises differences in behaviour and values and appreciates those differences as viable alternative solutions. Vanessa, for example, refers to 'giving them ideas' as an alternative as opposed to being an imposition:

> it's kind of like bringing them stuff from a different point of view . . . and giving them ideas that might just alter a little bit the way their lives go, you know and the way they think about things and stuff.
>
> (Vanessa [P2 GI4])

Very few students described how they facilitated opportunities that may be sustained in the longer term that did not depend upon their own contribution. One exception was how Olivia recalled including Roma children within planned activities

> they have got the experiences with each other as well not just with us . . . we tried to make the Roma children a part of everything as well now I don't know if that would stay, or that would go when we go.
>
> (Olivia [P4 FG2])

Although students recognised the value of 'being with' rather than 'doing for' partners overseas, they rarely associated their own habits of being, dispositions and orientation to the service work they were undertaking with the criteria with which they were judging their project a success. This suggests there is a need to explicitly recognise the purpose of ISL as a reciprocal exchange of ways of being and thinking.

Reconnecting with place

Students describe ongoing shifts in their identity and worldview following their ISL experience. The time immediately following ISL can be particularly disorientating. Some students, like Angela, report having their 'feet in both worlds'. Olivia describes this transition as 'making your head get from that place to this place'. When asked to outline future actions, many students referred to planned or completed international experiences. For some this was related to volunteering and public service and for others this was motivated by a sense of adventure and desire to see the world. The disorientation experienced by Olivia and others upon re-entry affirms the danger that those who travel everywhere, sometimes caricatured as the 'globe-trotting elite', become 'uprooted' and settled nowhere.

Re-entry is characterised not by contentment but by instability for some ISL participants, as they begin to question their sense of belonging to the

UK. Rachel described 'Never truly happy being here really . . . never truly happy . . . and always wanting to be there'. Similarly Angela, who subsequently returned to the site of her overseas service, reflected:

> It was totally different from what I was expecting . . . I felt more at home . . . there, than when I came here . . . I felt like I fitted in more there than I did here . . . I just can't explain it . . . you get off the plane, and I said to them this time, I feel like I've come home . . . I don't know . . . it's just everything, isn't it?
>
> (Angela [P1 I6])

For some students, particular habits of being assimilated overseas have been sustained upon re-entry. For example, Olivia and Cath continued to conserve water. Coleen's account also demonstrates an ongoing reconnection with the environment:

> There are other factors for instance your lights can be cut off back there in Malawi, and we did suffer some power cuts, whereas here I am putting off lights all the time . . . things like that, things that I wouldn't have done, but I do it now because its important.
>
> (Coleen [P2 GI2])

Tackling injustice

ISL exposes students to issues that matter deeply, such as how to tackle social injustice. Many students come to realise through ISL the limitations of short-term interventions to ameliorate poverty. For instance, a number of students show concern for whether their project will have a sustained impact beyond their departure.

Although some students experience a shift in orientation to their work with partners overseas from 'doing for' to 'being with', as described in Chapter 7, the language prevalent in student descriptions of their service is framed in terms of patronising notions of 'what we can do for you' or 'what we can give you'. Students referred to 'giving them' ideas and self-esteem. These phrases are indicative of the practice of power over, and 'leaping in' as opposed to 'power with' and 'leaping ahead'. These comments represent an ethnocentric perspective that views one's own culture as superior to others. This is epitomised by Sue for example who asked 'Do the teachers take on board what we have left them with?' These student reflections contrast dramatically with the principles of sustainable development as reflected in the literature, which draws upon the vocabulary of participation, bottom-up approaches, 'helping others to help themselves', empowerment, sustainability or 'handing over the stick' (Chambers, 1997: 156–7).

Some students begin to envision alternatives to the charitable model and work towards systemic change, for example through working closely not only with children but with local community members such as teachers. However, very few students referred to the mutually beneficial nature of exchanges with partners overseas: for example, discussion around pedagogical approaches.

Through ISL some students move beyond exacerbating or even tolerating injustice. This involves a shift away from patronising charitable approaches to ameliorating poverty to a concern for tackling systemic social injustices. Rahima, for example, explains the need to tackle the root cause of problems both overseas and at home:

> Yes money will help with the problem, money can buy you water, or seed, or whatever it is that the money can help, but you know you need to get to the root of the problem and not get in that problem again, and there is not enough of that throughout the world not just in Third World and developing countries, there is not enough of that in this country.
>
> (Rahima [P4 FG1])

For some students, tackling injustice is manifested through political action, such as demonstrating for particular causes, challenging stereotypes through their teaching and a desire to spread awareness of their new perspective on the world on to family, friends and the children in the UK, as in the notion of transformation by proxy introduced in Chapter 7.

On project completion Cath articulates a paralysis felt by a number of students as they struggle to identify actions they can take to 'make a difference':

> If you go to somewhere like the place we went, like Nigeria try not to get too emotionally involved, because the kind of stuff that you see out there it's heartbreaking, and there is so much of it that as one person there is nothing you can do about it, and you are going out there to make a difference in the first place, but you want to do so much more . . . it was heartbreaking knowing that you couldn't do that, it was just impossible.
>
> (Cath [P2 GI3])

Similarly Lucy was frustrated at not being in a position where she felt able to make a difference on re-entry. These frustrations are exacerbated by an inability to see beyond financial contributions as a way to 'make a difference'. Students do not always reassess their consideration of effective approaches for eradicating poverty. One student spoke of the 'satisfaction' of giving money to beggars on the streets of Delhi, indicating they had not been challenged to consider alternative solutions to such problems and move beyond traditional charitable perspectives. This demonstrates a failure to understand approaches to tackling poverty other than those that reinforce neo-colonial stereotypes of the South as needy and passive. A number of students, for example, continue to send money to those they met overseas.

> I don't think I've acted anymore on that . . . maybe when I'm in a position to act, and to contribute, in certain situations I'd be definitely more likely to do something . . . be a bit more proactive on helping causes such as that . . . it's just difficult at the moment, with not having the money, not having the flexibility to do that . . . but I think a certain part of my life, my income, whatever it will be, will probably forever be dedicated to that kind of cause.
>
> (Lucy [P1 I3])

Lucy's assumption that acting upon her experience overseas involves offering financial support suggests a failure to consider the root cause of problems as outlined earlier in this section by Rahima. It implies that Lucy does not recognise the importance of adopting virtuous dispositions and living a critical life as suggested by the findings of this study.

Barriers to cosmopolitanism

> I mean I went to India thinking I could make a huge difference to these children's lives, and give them some kind of hope of happiness but when I got there they actually taught me that their way of life was better than my way of life. They had more security, they had education what they wouldn't have got if they were still living on the streets with their parents, and they had hope in their life.
>
> (Sue [P1 I7])

This chapter demonstrates how students can replace one stereotype or incomplete perspective with another. Having expected squalor and unhappiness, they come into contact with people who are materially poor but apparently satisfied and content. Students then fail to critically challenge this incomplete frame of reference as demonstrated in the above quotation by Sue. Her account fails to acknowledge the diversity of lived experience both in the UK and overseas. Her ISL experience was with children living in an Indian SOS Children's Village who have a relatively comfortable standard of living. Students must move beyond homogenising the other and work with, rather than against, multiplicity.

> When you're mixing with children there, they're so happy, they don't know . . . any different, you know, from what we know, from our culture . . . and . . . you come back, and our children are just so . . . not satisfied with anything they get, and these children have hardly got anything and . . . you come back and you realise how lucky you are.
>
> (Angela [P1 I6])

The 'poor but happy' stereotype runs the risk of accepting current inequalities and assumes that the hopes and expectations of individuals are pre-determined by context. Recognising that resource-poor communities have not experienced a wealth of resources does not justify denying them these aspirations. However, without considering and evaluating evidence of the other capabilities required for human flourishing, the 'poor but happy' stereotype simplifies a complex situation and may be used to justify maintaining the status quo. Like Angela above, a number of students refer to feeling 'lucky' with their life in the UK:

> I think it does make you value everyone that you have got around you even more, because you think about it more and you realise how lucky you are to have the things that you do have.
>
> (Vanessa [P2 GI4])

The use of the word 'lucky' alludes to a perception that current inequalities have arisen by 'chance'. Student accounts rarely suggest they have considered the systemic and historical injustices which have led to this situation. The corollary is that students are arguably more likely to accept the status quo rather than work to identify and challenge causes of injustice. This is reflected in Alexia's account, shared in Chapter 6, of how she appreciates her life more on re-entry. She concluded: 'I am not guilty for the way I live either, because you realise that people live very differently and that's not to say that they are not enjoying the way they live in a different culture, but I just appreciate the life that we have.'

Rationalising injustice as the result of 'distant, unapproachable, implacable, unintelligent necessity' (Nussbaum, 2001: xxi) provides a justification for accepting the world as it is. Similarly, students apparently justify economic disparity as being tolerable 'because they don't know any different'. If we accept that we may play a role in changing this situation, we must also accept that we could have intervened to prevent the situation arising in the first place.

Understanding of how to provide ongoing support to overseas communities demands holding the virtues of benevolence and justice in tension. The dilemma of whether to give money to beggars provides an example of a situation where practising the virtues of benevolence and justice may prompt contradictory actions. For example, the decision to give money can be seen to propagate rather than challenge the systemic injustice which the act of begging represents, benevolent action characterised by the virtues of kindness, generosity and compassion therefore often conflicts with actions that promote justice as seen in the practising of the virtues of honesty, truthfulness and fairness. To illustrate this point further, supporting a drug addict with benevolence may involve providing them with money and accommodation, whereas acting with justice may involve reporting them to the police for shoplifting. Wallace depicts benevolence as a natural virtue based on a tendency people have to act because so doing fulfils an important need of another and contrasts this with acting in justice where our actions are influenced by a desire to get something right according to a standard or norm (1999: 82).

Certainly, students do not articulate an understanding that their own cosmopolitan learning and authenticity is an important feature of approaches to tackle injustice as claimed by this study. This is a view of justice grounded in character and relationships, where justice requires the acquisition and practice of the dispositions that have emerged in this study. This demands nurturing the beings and doings that people value and the freedom to achieve these.

References

Adorno, T. (1973) *The Jargon of Authenticity*. Guernsey: Guernsey Press Co. Ltd.
Appiah, K.A. (2006) *Cosmopolitanism: Ethics in a World of Strangers*. London: Penguin.
Aristotle (1925) *Ethica Nicomachea* [*The Nichomachean Ethics*]. In Aristotle, *The Works of Aristotle*, Volume IX (trans. W.D. Ross). Oxford: Oxford University Press.
Barnett, R. (2007) *A Will to Learn*. Maidenhead: Open University Press/SRHE.
Beck, U. (2006) *Cosmopolitan Vision*. Cambridge: Polity Press.
Chambers, R. (1997) *Whose Reality Counts? Putting the First Last*. London: ITDG.
Hill, J.D. (2010) Becoming a Cosmopolitan. Paper presented to ESRC Seminar Series 'Graduates as Global Citizens', 16 December, Royal Holloway, UK. Accessed 1 August 2015 at www.wlv.ac.uk/default.aspx?page=29721.
Jarvis, P. (2006) *Towards a Comprehensive Theory of Human Learning: Lifelong Learning and Learning Society Volume 1*. London: Routledge.
Mezirow, J. (1991) *Transformative Dimensions of Adult Learning*. San Francisco: Jossey-Bass.
Nussbaum, M. (2000) *Women and Human Development*. Cambridge: Cambridge University Press.
Nussbaum, M. (2001) *Upheavals of Thought: The Intelligence of the Emotions*. Cambridge: Cambridge University Press.
Phillips, D. and Schweisfurth, M. (2008) *Comparative and International Education: An Introduction to Theory, Method and Practice*. London: Continuum.
Rizvi, F. (2008) Epistemic Virtues and Cosmopolitan Learning. *Australian Educational Researcher* 35 (1): 17–36.
Wallace, J.D. (1999) Virtues of Benevolence and Justice. In Carr, D. and Steutal, J. (eds) *Virtue Ethics and Moral Education*. Oxon: Routledge, 82–94.

Part IV
Realising an ethical ecology of transformative learning

9 Realising an ethical ecology of transformative learning

Introduction

This book has been concerned both with development of knowledge regarding transformative learning and changing practice. Rather than overturning received notions of transformative learning, this book has sought to work within a tradition that takes transformative learning seriously. It is a response to Mezirow's call for an elaboration of concepts central to a notion of 'integral transformative learning' (2009: 28). Empirical data from the student experience of ISL has illuminated the interconnectedness between personal worlds, human community and natural environment, lending credence to Taylor's 'planetary view' of transformative learning (Taylor, 2008). Through interrogating the ethical dimension of learning, this book moves beyond this view. In doing so it meets the pressing challenge of developing an ethical framework for educational activity such as ISL.

An embryonic notion of an 'ethical ecology of transformative learning' was introduced in the segue to Chapter 3 and is explicated further in this concluding chapter. A systematic and comprehensive prescription *for* an ethical ecology of learning is antithetical to the idea of transformative learning developed here. This chapter will therefore attempt to orientate educators *towards* an understanding of what may be meant by an ethical ecology of transformative learning. It will outline the implications of this approach for how ISL in particular, and transformative learning in general, are conceived and constructed in education policy and practice.

Ecology is a 'thick concept' that works on different planes of meaning and is a particularly useful metaphor to deploy here. The ecological ideas of self-development, cross-pollination, fragility, evolution and sustainability are particularly pertinent to the understanding of transformative learning developed in this book. While recognising that metaphors are pervasive in the literature on travel and education, 'ecology' is used here as an illuminating concept that provides a 'key to giving an adequate account of understanding' (Lakoff and Johnson, 1980: ix). Furthermore, this use of metaphor is consistent with the principle guiding this study of allowing concepts to emerge.

An *ecology* of transformative learning elevates the importance of the context within which the learning self is embedded. Context is understood here not simply as the physical environment in which learning takes place. It is concerned with the totality of relationships nurtured by the learning self with knowledge, ideas, places, individuals and communities, locally and globally. This extends, but is consistent with, the first definition of *ecology* in print by the German zoologist Ernst Haeckel (1834–1919), as 'the relations of living organisms to their surroundings' (Haeckel, cited in Grundmann, 1991: 1). It is based upon the notion of *ecology* as 'being at home' in diverse settings, as outlined in the segue to Chapter 3, echoing Newman's claim that the educated person 'is at home in any society' (Newman, 1852/1959: 191).

An *ethical* ecology of transformative learning is concerned with how communities and societies flourish over time. It is concerned with how society learns about itself, and its many communities, such that those social learning processes are not merely sustained but enhanced, as demonstrated by the flourishing of participating individuals and institutions. As such, educators must be mindful of the well-being of this ecology at each level and in the relationships between the levels. An ethical ecology of learning has a systemic perspective that enables systemic change to be envisioned and enacted.

This chapter will further explore what may be meant by an ethical ecology of transformative learning, the challenges facing this approach to learning and how it can be embedded at the levels of practice, institutional ethos and partnership. The first section will explore what an ethical ecology of transformative learning looks like in practice. Embedding transformative learning does not involve simply thinking about how this form of learning can fit within existing educational institutions, but imagining the form of a school, college or university where learning is conceptualised as transformative. This entails envisioning not only what type of persons we want our students to become but also what sort of institutions we want to become. The second section will argue that transformative practice must permeate the ethos and structures of the institution. Furthermore, in the educational institution that wraps itself around transformative learning, the practice of transformative learning informs institutional development and the ongoing becoming of the institution. This demands particular institutional commitments that will be outlined here. The final section will explore an understanding of educational partnership that foregrounds the voice of the other and overcomes the barriers to recognition and cosmopolitanism suggested by this study.

In this final chapter the implications for each of the levels of practice, institutional ethos and partnership will be related to the understanding of transformative learning developed in this book: namely, that it involves the learning self in a process of becoming into three dimensions of authenticity which are in turn each underpinned by transformative aspects of knowing, being and doing (see Figure 9.1).

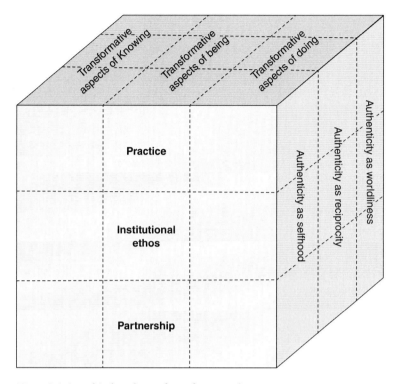

Figure 9.1 An ethical ecology of transformative learning

Practice

Nurturing the conditions for transformation

This book has drawn upon an eclectic group of philosophers and learning theorists to theorise an expanded conceptualisation of transformative learning with aesthetic, moral and relational dimensions. Following this investigation into the particular context of ISL, it is argued that transformative learning can be better understood as a holistic theory of learning concerned with both habits of mind and habits of being. Empirical data has been presented that suggests this includes rational, extrarational, affective, experiential and ethical dimensions of learning that depend upon the particular person engaged in the learning and the context in which they are embedded. It necessarily involves the education of the spirit, mind and body.

Chapters 6, 7 and 8 highlighted the fragility of readiness for transformation. Contextual aspects of educative experience were seen to enhance but also compromise transformation. For instance, a longing to complete ISL and determination to make the most of the experience may either accentuate or extenuate students' openness, receptivity and heightened sense of awareness.

Educators must therefore be concerned with how the conditions for transformation can be nurtured and created as much as with what happens when the conditions are in place.

Connectivity with self, others and the general other were highlighted as important conditions for transformation. For example, students were seen to develop integrity through connecting what they experience overseas to their ongoing everyday lives. Evidence here suggests that, as a prelude to transformative learning, students need to be supported in making such connections. Educators must scaffold students' experience of connecting and reconnecting with self, particular others and the general other in order to be enabled to do this on their own. This requires recognising the interdependency of the local and the global; 'the sense of the "global-in-the-local" and "local-in-the-global"' (Nixon, 2011: 8). Examples from the student accounts of ISL include relating the experience of begging overseas to understanding of poverty and homelessness at home. Creating the conditions, or capability, for becoming other-wise should be established as an important concern of a core curriculum that embeds 'education for global cooperation'. This presents an alternative vision of an internationalised curriculum for home students as developed elsewhere (Clifford and Montgomery, 2011).

The conditions, processes and dispositions of transformative learning are inter-related and often mutually reinforcing. For example, '*Perseverance, resilience and flexibility*' are conditions for transformation and, at the same time, outcomes of the transformative process. The transformative process can be seen to be self-sustaining: once established it builds upon itself. For example, resultant dispositions, such as the disposition towards '*Honesty and humility*', are the conditions for future transformative processes, such as '*Shared reflection*' and immersion. This reveals a paradox inherent within ISL illustrated by the discussion of the capability to overturn stereotypes in Chapter 8. It was described how students must be able to look beyond the superficial to avoid reinforcing stereotypes and suggested that some students only gain this capability as a result of their ISL experience. The fragility of the anticipated outcomes of such programmes, such as overturned stereotypes, has important implications for facilitating transformative learning in partnership with others. This raises questions about the readiness of students for potentially transformative experiences and reiterates the urgent need for educators to catalyse the transformative process.

There is evidence that service-learning participants in formal education are not representative of the wider student population (Bamber *et al.*, 2012) and that social capital is already greatest amongst affluent groups in society that are significantly more likely to volunteer (Civic Exchange, 2012: 63). This raises further questions for the role of educators in activating the transformative process. To ensure the participation of a more diverse group of students, optional programmes that encourage transformative learning must attend also to nurturing the conditions for transformation among all students. This demands intervention into the mainstream curriculum and a shift from viewing transformative experiences as enrichment for the few to being an entitlement for all.

Indeed, transformative learning is a pedagogical approach that provides opportunities to transcend individual disciplines. Rather than simply be considered a 'bolt-on', it has the potential to permeate the curriculum at all levels of formal education. This implicates institutional ethos for its advancement as will be discussed later in this chapter. At the same time, this vision of education does not exclude engagement with disciplinary knowledge. ISL, for example, demands students engage with concepts such as development, poverty and education as they become other-wise. In order to articulate what it means to become, for example, a historian, psychologist, mathematician or educator, teachers could begin by researching the processes of becoming oneself, persons-in-relation and other-wise as they relate to their discipline.

The conditions for transformation need to be made and remade

The focus on nurturing the conditions for transformation in this study provides a response to calls for research into understanding the barriers that inhibit transformative learning (Taylor, 2008: 12). Furthermore, this book concludes that a primary concern for educators must be to ensure the conditions for transformation are continuously made and remade. For instance, evidence has been presented here that just as stereotypes can be reinforced, what were once open and permeable perspectives can in time become ingrained and intransigent. Nurturing the 'habits of mind, disposition and will to become a more active learner' (Mezirow, 2003: 62) is clearly a complex but necessary endeavour. It demands nurturing habits of both being and mind that keep 'habit itself responsive, dynamic and expansive' (Hansen, 2011: 122). Discrete and atomised learning experiences and compartmentalised curricula propagate a view of learning as having particular start and end points and are detrimental to attempts to keep habit 'responsive, dynamic and expansive'. Educators must think beyond a relationship with students that begins on their first day of a programme of learning and ends upon course completion.

This book has sought to illuminate the unexpected and negative consequences of transformative experiences. It provides substantial empirical evidence of what has recently been termed 'regressive transformative learning' (Illeris, 2014: 93), although here the focus is on informal, rather than formal, adult education. The destabilising nature of ISL depicted in this study highlights the responsibility of practitioners, having catalysed the transformative process, to provide ongoing support for students. Transformative learning is a visceral form of holistic learning that may arouse strong feelings and emotions. It necessitates a duty of care for students who, as shown by this study, encounter physical, emotional and cognitive challenges which they have no option but to face.

The 'barriers' sections in each of the chapters in Part III of this book provide important empirical data of regressive transformation, substantiating the claim that this is always a possibility (Illeris, 2014). Practitioners must investigate and account for the destabilising aspects of transformative learning as reflected in the struggle to reconnect with others, highlighted in Chapter 7, and losing a sense of belonging, as discussed in Chapter 8. Furthermore, it must be recognised that disorientation may occur sometime following the transformative experience, as demonstrated by the narrative of Rachel presented in Chapter 5. Educators must recognise that transformative learning demands that students connect and reconnect their learning to other aspects of their lives, including relationships with friends, family and local and global communities. To ensure the conditions for transformative learning are continuously made and remade, further research is required into how students can be enabled to manage their own transformative learning and become self-sufficient in successfully encountering and overcoming disorientating dilemmas. Investigating the role of alumni networks and student support groups in supporting students to reconnect with self, others and the other should provide a fruitful line of enquiry.

Recognising value orientation

Definitions of ISL, as cited in Chapter 4, are relatively recent. It is argued in this book that ISL can be better understood as a form of ecological engagement with aesthetic, moral and spiritual dimensions that is enacted through participation in the lives and 'worlds' of those living in different countries, and which enables ethical reflection, enhances personal efficacy and seeks to engender a more just and sustainable society. Investigating the student experience of ISL has helped to reconceptualise transformative learning as a form of moral education. Transformative pedagogy, so understood, is never value-neutral or apolitical. Furthermore, practitioners must be completely transparent and acknowledge that they are working to promote particular values, understood broadly as 'enduring beliefs about what is worthwhile, ideals for which people strive and broad standards by which particular practices are judged to be good, right, desirable or worthy of respect' (Pike and Halstead, 2006: 24).

Declaring one's motivation and being prepared to disclose one's agenda is essential for students and tutors to act ethically. In the particular context of ISL, it is especially important given the history of relations between the developed and developing world. This study therefore also highlights the necessity for research and practice to recognise and account for the complex policy context in which it operates: for example, higher education policy in the UK currently propagates an understanding of individualism and 'education for global competitiveness', as outlined in Chapter 4, that impacts upon our understanding of the student experience of ISL.

This study suggests that disclosing one's value orientation augments a process of understanding the context, enabling researchers and practitioners to step outside of any 'hermeneutic circle', as will be explored further in the final section of this chapter. Through this process, individuals can become alert to outcomes they themselves had not anticipated and 'see what is questionable' (Gadamer, 1977: 13). Students have diverse and contrasting motives for enrolling upon particular educational programmes that promote transformation. Furthermore, data has been presented here that educational programmes may inadvertently strengthen unhelpful habits of mind and being. For instance, embedding a transformative learning programme within a 'Leadership Award' may incentivise students to participate but may potentially disrupt the achievement of particular goals of such a programme. Appealing to students to undertake ISL for individualistic reasons, such as enhancing employability or self-discovery, may have negative consequences if the primary objective is tangential – for example, supporting educational development in resource-poor communities. Evidence has been presented here that such programmes may nurture dispositions amongst students that impact negatively upon partnerships, for example by reinforcing power imbalances.

Educators must be careful not to establish programmes that predicate such gaps between 'intended' and 'experienced' ethos. Students undertaking transformative education primarily as a means to enhance their curriculum vitae or gain life experience should be encouraged to anticipate reciprocity and become prepared to be open with, and connect with, others: all important conditions for transformation, as explored in Chapters 6, 7 and 8. This provides a practical response to the challenge of balancing a broad range of sometimes competing outcomes within service-learning programmes, such as altruistic or community-focused objectives as well as reflective and individualised ones.

A corollary to this discussion is that educators have a responsibility to think carefully about the messages they deploy, both implicitly and explicitly, regarding the aims of their programmes. This demands clarity with students regarding the changes they intend to bring about. For instance ISL in itself is a deontic force: it propagates unspoken values and moral perspectives. Publicity will have certain intentions understood by those it addresses. Those who choose to participate will have particular expectations about what they are going to experience. Those who object to the idea that the educator's role is to mould certain kinds of people, as determined by the beliefs, values and attitudes they hold, must be reminded that education in general, and transformative learning in particular, is deeply value-laden and, whether consciously or unconsciously, values underpin practice. While educators may wish to avoid being accused of dogma or bias, 'the sobering reality is that all teachers are indoctrinators for a "doctrine" is a "teaching" and to "indoctrinate" is to lead others into that "teaching"' (Pike, 2011. 184).

In fact, through nurturing ethical reflection, educators facilitating transformative learning must enable their students to question their teachings. A pressing challenge for educators is to find ways of enabling young people to critically engage with the sources of the values they encounter (in the case of ISL, this includes their own, those of colleagues, those of providers, and those of the host communities), and to reflect upon the ethos of their experience (Bamber and Pike, 2013). Constructing an autobiographical account that interrogates one's own values and assumptions, although particularly challenging to complete, may be an important activity for those both facilitating and participating in transformative learning programmes. Through understanding our own worldview, and how this informs our practice, we can become ready to understand and facilitate the learning of others. To seek to provide a transformative experience, or even to facilitate reflection upon it, without exploring the implicit values of the particular programme is, ironically, to treat students in a somewhat colonial fashion. Methodologies such as critical literacy could be utilised as part of efforts to foster transformative learning through supporting students and staff with the difficult task of interrogating their values.

Educating dispositions

The longitudinal nature of the study drawn upon here provides evidence that transformative learning is experienced as an ongoing process of becoming. Through investigating the processes of transformative learning, it develops understanding of the role of educating dispositions and how the virtues can be educated. This is particularly timely given the current political interest in the UK, among all political parties, in character education (APPG, 2014; Birdwell *et al.*, 2015) and the founding of the Jubilee Centre for Character & Virtues at the University of Birmingham. As this concluding chapter demonstrates, transformative programmes such as ISL present opportunities for developing the moral agency of future teachers that resists reductive, formulaic models of teaching (Arthur *et al.*, 2015).

Holistic approaches to education are also explicitly foregrounded within UNESCO's latest vision for education for global citizenship (2014). This echoes a report by UNECE (2012) that argued that through education for sustainable development, educators must learn to know (develop understanding), learn to do (develop specific abilities), learn to live together (working together with others) and also learn to be (develop personal attributes). Who the educator is as a person is also a central component of a recent European framework for evaluating education for global citizenship (Fricke and Gathercole, 2015). It details the values (including 'justice, curiosity, diversity, empathy and solidarity') and dispositions (including 'care for and solidarity with people over-coming injustices and inequalities') that should be embedded within the teaching and learning process. This book takes this work forward through identifying and interrogating the theoretical perspectives that should underpin such proposals and providing important evidence of what this transformative learning looks like in practice.

In particular, this book has included evidence that physical immersion in an alternative context can lead to assimilation of different habits of being, as reflected in Rachel's account drawn upon in Chapter 5. For programmes such as ISL to reach their transformative potential, the discourse and language of capability and dispositions provides an important framework to enable practitioners and student participants to understand and articulate the impact of such experiences. This is a useful response to research which has identified that students return from ISL with a strong desire to act on what they have witnessed but lack a framework to express their own learning (Kiely, 2005) or their contribution to host communities overseas (Birdwell, 2011).

The student accounts of ISL presented here echo the discourse within global citizenship education and development education that postulate the existence of a continuum of participation from awareness of issues to action that challenges injustice. For instance, students demonstrate an acute awareness that having gained awareness of poverty and the lives of others through ISL, they are expected to subsequently take action against social injustice. Students experience feelings of guilt when they conclude, as Lucy did, that 'there is nothing much I can do about that right now'. An understanding of transformative learning concerned with cultivating virtues, as elaborated in this study, refocuses this debate upon aspects of the learners' being alongside their agency. It acknowledges the real-world constraints on, or barriers to, moral action (Merry and Ruyter, 2011), which are highlighted in Chapters 6, 7 and 8 of this study. Rather than creating the expectation that students undertake particular actions, an ethical ecology of transformative learning prioritises the nurturing of the learner's capabilities and their becoming a certain kind of person. Sport provides a useful analogy to understand the distinction between doing and being that has emerged here. While a cricketer may occasionally play a good shot, a good cricketer produces good shots regularly, although not all of the time. Just as the best cricketers recognise it would be impossible to play good shots all of the time, students who seek to challenge injustice must develop a sense of social realism that helps to eliminate paralysis, frustration and despair. Researchers and practitioners must therefore find new ways to understand the students' being rather than their doing and in particular their being 'until it becomes them'. It demands a renewed focus upon students as ends-in-themselves.

This book therefore substantiates a report by third sector organisations in the UK that concluded 'we need to shift the balance of NGO public engagement activities away from "transactions" and towards "transformation"' (Darnton and Kirk, 2011). This demands less emphasis on simple campaigning actions, and more emphasis on providing supporters with opportunities to engage increasingly deeply over time through a 'supporters' journey' (Darnton and Kirk, 2011: 10). Consequently, sending organisations such as Voluntary Service Overseas should resist demands to support returned volunteers to draw upon their experience through their future work (Bentall et al., 2010: 2) in ways that are perhaps easy to identify and measure. Elevating the importance of the person the returned volunteer is becoming places value on informal ways in which an overseas experience can have an ongoing impact.

At the same time, focusing upon the types of persons our students are becoming does not excuse unethical behaviour. While acknowledging participants will encounter complex and ambiguous problems in programmes such as ISL, where no clear course of action is sometimes obvious, it is through balancing conflicting needs and being alert to the unintended consequences of any action that they can act ethically. For example, an ongoing disconnect between

190 *Realising an ethical ecology*

what students value and what they actually do, as highlighted by returned ISL participants here in Chapters 6 and 7, can be deeply damaging. It has been suggested that such incongruence 'corrodes . . . concern, love and commitment to others in their care and is storing up tensions and stresses within individuals and within [school] communities who are pushed towards a culture of isolationism, individualism and self-interest' (Clarke, 2009: 187). Through a deeper understanding of their own values, educators and their students can become more clearly aware of this disconnect and develop strategies to align their values and actions. This book has also developed understanding of the contextual affordances and constraints external to the student which neither they nor their tutors can determine but of which they must be cognisant, such as return to consumer culture on completion of ISL.

This book has highlighted that contentment and comfortableness in oneself, as described in *reconnecting with time*, while in themselves hardly a stimulus for social action, are a valuable outcome of transformative learning. This is aligned to the work of liberation theologians who resist the prescription of specific rules for how to challenge injustice and instead emphasise lives lived in solidarity with the poor. This framework for transformative learning elucidates the complexity of the interdependence between thought and action and suggests it is successfully mediated through reflexivity and relationships. The argument here is that the paradigms of service and social change discussed in Chapter 4 have the potential to be mutually reinforcing, as opposed to being complementary or antagonistic, through attention to the students becoming oneself, persons-in-relation and other-wise.

The poverty of pre-specifying learning outcomes

At the heart of this approach to transformative learning are processes such as shared reflection, immersion, deliberation and exchange which are inimical to pedagogies and curricula which pre-specify learning outcomes. For example, searching for an 'authentic experience' of the other may predispose the learner to simply confirm previously held suppositions. Instead, transformative learning emerges: it occurs when it is least expected. Values and virtues emerge through lived experience. From this view, 'not looking' for learning becomes strength. This places demands upon educators who must be able to identify this learning as it becomes manifest. Educators must become accustomed to living alongside and sharing experiences with their students in order to fully understand them. It requires a focus on both the aesthetic (understood as what is being lived through) and the efferent (understood as what is carried away or retained after the experience). Moreover, this study highlights the importance of further research that moves beyond retrospective articulation and rationalisation of the learning process in which students have been involved. Future research into the tacit and aesthetic aspects of transformation should not rely solely on interviews and self-report, but should also include methods such as observations, learning journals, blogs and videotaping. This will help capture, for example, emotive and embodied aspects of reflection, as will be discussed in the next section.

An ethical ecology of learning does not require students, teachers or researchers to seek correct answers. It involves a spectrum of possibility rather than a search for one particular thing. It demands finding a space for the unexpected and the tacit, aesthetic and relational aspects of learning as outlined in Chapter 2. This is a significant challenge within current educational structures that are resistant to change and often prevent the envisioning of alternatives. Amidst a culture of accountability and measurability in formal education, this understanding of transformative learning has implications for assessment of learning that demands radical solutions. Indeed, assessing resultant dispositions is not straightforward: students have been found to ape key skills as they have been assessed (Barnett, 2007: 109–10). Moreover, practitioners must develop creative and innovative strategies to overcome the constraints of institutional assessment mechanisms and move beyond individual assessment. They must facilitate and assess cooperative learning and forms of knowing, being and doing that emerge through working collaboratively. Formative, as opposed to summative, assessment which nurtures the learners' ongoing becoming should be deployed. Educators will require professional development in structuring and facilitating tasks such as these with which they are unlikely to be familiar.

The importance of aesthetic engagement

Through transformative learning, students experience (to borrow a term from aesthetic theory) an altered 'horizon of expectation' (Jauss, 1982: 25). Response to a new encounter augments or reconfigures the student's experience and results in a 'change of horizons' (Jauss, 1982: 25) and new ways of 'reading' of one's world. In describing the importance of aesthetic experience, the poet W.H. Auden suggests each of us inhabits both a 'primary world' of experience and a 'secondary world' of imagination or aesthetic response. There is much here that might inform our understanding of transformative learning:

> Present in every human being are two desires, a desire to know the truth about the primary world, the given world outside ourselves in which we are born, live, love, hate and die, and the desire to make new secondary worlds of our own or, if we cannot make them ourselves, to share in the secondary worlds of those who can.
>
> (Auden, 1968: 49)

Transformative learning, rightly conceived, must enable students not only to negotiate both worlds but to acknowledge their interdependence. Destinations must not be understood as separate from, but rather related to, our primary world. Analogously, learning in our primary world is always an expansion or development of what we already know. Through contact with a secondary world, we check our prior understanding of ourselves and of our primary world. Exposure to an unfamiliar secondary world may challenge deeply held assumptions and ways of interacting and helps students come to a more integrated perspective and way of being in their primary world. This takes place until the secondary world 'becomes you', morally, ethically, spiritually. Further, the ways in which one reflects upon, interprets and responds to experiences in any secondary world is rather important. In *Art as Experience* (1934), Dewey argues that we should recover 'the continuity of esthetic experience with normal processes of living' (p. 10) and ethical ISL should reflect the continuity between different worlds. This book has outlined a series of potentially dangerous dichotomies, such as 'primary' and 'secondary' worlds, 'here' and 'there', 'us' and 'them', 'real' and 'man-made' worlds, that are resisted within an ethical ecology of transformative learning.

For Dewey, aesthetic experiences are 'consummatory' because they attain union and harmony or 'experience in its integrity' and the artist 'does not shun movements of resistance and tension' (1934: 14). This is important because transformative learning is rarely a comfortable experience. If the function of art as 'a central and essential human and social activity' (Stibbs, 1998: 202) involves 'art's ability to shock and inspire, to change vision, ideas and feelings' (Stibbs, 1998: 210), we need to consider further the ethics and the aesthetics of the changes experienced by students. This should provide the focus for future transformative learning research.

If transformative learning is to be construed as a form of aesthetic engagement, practitioners and participants may draw upon creative pedagogic approaches such as the use of images, music, role play, poetry and reflective journals composed in different contexts (see, for example, Bamber and Westrup, 2012). For example, the quotation, 'We don't see things as they are, we see things as we are' attributed to the French writer Anaïs Nin may encourage students to interrogate the sources of their deeply held values and perceptions. Similarly, Harper Lee's *To Kill a Mockingbird* may provoke group discussion as students learn to live alongside others in diverse communities. In particular, Atticus Finch's advice to his daughter, Scout, 'You never understand a person until you consider things from his point of view. Until you climb into his skin and walk around in it' (1960: 30), may help nurture the importance of empathy among students.

Pedagogic approaches derived from reader response criticism may also help realise the potential synergy of the personal and poetic. For instance, an instructor or programme director can design annotation, paired-talk and group-talk activities focused on extracts from participants' diaries kept during a transformative experience. The diary text can function as a 'stimulus activating elements of the reader's past experience' (Rosenblatt, 1978: 1) and the reading of it will often have aesthetic and ethical characteristics not least because 'in the aesthetic transaction the reader's attention is focussed on what he is living through during the reading event' (Rosenblatt, 1985: 38). In other words, what the diary means in a different place and at another time to the one in which it was written. Such diary extracts might well evince qualities of Wolfgang Iser's literary work, which 'diverges from the ordinary experience of the reader in that it offers up views and opens up perspectives in which the empirically known world of one's own personal experience appears changed' (Iser, 1971: 7). This 'aesthetic distance' (Jauss, 1982) between the 'world' in which the diary entry was penned and the current physical location of the reader could map out the landscape across which learners make 'spiritual' journeys (Pike, 2002). A similar approach can be taken with photographs and can generate 'ekphrasis' (Benton, 2000) and moral reflection (Pike, 2011).

Institutional ethos

The student experience

Virtue ethics provides the foundations for an ethical ecology of transformative learning as it provides a framework to understand the moral aspects of our becoming. It is concerned less with the principled ethics of duty or utility and more with our becoming through the cultivation of inclinations, dispositions and good judgements. The words ethics is derived from ethos, which forms the root of the Greek word *ethikos*, meaning 'moral character, nature, disposition, habit, custom'. Ethos, pathos and logos were identified by Aristotle as important means of persuasion, or rhetoric. Institutional ethos therefore relates to the rhetorical, or persuading nature, of the institution. Those who encounter an institution can expect to find their values, attitudes and dispositions influenced by its ethos.

The current preoccupation with student experience, voice and satisfaction in formal education policy and practice is antithetical to transformative practice grounded in partnerships and reciprocity. In relation to higher education, the present situation has led to what has been described as a University Legitimation Crisis (White, forthcoming). In the context of ISL, it reinforces a focus on satisfying the needs of those who inhabit the developed world rather than listening to the needs of those in the developing world.

Recent changes to higher education in the UK have been driven by the principle that students are best placed to decide what they want to get from their higher education. However, the notion of student as consumer is potentially damaging to transformative practice. While opportunities for 'personal development' are the seventh most important reason for undertaking undergraduate study, it is the second-most benefit identified by graduates (Arthur, 2010: 75). Indeed, 'the paradox of real learning is that you don't get what you "want" – and you certainly can't buy it' (Collini, 2011: 12). Transformative learning places demands upon students and is often frustrating, destabilising and uncomfortable in ways which cannot be predicted or accounted for. In offering learning experiences which are uniform, describable and predictable educators capitulate to the 'student experience' mantra. A richer understanding of student satisfaction must nurture clear expectations amongst students of the epistemological and ontological challenges they will face during their study and resist sanitising the learning experience as will be explored later in this chapter.

Transformative learning is one way to develop civic and moral values. It provides a vision for education concerned less with acquisition of academic knowledge and technical skills but, more fundamentally, with the cultivation of virtues and the kind of person each student is becoming. Educational institutions at all levels must nurture a climate for vocational education, understood as enabling students to find their calling or purpose in life. This demands resisting instrumental and functional approaches to education that derogate students to being simply instruments or tools in social processes. It demands a return to education as public service rather than a private good. In embedding transformative learning, as it is understood here, universities would be attempting a return to the original purpose of higher education: preparation for a life of involved and committed citizenship.

Practitioners and researchers must take time to understand the affordances and constraints within any particular context for nurturing transformation. This process reaffirms the role of the good teacher in transferring authority to the student (White, forthcoming). Furthermore, for higher education to meet its transformative potential, all aspects of student interaction with the university have a role to play in the becoming of the student. This elevates the work of broader student support, including pastoral care, social and sports groups, chaplaincy and library services. The diverse and changing nature of higher education ensures increasing numbers of students live at home, study online courses at a distance or work part-time to pay for fees. Whilst presenting pedagogical opportunities for universities, these shifts may be detrimental to higher education as a 'unity of experience' (Dewey, 1934: 10). Universities must develop creative pedagogical initiatives that support all students, regardless of their form of study, to connect with self, others and the other.

Using the language of the marketplace into which many educational establishments have been propelled, the products of education must be seen not as particular courses that are chosen but the graduates who emerge with associated attributes and dispositions. At the same time, education must never be something which is done to the student, but through a reciprocal process, with the student. Nevertheless, listening to 'student voice' does not necessitate students and tutors be viewed 'all on the same level' (White, forthcoming), but it must involve attending not only to the beings and doings that students choose to value but, more importantly, their capacity to develop the functioning of these dispositions. This involvement of students in the development of a transformative curriculum presents a particular challenge to those who mistrust young people and under-estimate their ability to meaningfully contribute to policy making processes in education.

Focus on purpose and process

In a managerialist world of targets, avoidance of ultimate questions is all too common. Educational institutions must dedicate some of their time and resources to seeking the answer to 'first-order questions'. For instance Boyer pleaded for higher education to focus on purpose and process rather than action: 'what is needed is not just more programs, but a larger purpose, a larger sense of mission, a larger clarity of direction' (1994: A48). Just as ISL encourages participants to ask existential questions, a culture must be nurtured within education which encourages staff and students to ask questions such as, why are we doing this, what is the purpose? For example, this study presents evidence that educational projects with communities in the developing world, without being problematised, can be damaging. An ethical ecology of transformative learning must recognise the teleological nature of education and ensure questions of effectiveness, or 'what works', are secondary to questions of purpose (Biesta, 2010).

Educators must resist the temptation to overlook challenging questions about purpose through focusing on organisational and practical aspects of curriculum and pedagogy. For instance, practitioners can easily become consumed by the complex logistics required to facilitate ISL. From this view, what is gone through is as important as any particular outcome. It is through deliberation around the purpose and process of transformative learning that we guarantee congruence between means and ends. This demands awareness of the horizons of significance against which activity is being conceived, structured and enacted. It has been argued here that the capability approach provides a horizon of significance (Taylor, 1991) by which educators can judge what counts as purpose-full education. In particular, nurturing the authenticity of others provides a horizon of significance to conceptualise ISL in particular and transformative learning in general. Future research and practice should be orientated to help understand how a particular activity or process contributes to the development of participating student's own well-being and the well-being of others.

The methodology adopted here of elucidating the concepts central to transformative learning through analysis of the student experience may be a useful process for supporting educators to clarify the purpose of the work with which they are engaged. The conceptual framework that emerged illustrates not what always happens but what is possible to happen. In discussing the beings and doings that they value, educators can develop their own aspirations for the purposes, processes and outcomes of transformative pedagogy. Furthermore, as discussed in the previous section, through attending to student voice, the outcomes and processes of learning can be more fully understood.

Once the purposes of any form of education are understood, transformative learning can be enacted through processes that act upon the insight. This is, however, not a search for a 'quick-fix' or 'one-size-fits-all' solution but comprises processes that attend to the complexity of practice and educational research. This involves accounting for contingencies including the contextual factors that influence the conditions for learning for different individuals. Just as students must continuously remake the conditions for transformation, so must educators and institutions. This demands a reflexive approach to pedagogical practices. Just as the external context changes, for example in the case of ISL the socio-cultural context in which students volunteer overseas, so does the nature of the student experience.

Institution as role model

Transformative learning has the potential to challenge and change dominant culture and practice within educational institutions and society more broadly. Chapters 1 and 2 outlined the urgent need to develop a discourse around pedagogical languages and practices concerned with education that is critical, democratic, relational and ethical, rather than simply valorising 'key skills', 'attributes' or 'deep' individual learning. Whilst being mindful that 'excessive homage to a narrow disciplinary guild and the presumption of neutrality has robbed the academy of its ability to effectively challenge society or to create change' (Saltmarsh *et al.*, 2010: 396), it may be that, for now, institutional leaders can only secure legitimacy by accommodating their efforts within the traditional values of the academy. To ensure 'transformative learning' does not simply become a 'floating signifier' (Illeris, 2014: 15), an open and critical debate is required around transformative pedagogy and its place within the core curriculum. This will challenge educators to rethink their teaching practice and relationship to the wider community. The porosity of educational institutions, both temporally and spatially, must be acknowledged. For instance the transformative processes of reconnecting with self, others and the other demand that universities recognise an ongoing commitment to their students beyond both graduation and news that alumni have secured employment.

Transformative pedagogy is concerned with the body and spirit as well as the mind. It requires educators to engage with the wholeness of their own and learner's lives. Attending to capabilities in all aspects of student lives can help redress the schism between research, teaching and formation of students detailed in Chapter 1. Since educators who understand the multiple selves of their students are best placed to facilitate transformative learning, professional development is required around strategies to support students to become oneself, persons-in-relation and other-wise. At the same time, transformative learning is not simply concerned with the student's emergent identity and self-image (see, for example, Illeris, 2014). In becoming 'persons-in-relation' and 'other-wise', students are challenged to come to a deeper understanding of their world and how they live within it. In the case of ISL, this involves developing critical understanding of concepts such as education, poverty and development. An ethical ecology of education highlights the importance of developing, with others, ways of understanding such concepts through, rather than separated from, experience.

A concern for the students' becoming demands educational institutions value the becoming of role models entrusted with this endeavour. The dispositions of staff and ethos of the institution impact upon the ecology of learning in non-trivial ways, demonstrating the fragility of this endeavour. Indeed, as students discover through transformative experiences such as ISL, their own well-being is intimately inter-related to the well-being of others. This highlights the necessity of institutional efforts to nurture the authentic self of academic and support staff. Newman's description of the university as an 'alma mater' must be extended to incorporate all staff being known 'one by one' by senior members within the institution. Further research is required into the capabilities educators need to facilitate such programmes and how these can be engendered.

While students often describe the ISL experience as spiritual, there is only limited evidence here, outlined in Chapter 6, that students relate this to the Christian tradition or a renewal of faith. It is argued here that ISL nurtures virtues which are good for everyone (regardless of faith). Just as particular educational programmes must be transparent about their underpinning rationale, there is an urgent need for educators and institutions in general to be open about their values. This demands recognition that educators propagate certain messages in their work and that they, and their students, must be supported to interrogate the assumptions about meaning-making that are made in their institution.

Allowing learning to emerge requires a bottom-up approach to curriculum development that nurtures the conditions of openness and connectivity with self, others and the other. This involves creating the conditions within a community of learners 'where ideas can be voiced freely, where people can meet regularly to reflect and reconstruct their thoughts with others and where people could bring new ideas and interests to share and expand upon with colleagues' (Clarke, 2009: 184). Transformative learning so envisaged demands social relations, deliberation, immersion and reflection, and provides a response to claims of crisis in the academy:

> What is at stake in the academy is the erosion of not just academic freedom and autonomy, but also of collegiality, and we might say care, that is extended to co-workers, students and the wider public.
> (Kreber and Fanghanel, 2012: 131)

Educational institutions must model ways of working in partnership, as will be elaborated upon in the final part of this chapter. Attending to '*Openness with*' and '*Connectivity with*' self, others and the other will help ensure institutions become 'open reflectively to the new and loyal reflectively to the known' (Hansen, 2011: 36). Like individual students, institutions must cultivate these conditions of transformation by both standing behind their convictions and also taking seriously others' doubts about them. This demands recognising the institution's past and present whilst envisioning possible and preferable futures.

Fragmented disciplinary knowledge has been found lacking when confronted with the nature of the complex social, political, cultural and ethical problems of our globalised world (UNESCO, 2010: 349). The form of transformative learning outlined here has the potential to bring together educators and academics from different disciplines in a common endeavour, contributing to what Maxwell (2010) describes as a shift from knowledge inquiry to wisdom inquiry. Innovative models of knowledge, teaching and research, such as transformative learning, necessitate cross-curricular and trans-disciplinary engagement with diverse cultures, indigenous ways of knowing and systems of values and beliefs. This must recognise the co-production and meaningful public dissemination of knowledge. This can be achieved, for example, through schools, colleges and universities working with NGOs and other public and private bodies, across sectors, to research social issues in order to alleviate suffering and disadvantage. This can be achieved through connecting the local with the global and vice versa, finding a space for both the marginalised and the other, nurturing inter-connectedness across the disciplines and provision of a student experience that embeds civic engagement.

Finally, in highlighting the role of transformative learning in supporting students to reconnect with place and the planet, this book is consistent with the work of Bateson and deep ecologists, who would argue that environmental issues cannot be separated from an overall ecology of human relations. Transformative pedagogy must be considered alongside recent attempts to reduce the carbon footprint of education institutions within the UK. Researching pedagogical interventions that do not necessitate travel to other countries will further develop understanding of a more sustainable ecology of learning where values and actions can become more closely aligned. This raises particular challenges given the evident importance, highlighted by this study, of physical immersion and personal encounter. Nevertheless, virtues such as prudence, compassion, patience, honesty and practical wisdom are particularly relevant to education for sustainable development and worthy of future research.

Partnership

Balancing the multi-faceted nature of transformation

Attending simultaneously to becoming oneself, persons-in-relation and otherwise elevates the role of the particular and general other and consequently the importance of partnership to learning. If practitioners were to focus solely on 'becoming oneself', students may develop self-confidence, perseverance and courage but not value other forms of knowing, and fail to become other-wise. This illustrates the dangers of the current preoccupation of policy makers in the UK, with character education focused upon performance virtues such as grit and resilience (DfE, 2015). Indeed, transformative learning, as it is understood here, cannot simply be a vehicle for self-discovery. A sole focus on becoming oneself in ISL may propagate a narrative that accentuates the differences between life in the UK and overseas as detailed in Chapter 6. Similarly, a focus upon overcoming physical, practical and emotional challenges can reinforce stereotypes and differences between 'us' and 'them' as outlined in Chapter 8.

The three dimensions of authenticity must be viewed as overlapping and reinforcing rather than mutually exclusive. For example, selfhood and reciprocity interact in that developing self-esteem often provides students with the confidence to meet and be with other adults and vice versa. In this study, certain dispositions have been shown to catalyse the development of others: '*Honesty and humility*' (a disposition related to becoming oneself) helps individuals gain a '*Felt sense of the worlds of others*' (becoming persons-in-relation) which, in turn, helps develop a disposition towards '*Valuing other ways of knowing*' (becoming other-wise). In an attempt to capture the relationship between the three organising concepts of authenticity, this example suggests a spiral (as depicted in Figure 9.2) illuminates and provides insight into the learning self's process of becoming authentic, and is worthy of further investigation.

This book has emphasised the multidimensional, or holistic, nature of transformation. For instance, it concludes that critical reflection, understood as a rationalist ideal, is necessary but not enough in itself to secure transformative learning. The focus has, instead, been on ethical and aesthetic aspects of reflection. This presents an alternative to Mezirow's understanding of 'moral-ethical critical self-reflection' (1998: 190) that is concerned solely with critiquing the norms of one's ethical decision making. Evidence has been presented here of the role of the tacit and unconscious within reflection. Further research is needed into conceptualisations of reflection that accommodate emotions, immersion and encountering other people, places and ideas.

More broadly, this book highlights the sophisticated balance required in educational endeavour. For instance, transformative learning is conceptualised here as being deeply relational yet dependent upon space for individual reflection. The importance of balancing distanciation and participation supports evidence that we can reach the wrong conclusions by 'too much rational detachment' as much as by 'insufficient emotional attachment' (Carr, 2007: 375). In relation to ISL, providers may even sterilise the potency of immersion in a new context through over-preparation, including the use of images, videos and first-hand accounts that embeds expectations and colonises an environment that conflicts with the holistic, indefinable and unpredictable nature of the experience. On the other hand, an emphasis on the immediacy of experience and immersion is likely to miss important ethical considerations. Certainly Aristotle's 'doctrine of the mean' (Aristotle, 1925: 1107a 6–8), might inform students' rational ordering of, and reflection upon, their actions both during and after transformative experiences. Deeper understanding of the notion of balance in educational endeavour, perhaps drawing upon Aristotle's work, may provide a fruitful frame for future educational research.

Authentic relationships

This book has developed understanding of ways in which personal transformation informs social transformation and social change. Transformative learning as it has been conceptualised here is founded upon connectivity. It is not concerned solely with individual agency but what we can do together. It suggests

200 *Realising an ethical ecology*

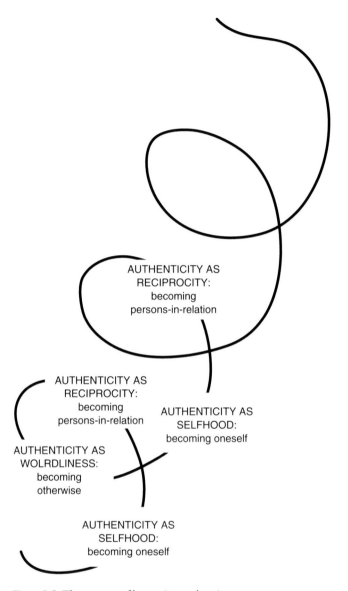

Figure 9.2 The process of becoming authentic

transformation occurs not through solely reasoning on our own but through deliberation and working in partnership.

Pedagogical approaches such as ISL must be careful not to objectify and dehumanise things that do have being through I–It relationships (Buber, 1961: 127). This demands a shift from a mode of having to a mode of being as outlined in Chapter 6. A focus on authentic relationships provides an alternative pedagogical response to recent calls for global partnerships to be underpinned by postcolonial theory (Martin and Griffiths, 2012). With respect to higher education, the power and politics of expert academic knowledge has been described as 'the largest obstacle in higher education to authentic engagement with communities and the public world' (Boyte, 2008: 108). Furthermore, the current emphasis on student satisfaction and the student experience increases the likelihood of partnerships underpinned by exploitative I–It, as opposed to I–Thou, relationships. School linking provides an example of a new form of colonialism whereby institutions exercise *power over* those with whom they are engaged, and the experiences of members of resource-poor communities are used to resource the curriculum of relatively wealthy schools.

An ethical ecology of education must be founded upon authentic relationships that nurture *power with* rather than *power to* or *power over* as discussed in '*Recognising others*' in Chapter 7. In *power over* relationships, one partner control resources and decision making and may benefit at the expense of others. *Power with* is instead underpinned by shared agency and is mutually transforming. In transformative learning educators demonstrate *power with* as they resist 'leaping in' and instead 'leap ahead' when engaged with students and partners in conversations about practice. In this way, they become disposed towards 'being with' rather than 'doing for' or even 'doing to'. Institutions must model this way of working in partnership through nurturing engagement with the publics they serve founded upon mutuality and reciprocity.

Transformative learning so conceived has the potential to transform development initiatives that have reduced partnerships to simply an exchange of money from North to South. Implicitly acknowledging the importance of '*power with*', a recent report initiated by the international NGO Oxfam (Darnton and Kirk, 2011) advocated a shift in the principles guiding such projects from aid to mutual support, from charity to justice, and from development to well-being and freedom. This study augments recent calls for North–South partnerships between schools and other organisations to be grounded in conceptualisations of knowledge, the curriculum and pedagogy that are based on a more relational ontology (Martin, 2011). The focus here is on nurturing and sustaining authentic relationships at the level of individuals and institutions. Just as this study recommends students '*Reconnect with others*', attempts must be made to maintain and sustain institutional partnerships over time.

There is an urgent need to recognise fully the role of all partners in the transformative process. The conditions and processes of transformation depend upon engagement with others. It is through exposure to the capabilities of the lives of others that students are able to reflect upon their own well-being and flourishing. The mutuality this depends upon must be explicitly acknowledged: openness with others is dependent upon openness to others as well as openness of others. This demands moving beyond a deficiency view of partners, as demonstrated in ISL through focusing upon what overseas partners have not got in terms of material resources, to understanding more fully their involvement in and contribution to transformation.

The notion of authentic relationships developed here provides a timely contribution to an emergent discussion around pedagogical approaches underpinning counter-cultural and critical service programmes aligned with the radical principles of Catholic social teaching (Bamber, 2011). Viewing partners as objects of our generosity, as represented by traditional charitable perspectives, is inconsistent with an authentic relationship. Partners must instead be recognised as people with their own dignity, concerns and opinions who are themselves involved in a process of becoming. The situation and context of partners must be fully acknowledged. Transformative learning research and practice cannot be solely concerned with the learning outcomes for participating students since they are deeply related to the particular and general other.

Community partners must be recognised as educators pivotal to the transformative process. This involves, for example, being open and honest about their role in challenging student stereotypes. Moreover, community partners must take a central role in the development and provision of the curriculum with which they are associated, including decisions around the purposes and values underpinning a particular programme as discussed earlier. This involves deliberation around the dispositions, or beings and doings, which are valued in a particular learning context. Being transparent and explicit about what transformative learning is trying to achieve, as outlined in this chapter, enables the contributions of, and demands placed upon, partners to be more fully understood and acknowledged.

This conceptualisation of authentic relationships offers a rich lens for understanding the research process itself. For instance, in order to anticipate and nurture reciprocity, future research into transformative pedagogy should involve participants more fully in the research process. For instance, response validation deliberation may have developed further understanding in this study regarding the beings and doings that students choose to value and indeed live out in practice. Just as the arguments here have drawn upon the capability approach, used initially to reconceptualise poverty in resource-poor countries, research into transformative pedagogy would benefit from drawing upon established participatory research methodologies in the field of development studies. Furthermore, partners must be involved in the generation of concepts guiding similar studies to ensure their development is not constrained by Western 'learned ignorance' (Santos, 2009). Fully recognising indigenous ways of knowing in this process opens up the potential for a more genuine 'ethical hermeneutics' (see, for example, Dussel, 2003).

A cosmopolitan outlook

Educators must acknowledge their role within economic, social and cultural processes locally, nationally and internationally and the ways in which they are implicated in intensifying social injustices and exacerbating inequalities in the classroom, on campus and in wider communities. This research highlights that ways of knowing, being and doing in educational institutions are shaped by but are also able to shape this context. The 'bigger-than-self' challenges facing society require 'bigger-than-self' solutions. For Ulrich Beck, in a world of global crises, the human condition has already itself become cosmopolitan (2006: 2). It is the same for the university in that:

> it is not that there are many crises in society and across the world and that the university has a responsibility to respond to them. It is rather that the university, through its activities in learning, inquiry and development, is already inter-connected with this world.
>
> (Barnett, 2011: 145)

Transformative learning enables educators to recognise their responsibility for the well-being not only of the students in their care, but also towards the broad range of communities with which they are engaged. Furthermore, it can also be argued that students must be enabled to engage in transformative learning not as a means to an end (either for institution or students) but, as argued in Chapter 1, because it is the right thing to do. Whilst this may involve moves away from benevolence (preserving and enhancing the welfare of those with whom one is in frequent personal contact) to universalism (understanding, appreciation, tolerance and protection for the welfare of all people and for nature) (Darnton and Kirk, 2011: 51–2), it also demands holding in tension similarities and differences.

While overemphasising the 'otherness' of those we encounter is likely to embed stereotypes and power imbalances, focusing upon inter-connections rather than distinctions can lead to a denial of difference which neglects the myriad of variations in the human condition. However, 'Otherness' remains problematic and this approach to transformative learning enables educators to avoid 'a respect of differences that maintains differences, and notions of "multiculturalism" that hold on to tightly scripted and immobile views of self and identity' (Fanghanel and Cousin, 2012: 41). This is addressed by this framework in acknowledging the importance of becoming other-wise and valuing other forms of knowing. Transformative learning, so understood, supports the recognition of difference that acknowledges and respects ethno-cultural identities but also encourages mutual engagement across difference (Blum, 2014). Just as it has been argued here that institutions themselves must nurture the habits of ethical reflection, this recognition of difference demands individuals have a sense of both pluralism and fallibilism (Merry and Ruyter, 2011: 9–10).

Given contemporary concerns about the treatment of difference and otherness, acutely expressed in the moral panic and public hysteria surrounding fundamentalism, an ethical ecology of transformative learning can be seen to exemplify the important practice of 'entoleration' (Lundie and Conroy, 2015), whereby individuals and groups engage with sympathetic and transformative encounters with others' beliefs. Moreover, in focusing upon nurturing and catalysing dispositions which could be described as 'features of humanness', transformative learning is a foundational pedagogical approach that transcends cultural boundaries and, simultaneously, recognises the liquidity and evolution of difference.

The role of nurturing the authenticity of others is alluded to in David Held's definition of cosmopolitanism as the 'ethical and political space which sets the terms of reference for the recognition of people's equal moral worth, their active agency and what is required for their autonomy and development' (Held, 2010: 49). This substantiates the pertinence of cosmopolitanism to a holistic conceptualisation of transformative learning. Similarly, developing understanding of transformative learning as a form of aesthetic engagement lends credence to research that claims cosmopolitan education has a distinctly aesthetic dimension (Hansen, 2011).

Conclusion

Given the centrality of values, purpose and relationships to this view of transformative learning, the label of 'learning' inadequately captures the extent and depth of the discussion (see, for example, Biesta, 2015). Moreover, through considering the implications for educational programmes and institutions, the ambitious proposals contained here are perhaps better captured in the broader notion of 'an ethical ecology of education'.

This book has aimed to create an 'imaginative interpretation' (Charmaz, 2006: 181) of transformative learning, and gain a sense of 'what this requires of us' (Gadamer, 2004: 41). The conceptual framework that emerged captures practical ways in which transformative pedagogy can be grounded in both ways of knowing and being:

> the whole point of the project . . . it encourages you to think . . . to think, for a change.
>
> (Becca)
>
> I think I only wrote about two emails. It's something that I do now when I'm going away; I kind of cut off and get in to where I'm going.
>
> (Lucy)

This book offers the conceptual tools to assist students, practitioners and researchers as they seek to 'get out' of their current ways of thinking and being through a form of 'critical hermeneutics'. Beyond solely 'thinking for a change', it highlights the importance of 'getting in' to where they are going through reconnecting, immersion and gaining a felt sense of the worlds of others. Similarly, the conditions of '*Connectivity with*', '*Openness with*' and '*Anticipating reciprocity*' are all capabilities required by educational researchers seeking to challenge social injustice.

A cosmopolitan outlook, characterised by both habits of mind and being, is central to the understanding of transformative learning developed here (Bamber, 2015). Transformative pedagogy has the potential to nurture local, national and global aspects of citizenship as understood in frameworks for cosmopolitan citizenship. Understanding education for cosmopolitan citizenship as nurturing a process of becoming has the potential to refocus debate around global and national citizenship in general (Heater, 2002). It is through partnerships that cultivate the conditions, processes and dispositions embedded within an ethical ecology of transformative learning that the cosmopolitan citizen can be realised, supporting moves towards a more equitable and sustainable world.

References

All-Party Parliamentary Group on Social Mobility (APPG) (2014) *Character and Resilience Manifesto*. London: HMSO.
Aristotle (1925) *Ethica Nicomachea* [*The Nichomachean Ethics*]. In Aristotle, *The Works of Aristotle*, Volume IX (trans. W.D. Ross). Oxford: Oxford University Press.
Arthur, J. (2010) *Of Good Character: Exploration of Virtues and Values in 3–25 Year Olds*. Exeter: Imprint Academic.
Arthur, J., Kristjansson, K., Cooke, S., Brown, E. and Carr, D. (2015) The Good Teacher: Understanding Virtues in Practice Research Report. Birmingham: The Jubilee Centre for Character & Virtues, University of Birmingham.
Auden, W.A. (1968) *Secondary Worlds*. New York: Random House.
Bamber, P. (2011) The Transformative Potential of International Service-Learning at a University with a Christian Foundation in the UK. *Journal of Beliefs and Values* 32 (3): 343–59.
Bamber, P. (2015) Becoming Other-Wise: Transforming International Service-Learning Through Nurturing Cosmopolitanism. *Journal of Transformative Education* 13 (1): 26–45.
Bamber, P. and Pike, M. (2013) Towards an Ethical Ecology of International Service-Learning. *Journal of Curriculum Studies* 45 (4): 535–59.
Bamber, P. and Westrup, R. (2012) Finding a Shared Path: Journal Writing, Reciprocity and International Service-Learning. In Baca, I. (ed.) *Service-Learning and Writing: Paving the Way for Literacy(ies) through Community Engagement*. Boston: Brill, 129–54.
Bamber, P., Bourke, L. and Lyons, M. (2012) Global Citizens: Who Are They? *Education, Citizenship and Social Justice* 7 (2): 161–75.
Barnett, R. (2007) *A Will to Learn*. Maidenhead: Open University Press/SRHE.
Barnett, R. (2011) *Being a University*. Oxon: Routledge.
Beck, U. (2006) *Cosmopolitan Vision*. Cambridge: Polity Press.
Bentall, C., Bourn, D. and Blum, N. (2010) Returned Volunteers and Engagement with Development. London: Institute of Education. Unpublished report.
Benton, M.G. (2000) *Studies in the Spectator Role*. London: Routledge.
Biesta, G. (2010) Why 'What Works' Still Won't Work: From Evidence-Base Education to Values-Based Education. *Studies in Philosophy of Education* 29: 491–503.
Biesta, G. (2015) What is Education For? On Good Education, Teacher Judgement, and Educational Professionalism. *European Journal of Education* 50 (1): 75–87.
Birdwell, J. (2011) *Service International: This is the Big Society without Borders*. London: DEMOS. Accessed 1 August 2015 at www.demos.co.uk/files/Service_International-web.pdf?1311850342.
Birdwell, J., Scott, R. and Reynolds, L. (2015) *Character Nation*. London: DEMOS.
Blum, L. (2014) Three Educational Values for a Multicultural Society: Difference Recognition, National Cohesion and Equality. *Journal of Moral Education* 43 (3): 332–44.

Boyer, E. (1994) Creating the New American College. *The Chronicle of Higher Education* A48.
Boyte, H. (2008) Against the Current: Developing the Civic Agency of Students. *Change*, May/June. Accessed 11 April 2012 at www.changemag.org/Archives/Back%20Issues/May-June%202008/full-against-the-current.html.
Buber, M. (1961) *Between Man and Man*. London: Collins.
Carr, D. (2007) Character in Teaching. *British Journal of Educational Studies* 55 (4): 369–89.
Charmaz, K. (2006) *Constructing Grounded Theory*. London: Sage.
Civic Exchange (2012) The Big Society Audit 2012. Accessed 1 August 2015 at www.civilexchange.org.uk/wp-content/uploads/2012/05/THE-BIG-SOCIETY-AUDIT-2012_Civil-ExchangeFinal8May.pdf.
Clarke, P. (2009) A Practical Guide to a Radical Transition: Framing the Sustainable Learning Community. *Education, Knowledge and Economy* 3 (3): 183–97.
Clifford, V. and Montgomery, C. (2011) Introduction: Internationalising the Curriculum for Global Citizenship in Higher Education. In Clifford, V. and Montgomery, C. (eds) *Moving towards Internationalisation of the Curriculum for Global Citizenship in Higher Education*. Oxford Brookes University: The Oxford Centre for Staff and Learning Development, 13–24.
Collini, S. (2011) From Robbins to McKinsey. *London Review of Books* 33 (16): 9–14. Accessed 1 August 2015 at www.lrb.co.uk/v33/n16/stefan-collini/from-robbins-to-mckinsey.
Darnton, A. and Kirk, M. (2011) *Finding Frames: New Ways to Engage the UK Public in Global Poverty*. London: BOND for international development. Accessed 20 April 2012 at http://findingframes.org/.
Department for Education (DfE) (2015) Rugby Coaches to be Drafted in to Help Build Grit in Pupils. Accessed 31 May 2015 at www.gov.uk/government/news/rugby-coaches-to-be-drafted-in-to-help-build-grit-in-pupils.
Dewey, J. (1934) *Art as Experience*. New York: Perigee Books.
Dussel, E. (2003) *Philosophy of Liberation*. Pasadena: Wipf and Stock.
Fanghanel, J. and Cousin G. (2012) 'Worldly' Pedagogy: A Case Study on Learning across Conflict at University. *Teaching in Higher Education* 17 (1): 39–50.
Fricke, H.J. and Gathercole, C. (2015) *Monitoring Education for Global Citizenship*. Brussels: DEEEP.
Gadamer, H.G. (1977) *Philosophical Hermeneutics* (ed. and trans. D.E. Ling). Berkeley, Los Angeles and London: University of California Press.
Gadamer, H.G. (2004) *Truth and Method* (trans. J. Weinsheimer and D.G. Marshall) (2nd Revised Edition). London and New York: Continuum.
Grundmann, R. (1991) The Ecological Challenge to Marxism. *New Left Review* 187 (May–June): 103–20.
Hansen, D. (2011) *The Teacher and the World: A Study of Cosmopolitanism as Education*. London and New York: Routledge.
Heater, D. (2002) *World Citizenship: Cosmopolitan Thinking and Its Opponents*. London: Continuum.
Held, D. (2010) *Cosmopolitanism: Ideals and Realities*. Cambridge: Polity Press.
Illeris, K. (2014) *Transformative Learning and Identity*. London and New York: Routledge.
Iser, W. (1971) Indeterminacy and the Reader's Response in Prose Fiction. In Miller, J. Hillis (ed.) *Aspects of Narrative*. Columbia: Columbia University Press, 3–30.
Jauss, H.R. (1982) *Toward an Aesthetic of Reception*. Minneapolis: University of Minnesota Press.
Kiely, R. (2005) A Transformative Learning Model for Service-Learning: A Longitudinal Case Study. *Michigan Journal of Community Service Learning* 12 (1): 5–22.

Kreber, C. and Fanghanel, J. (2012) Knowing and Being in the Academy: Exploring Local Approaches for Transformative Learning. In Adamson, J., Nixon, J. and Su, F. (eds) *The Reorientation of Higher Education: International Perspectives*. Hong Kong: Comparative Education Research Centre (CERC) University of Hong Kong/Springer, 214–33.

Lakoff, G. and Johnson, M. (1980) *Metaphors We Live By*. Chicago: University of Chicago Press.

Lee, H. (1960) *To Kill a Mockingbird*. New York: HarperCollins.

Lundie, D. and Conroy, J. (2015) 'Respect Study': The Treatment of Religious Difference and Otherness: An Ethnographic Investigation in UK Schools. *Journal of Intercultural Studies* 36 (3): 274–90.

Martin, F. (2011) Global Ethics, Sustainability and Partnership. In Butt, G. (ed.) *Geography, Education and the Future*. London: Continuum, 207–24.

Martin, F. and Griffiths, H. (2012) Power and Representation: A Postcolonial Reading of Global Partnerships and Teacher Development through North-South Study Visits. *British Educational Research Journal* 28 (6): 907–27.

Maxwell, N. (2010) Does Science Provide Us with the Methodological Key to Wisdom? Accessed 4 August 2015 at http://philpapers.org/archive/MAXDSP.2.doc.

Merry, M. and Ruyter, D. (2011) The Relevance of Cosmopolitanism for Moral Education. *Journal of Moral Education* 40 (1): 1–18.

Mezirow, J. (1998) On Critical Reflection. *Adult Education Quarterly* 48 (3): 185–98.

Mezirow, J. (2003) Transformative Learning as Discourse. *Journal of Transformative Education* 1 (1): 58–63.

Mezirow, J. (2009) Transformative Learning Theory. In Mezirow, J. and Taylor, E. (eds) *Transformative Learning in Practice: Insights from Community Workplace and Higher Education*. San Francisco: Jossey-Bass, 18–32.

Newman, J.H (1852/1959) *The Idea of a University*. New York: Image Books.

Nixon, J. (2011) Interpretive Pedagogies for a Globalised World: Converse or Perish. Paper presented to ESRC Seminar Series, 'Graduates as Global Citizens', 14 October, University College London, UK. Accessed 21 April 2012 at www.wlv.ac.uk/default.aspx?page=29718.

Pike, M.A. (2002) Aesthetic Distance and the Spiritual Journey: Educating for Morally and Spiritually Significant Events across the Art and Literature Curriculum. *International Journal of Children's Spirituality* 7 (1): 9–21.

Pike M.A. (2011) Ethical English Teaching and Citizenship Education: Promoting Democratic Values or the Tao? *Changing English: Studies in Culture and Education* 18 (4): 351–9.

Pike, M.A. and Halstead, M.J. (2006) *Citizenship and Moral Education: Values in Action*. London: Routledge Falmer.

Rosenblatt, L. (1978) *The Reader, the Text, the Poem: The Transactional Theory of the Literary Work*. Carbondale: Southern Illinois University Press.

Rosenblatt, L. (1985) The Transactional Theory of the Literary Work: Implications for Research.

In Cooper, C. (ed.) *Researching Response to Literature and the Teaching of Literature*. Norwood: Ablex, 33–53.

Saltmarsh, J., Hartley, M. and Clayton, P. (2010) Is the Civic Engagement Movement Changing Higher Education? *British Journal of Educational Studies* 58 (4): 391–406.

Santos, B.S. (2009) A Non-Occidentalist West? Learned Ignorance and Ecology of Knowledge. *Theory, Culture & Society* 26 (7–8): 103–25.

Stibbs, A. (1998) Language in Art and Art in Language. *Journal of Art and Design Education* 17 (2): 201–9.

Taylor, C. (1991) *The Ethics of Authenticity*. London: Harvard University Press.
Taylor, E.W. (2008) Transformative Learning Theory. *New Directions for Adult and Continuing Education* 119 (Fall): 5–15.
United Nations Economic Commission for Europe (UNECE) (2012) Learning for the Future – Competencies in Education for Sustainable Development. Geneva: UNECE.
United Nations Educational, Scientific and Cultural Organisation (UNESCO) (2010) World Social Science Report: Knowledge Divides. Paris: UNESCO Publishing. Accessed 1 August 2015 at http://unesdoc.unesco.org/images/0018/001883/188333e.pdf.
United Nations Educational, Scientific and Cultural Organisation (UNESCO) (2014) Global Citizenship Education: Preparing Learners for the Challenges of the 21st Century. Paris: UNESCO.
White, M. (forthcoming) Student Partnership and a University Legitimation Crisis. In Bamber, P. and Moore, J. (eds) *Teacher Education in Challenging Times*. London: Routledge.

Appendix
Mapping of data collection

Table A.1 Phase One research participants

Data code	Pseudonym	Year of ISL experience	Location of project overseas	Current employment
P1 I1	Rachel	1993	India (Tibetan community)	Primary school teacher, UK
P1 I2	Ann	1999	India (Tibetan community)	Secondary school teacher, UK
P1 I3	Becca	2001	Malawi	Secondary school teacher, UK
P1 I4	Katie	2003	India (Tibetan community)	Mental health charity, UK
P1 I5	Lucy	2004	Malawi	University part-time worker, UK
P1 I6	Angela	2005	Sri Lanka	Primary school teacher, overseas
P1 I7	Sue	2004 and 2005	India (Hindu community) and South Africa	Primary school teacher, UK

Table A.2 Phase Two research participants

Data code	Pseudonyms	Year of ISL experience	Location of project overseas
P2 GI1	Rita and Alice	2007	India (Tibetan community)
P2 GI2	Mary and Coleen	2007	Malawi
P2 GI3	Jenny, Megan and Cath	2007	Nigeria
P2 GI4	Vicky and Vanessa	2007	Brazil
P2 GI5	Carol and Lisa	2007	Uganda
P2 GI6	Alexia, Andrea and Liz	2007	India (Tibetan), India (Hindu) and Sri Lanka

Table A.3 Phase Three research participants

Data code	Pseudonym	Year of ISL experience	Location of project overseas
P3 I1	Lin	2009	Brazil
P3 I2	Melanie	2009	India (Hindu community)
P3 I3	Olivia	2009	Romania
P3 I4	Rahima	2009	Malawi
P3 I5	Gwennan	2009	Romania
P3 I6	Isabelle	2009	Caux, Switzerland

Table A.4 Phase Four research participants

Data code	Pseudonyms	Year of ISL experience
P4 FG1	Lin, Rahima and Isabelle	2009
P4 FG2	Melanie and Olivia	2009

Index

absorption *see* internalisation
active learning 21, 58, 68, 69
adaptive preferences 44, 126
Adorno, Theodor W. 57, 155
Adrian, William 80
adult learning 4, 17–18, 22–6, 185
aesthetic knowledge 29–32 *see also* knowing
aesthetics: agency 46; authenticity and selfhood 54–5; being and becoming 37; engagement and transformation 108, 114–15, 163, 191–3, 204; ISL, definition 6, 70, 186; knowing, aspects of 29–32; transformative learning, model of 5, 91, 183, 190–1, 199, 204
affectivity 16, 18, 23–6, 38–9, 105, 140–1; *see also* emotions
agape (love) 87
agency: being and knowing 52–7, 189; capability approach 43–7; civic 77; integrity 126–9; learning theory 20, 23; reciprocity and mutuality 149–51, 199, 201
agency freedom 45 *see also* capability approach
agent-centred education 41
aid 71
altruism 87, 135
anaesthetic experience 31, 54, 114 *see also* aesthetics
Anglicanism 85–6 *see also* Catholicism; Christianity; faith; religion; spirituality
Annette, John 78–9
anxiety 39
Aquinas, Thomas
Arendt, Hannah 44–5
Argyris, Chris 17
Aristotle 39–42, 60, 67, 79, 156, 193, 199
Arthur, James 87

assessment 191
Augustine, St. 71–2
autobiography 91, 187 *see also* biographies, personal
autonomy: authenticity 7, 53, 107, 204; capability approach 43, 47, 57; learning 22, 24, 35, 58
awareness: focal 32–4, 55, 114; subsidiary 32–4, 114

Barnacle, Robyn 31
Barnett, Ron 24, 34, 39, 55–6, 125
Barnett, Samuel 75
barriers: agency and capability approach 44, 57; cosmopolitanism 170, 176–8; integrity 126–9; reciprocity 152–3; transformative learning, model of 185–8, 189
Bateson, Gregory 17, 23, 62, 198
Beck, Ulrich 156, 203
becoming: being as process of becoming 37–9; virtue ethics and becoming 39–43; *see also* cosmopolitanism (worldliness); integrity; reciprocity
Being 33 *see also* being; Heidegger, Martin
being: authenticity and reciprocity 117–9, 201; authenticity and selfhood 52–7, 121–2; mode of 56, 108, 121, 126, 157; as process of becoming 37–9; virtue ethics and becoming 39–43; *see also* 'being with'; habits of being
'being with' 117, 132, 141, 147–9, 172–4, 201
Belenky, Mary Field 36
benefit, socio-economic 69, 75, 77
benevolence 45, 177, 203
Big Society 67, 78
biographies, personal 108, 110, 111 *see also* autobiography

bodies: capability approach 45; holistic learning 24–6; tacit knowing 32, 34; transformative learning, conception of 183, 196; lack of trust in; 22; *see also* knowing, embodied
Bonhoeffer, Dietrich 60
Boyer, Ernest 59, 69, 194–5
Brookfield, Stephen D. 20, 25
Browne Review (2010) 77
Buber, Martin 35–6, 132, 147, 151, 200
Byron, William 78

Calhoun, Cheshire 129
Campus Compact (US) 68–9
capability approach 43–7, 57, 81, 126, 195, 202
cardinal virtues 40, 87; *see also* virtue
care 131–2, 134, 150, 166, 188
care theory 41
career choice 108, 110, 111
Carr, David 39–41, 46–7, 199
Carusetta, Ellen 52
Catholicism: Liverpool Hope University 85–6; social teaching 61, 67, 80–1, 202; student narratives 96, 99 *see also* Christianity; faith; religion; spirituality
Central America 20
challenge: becoming authentic 114–16, 158
character education 40–1, 136, 188, 198
charity 45, 61, 80–1, 151, 155, 174–5; reciprocity 134–5, 201–2; theological virtue 39
Choglamsar, Ladakh, India 93–6
Christ *see* Jesus
Christianity 40, 60, 79–81, 112; Anglicanism 85–6; Catholicism 61, 67, 80–1, 85–6, 96, 99, 202; *see also* faith; religion; spirituality
Christ's College 86
Church of England 85–6 *see also* Catholicism; Christianity; faith; religion; spirituality
citizenship: active 72, 76, 78; cosmopolitan 204–5; higher education 75–6, 78–9, 194; service-learning 69; *see also* global citizenship
civic role, universities 74–9
codes of practice 72
colonialism, new 22, 60, 70, 201
combined capabilities 44 *see also* capability approach
commodification: education 3, 38, 79, 81 *see also* consumerism; marketisation
communicative action 16

communities of practice 22–3, 42
community *see* reciprocity; relationality
Community Action Partnership (US) 68
community engagement 5, 9, 75, 77–8, 87
community service 67–9 *see also* International Service-Learning; Service-Learning
compassion 151–2
competence, global 3–4
conation 16, 18
conceptual framework, transformative learning 91–2, 103–4, 195, 204
conditions, transformative learning 103–5: cosmopolitanism 155–62; integrity 108–13, 125, 128–9; model, ethical ecological 183–7, 195, 197, 201, 204–5; reciprocity 131, 133–7
confidence: development 100, 124–5, 143, 198–9; lack of 120, 135, 152
connectivity: with 'the other' 160–2; with others 135–7; with self 111–12; conscientisation 17, 19–21, 47, 86
consciousness, critical 20
consciousness, relational 131
consequences, unexpected 45, 71, 117, 129, 165, 168, 185
Conservative government (UK) 69
constructivism 18, 22, 53, 68
consumerism 77, 79, 170, 190, 193; service-learning and volunteering 68, 71
cosmopolitan learning: definition 156 *see also* cosmopolitanism (worldliness)
cosmopolitanism (worldliness): barriers to 176–8; citizenship 74, 204–5; conditions for 156–62; dispositions toward 168–76; processes underpinning 162–8; transformative learning, model of 182–3, 202–5; worldliness and authenticity 60–1, 155–6 Cousin, Glynis 44
Crabtree, Robbin D. 73
Cranton, Patricia 19, 52
critical consciousness 20
critical pedagogy 25, 39, 81 *see also* Freire, Paulo
critical theory 20
critical thinking: alongside immersion 162–5; capacity 158–60; Freire 20, 47; higher education 58, 75, 78; learning theory 18–19, 21–4, 158, 160, 199; tacit knowing 34; value orientation, recognising 186–8; *see also* practical reason; reflection, shared; self-reflection
curriculum 67–8, 84–5, 184–5, 194, 196–7, 201–2

Dall'Alba, Gloria 31
Dasein 33, 54–5, 118 *see also* Heidegger Martin
data: collection and analysis 90–2
Dautoff, Diane 72, 73
Dearing Report 76
deep ecology 63
Department for Education and Skills (DfES) 76
dependency, culture of 165, 171
Descartes, René 26
development: personal 17, 60, 88 158; higher education 58, 61, 74–5, 193
development education 72, 189
development, sustainable 3, 174, 188, 198
Dewey, John 21, 23, 35–6, 40, 75, 142, 192; aesthetic aspects of knowing 29–30, 54–5; experience, unity of 30, 55, 58, 92, 194; service-learning, development 68–9
Dirkx, John 17–18, 19, 25, 39
discontinuity 62, 108, 110
dispositions 103–5: capability approach 47; towards authentic selfhood 111, 113, 120–6, 128–9; towards cosmopolitanism 168–76; towards reciprocity 146–52, 156; transformative learning, model of 184–5, 187, 188–91, 194–4, 196, 199, 202–5; virtue ethics 39–41
dissonance 38–9, 81
distal, the *see* focal, the
distanciation/participation 165, 199 *see also* immersion
'doing for' 117, 132, 141, 147–9, 150, 172–4, 201
double loop learning 17
dualism, West/non West 24–5
Dunne, Joseph 41
dwelling 32–3, 55, 62, 123 *see also* indwelling

ecology 62, 181–2 *see also* ethical ecology
education, experiential 21–5, 30–1; service-learning 68
efficacy, personal 70, 75, 124–6, 129, 143, 152, 186
Eisner, Elliot 43
Eliot, T.S. 69–70
elite/elitism 74, 173
Ellsworth, Elizabeth 39
emotion: aesthetic aspects of knowing 30–1, 55, 163; capability approach 45; cosmopolitanism 157, 160, 163, 168, 175; integrity of self 111, 114–16, 120, 125, 128; learning 16, 24, 39; mission, Liverpool Hope University 58; reciprocity 137, 139–41, 143–4, 146, 151; transformative learning, model of 185, 198–9
empathy 132, 151–2, 192 *see also* reciprocity
employability 69, 75–8, 82, 88, 187
empowerment 20, 68, 174
England 75, 85, 169 *see also* Liverpool Hope University
entoleration 203
epistemology *see* knowing
ethical ecology: concept of 6–7, 62–3, 181–3, 204–5; institutional ethos 193–8; partnership 198–204; practice 183–93
ethics: higher education 59, 69, 75, 78; (I)SL 5–6, 60, 70–1, 75, 78, 192, 199; knowledge, relational 35; LHU and ISL, 87, 89; reflection 117, 158, 186, 199; student experience, dilemmas 127, 165, 199; teaching 45; value reorientation, recognising 186–8; virtue ethics 39–43, 136, 193
ethnocentricity 73, 174
ethnorelativity 73, 173
ethos 35, 39–40, 40, 42–3, 187–8; institutional 183, 193–8; Liverpool Hope University 85–9
Europe 72–3
evaluation, of service 116–18
everydayness (Heidegger) 54
exchange, cultural 140–2, 152, 161 *see also* reciprocity
existential questions 118–19 ,121
expectations: ISL 58, 109, 126, 187, 193, 199; defined by own 58, 114, 142, 164
experiential education 21–5, 30–1; service-learning 68
exploitation 36, 60, 70–1, 132, 151, 201
externalisation 34, 113–15 *see also* internalisation; knowing, tacit

faith: learning 78, 79–81, 87; student experience, ISL 112, 118, 119, 197; theological virtue 39–40, 87; *see also* Christianity; religion; spirituality
faith-based education 78, 79–81, 87
fallibility 68–70, 169
false consciousness 20
fees, tuition 76–7, 196
feminism 36
flexibility 110–11, 124, 184
focal, the 32–4, 55, 114
frames of reference (Mezirow) 17–18, 24
freedoms *see* capability approach

Freire, Paulo 17, 19–21, 47, 58
functionings 43–5, 57 *see also* capability approach
'Future of Higher Education, The' (white paper) 76

Giddens, Anthony 54
Gilligan, Carol 36
GiveBacc (UK) 69
Glanzer, Perry 87
global citizenship: construal 2–3; ethical ecology 189, 205; ISL 5–6, 67, 70, 72–4, 189; Liverpool Hope University 88; service-learning and higher education 76, 78; UNESCO 3–4, 188; *see also* citizenship
global competence 3–4
Global Hope 86
globalisation 1–4, 76, 155–6, 157
'good life': authenticity 56, 58, 60, 108, 117–18, 125, 129; capability approach 44, 47; virtue ethics 39–40, 42
government (UK) 69, 72, 76
Greene, Maxine 19
Guattari, Felix 62
guilt 96, 122, 126, 135, 143, 177, 189

Habermas, Jürgen 16, 21
habits of being 38, 55, 183, 188; student experience 105, 110, 113, 116, 123–4, 144, 173–4
habits of mind 17, 91, 183, 185, 187, 204; being and becoming 38, 40, 55; student experience 113, 140
Haeckel, Ernst 182
Harré, Horace 107
Hart, Mechthild 25, 43–4, 47
having, mode of 108, 121, 126, 157
hegemony, questioning 158, 160, 170–1, 173
Heidegger, Martin: authenticity 54–5, 58, 118, 123, 150, 164; being and becoming 37; knowledge, tacit 33–4
Held, David 204
hermeneutics 37, 91, 186, 202, 204
Heron, John 29–30
higher education: American 68–9; anxiety 39, 45; authentic relations 200–1; selfhood and authenticity 58, 125; ethos, institutional 193–8; faith-based 78, 79–81, 87; internationalisation 61; service-learning 69, 72, 74–9; tacit knowledge 34 *see also* Liverpool Hope University; universities; worldliness and authenticity 51

Higher Education Active Community Fund 77
holism: capability approach 45; ethical ecology 62, 183, 185, 188, 199, 204; knowing, ways of 30, 38, 55–6; 'Learning Age, The' (green paper) 76; learning, models of 5, 16, 23–6, 39, 131; honesty 120–1
hope: theological virtue 39, 87
Hope One World 86
horizon of expectation 191
horizons of significance 58–9, 116–18, 148–9, 195
Hull House 75
humility 120–1

identity, religious 87
ideology critique 19
idolisation, individuals 136
I-It relationships 36, 132, 151, 200–1; *see also* Buber, Martin; I-Thou relationships
Illeris, Knud 47–8
immersion: aesthetics and knowing 30–1, 55, 108; reciprocity and authenticity 55, 133, 136, 138, 140; selfhood and authenticity 113–14, 115–16, 118; transformative learning, model of 188, 190, 197, 199, 204; worldliness and authenticity 157, 160, 162–5
impact, on participants 95, 112, 116, 140–1, 145–6, 166–9, 188–9 *see also* habits of being; habits of mind
Incheon Declaration (UNESCO, 2015) 3
India: service-learning 72
individual: learning models 22–4, 35, 196
individualism: learning models 24, 35, 58, 186–7, 189; service-learning, growth of 6, 68; student experience 112, 126
indwelling 32–3, 55, 114
informal learning 26, 147, 185
injustice, social: ISL and authenticity 118, 122, 126–7, 155, 165–168, 171, 174–8; SL, nature and role 6, 63, 68, 70, 72, 78, 85–6; transformative learning, model 189, 202–4; *see also* justice; poverty
internal capabilities 44–5 *see also* capability approach
internalisation 16, 33, 40 *see also* knowing, tacit; externalisation
International Assocation for Research on Service-Learning and Community Engagement 73

International Citizen Service (UK) 69, 72
International Partnership for Service-Learning and Leadership 73
International Service-Learning: concepts and practices 67, 69–75; ethical framework for 6–7; service-learning, development 67–9; service-learning and faith-based education 79–81; service-learning and higher education 74–9 *see also* student experience, ISL
internationalisation 61, 78
internationalism 61, 78, 83
Irish Potato Famine 85
Iser, Wolfgang 192–3
I-Thou relationships 36, 132, 147, 151, 200 *see also* Buber, Martin; I-It relationships

Jarvis, Peter 56, 59
Jesus 45, 80, 87
Jubilee Centre for Character & Virtues, Birmingham 188
justice, social: conscientisation 20, 86; ISL and authentic selfhood 58; ISL and cosmopolitanism 60; ISL and recognition 73–4, 177–8; transformative learning, model 201; *see also* injustice; poverty

Kapuscinski, Ryszard 131
Kasl, Elizabeth 19, 23, 24, 30, 36
Kegan, Robert 19
King, Patricia 18
Kitchener, Karen 18
knowing, embodied 23–5, 30–4, 38, 42, 55, 115, 191
knowing/knowledge: aesthetic 29–32; authentic self 52–7; being and becoming 5, 16, 24, 34, 37–9, 43; capability approach 46; embodied 23–5, 30–4, 38, 42, 55, 115, 191; holistic 5, 16, 23–6, 38–9, 55–6; learning and experience 21–3; learning, transformative dimensions 16–19; limitations, acknowledging 168–70; other ways, valuing 171–3, 202–3; practical 29, 32–4; presentational 29–30; propositional 29–30; reciprocity and authenticity 131–2; relational 34–7; scientific 32; separated 132, 138; service-learning 68; tacit 32–4, 50, 114; transformative learning, model of 5, 182–3, 185, 191, 194, 197–9, 201–4
knowledge economy 3, 76

Kolb, David A. 21–2, 68
Kwa Zulu Natal, South Africa 86

Lahroodi, Reza 40
Land, Ray 39
Lather, Patti 39
Lave, Jean 22–3, 42, 46
Le Cornu, Alison 33–4
'Learning Age, The' (green paper) 76
learning cycle (Kolb) 21–2, 68
learning outcomes 190–1, 37,8, 105, 202
Lee, Harper 192
Leitch Review of Skills 76
Levinas, Emmanuel 131–2
Lewis, C.S. 38
liberal arts 58
liberalism 35, 47, 79
liberation theology 60, 190
liminality 39
Liu, Goodwin 35
Liverpool Hope University: authentic selfhood 58–9; ISL, development and nature 85–9; Ladakh, India, student narrative 92–6; reciprocity and relationality 59–61; Sarata, Romania, student narrative 96–100; student experience of ISL, investigation 89–92
Liverpool Institute of Higher Education 86
logos 39, 193
love: theological virtue 87
Luther, Martin 60

MacIntyre, Alasdair 42, 46
Magician's Nephew, The (C.S. Lewis) 38
Mandela, Nelson 38
Marcuse, Herbert 30
marketisation: of education 3, 38, 67–9, 81, 88 *see also* commodification
masculinism 22
materialism: cosmopolitanism and authenticity 159, 168, 170; integrity of self 111, 115–16, 119, 121–2; participant narrative, Ladakh 96; reciprocity and authenticity 145
meaning-making: Kolb 21–2; Mezirow 16–17, 22
Mello, Anthony de 135
methodology 89–92
Meyer, Jan 39
Mezirow, Jack: critical reflection 18–19, 20, 158, 160, 199; knowing, modes of 34, 38–9; transformative learning, models of 4–5, 16–20, 22, 24
mission: faith-based education 79, 81; Liverpool Hope University 58–9, 85–8

Index

Mitchell, Tania 81
mode of being 56, 108, 121, 126, 157
mode of having 108, 121, 126, 157
morality: authenticity as ideal 56; cosmopolitanism and ISL experience 165–6; faith-based education 79; integrity and ISL experience 108, 128; ISL, understanding of 5–6, 70, 186–8; learning theory 5, 16, 24; LHU and ISL 59–60; reciprocity and ISL experience 132; SL and higher education 75–6; transformative learning, model of 183, 186–9, 192–4, 199; *see also* ethics; virtue ethics; virtues
motivations, undertaking ISL 74, 89, 134–5, 186–7
Myth of Sisyphus 17

National Citizen Service (UK)
National Committee of Inquiry into Higher Education 75
New Labour government (UK) 76
Newman, John Henry 60, 79–80, 182, 197
Nietzsche, Friedrich 135
Nin, Anaïs 61, 192
Nixon, John 45
Noddings, Nel 36, 41
Non-Government Organisations (NGOs) 5, 189, 198, 201
North 71, 80–1, 89, 152–3, 201 *see also* South
North America 4
Notre Dame College 86
Nussbaum, Martha 41–2, 53–7, 74, 117, 134
Nye, Rebecca 131

O'Carroll, Sr Maureen 86
O'Neill, Onora 45
ontology *see* being
openness: presencing 31–2; reciprocity 132–4, 140–1, 145–6; transformative learning, model of 197, 201, 204; with the other 156–8, 162; with self 108–110
Our Lady's Training College 85
Oxfam 72, 201

Palmer, Parker J. 35–6, 38
Parker, Barbara 72, 73
Parks-Daloz, Laurent A. 38
participant narratives 92; Olivia (Transylvania, Romania, 2009) 96–100; Rachel (Ladakh, India, 1993) 93–100
participation/distanciation 165, 199 *see also* immersion

participation, widening 75
partnership: with community, in development of service-learning 69; Liverpool Hope University 59; North-South 201; universities, with stakeholders 75
paternalism 61, 81 *see also* patronisation
pathos 39, 193
patronisation 2, 71, 135, 174–6 *see also* paternalism
Peace Corps (US) 68
perseverance 110–11
personal transformation 18–20, 73, 133, 199
perspective transformation 4, 17–19, 21, 34
phenomenology 23, 91
philia (brotherly love) 87
phronesis 40–1, 117, 140 *see also* practical reason
pity 132, 135, 151
place, reconnecting with 173–4
points of view (Mezirow) 17
Polanyi, Michael 32–4, 55, 114
positionality 91
positivism 37
postmodernism 53
poverty: capability approach 43; globalisation 2; ISL and authentic selfhood 58, 111, 118, 126–8; ISL and cosmopolitanism 155, 157, 159–62, 163–4, 169–70, 174–6; service-learning, nature and role 6, 63, 68, 70; transformative learning, model 184–5, 189, 196; *see also* injustice; justice
power: agency and functioning 44; hegemony, questioning 158, 160, 170–1, 173; imbalance, perpetuation and reinforcement 61, 71, 152, 170–1, 187, 203; imbalance, recognition 156, 158; 'learning theories 18–20, 24; 'over' 149–50, 152, 174, 201; 'to' 150, 201; 'with' 132, 149–50, 152, 174, 201
practical knowledge 29, 32–4
practical reason 41–2, 45, 47, 117, 128, 166
practical wisdom *see phronesis*; *see also* practical reason
pragmatism (Dewey) 21, 23, 35–6, 69, 142
presence-to-hand 33–4, 54, 113–14 *see also* Heidegger, Martin
presencing 31, 55, 109
presentational knowledge 29–30
processes, cosmopolitanism 162–8; integrity 112–20; model, ethical ecological 184–5, 188, 190, 194–6, 202, 205; reciprocity 137–46; transformative learning 103–5

Programme for International Student Assessment 3
propositional knowledge 29–30
proximal, the *see* subsidiary, the
psychology 21, 24, 35–6
purpose, higher education 194–6; *see also* higher education, service-learning; universities, idea of (Newman)
Pusch, Margaret 73
Putnam, Robert 69
Putting the World into World Class Education (DfES) 76

readiness-to-hand 33–4, 113–14 *see also* Heidegger, Martin
realism, social 189
reciprocity: authenticity 53, 57–8, 59–60, 61, 103–4, 131–2; barriers to 152–3; capability approach 43, 45; conditions for 133–7; dispositions toward 146–52; (I)SL 68, 73, 87, 89, 92; processes underpinning 137–46; transformative learning, model of 62, 183, 187, 193, 198–9, 200–2, 204 *see also* relationality
reciprocity and authenticity 135, 140, 143–6, 147–8, 151
recognition 132–3, 141, 150–3, 161, 182 *see also* reciprocity
reconnection: with the other 166–8; with others 143–6; with place 173–4; with self 108, 119–20; with time 108, 123
reflection, shared: 142–3; 165–6; *see also* critical thinking; self-reflection
reflexivity: authenticity 54, 58, 117, 149, 156; Mezirow 18; transformative learning, model of 190, 195 *see also* self-reflection
reification, indigenous culture 162
relational consciousness 131
relationality: being 37–8, 201; cosmopolitanism 156; (I)SL 73, 91; knowing 29, 34–7, 56, 73, 132; learning 16, 22–6; transformative learning, model of 62, 183, 191, 199, 196, 201, virtue ethics 41–2 *see also* reciprocity
relations, tutor-student 100, 135–7, 139, 143, 152, 194
relativism 42, 142, 173
religion 68, 74, 80–1, 87, 111–12, 118–19 *see also* Christianity; faith; spirituality
research 72–3, 78–9, 185–6, 188–92, 194–9, 202
resilience 110–11
return home: cosmopolitanism 166–9, 173–5, 177; integrity of self 110, 113, 116, 119–120, 122–8

Ricoeur, Paul 37, 107, 132
Rizvi, Fazal 156
role models 46, 138, 196–8
Russell Commission 77

Saltmarsh, John 36, 196
Sarata, Romania 96–100
Scharmer, Otto 31–2, 55, 109
scholarship of engagement 59, 69
Schön, Donald 17
scientific method 54
self-awareness 31, 55, 135; of strengths and weaknesses 110, 120, 124
self-fulfilment, instrumental 56, 61, 149
self-reflection 109, 112–14, 128, 133–4, 160, 163, 199 *see also* critical thinking; reflexivity
Sen, Amartya 43, 45–6
service: definition 68; evaluation of 116–17
Service and Leadership Award, LHU 87–9, 187
service apathy 6, 68
Service-Learning 67–9; faith-based education 79–81; higher education 74–9 *see also* International Service-Learning
settlement movement 75
Sherman, Nancy 41
Sisters of Notre Dame 85–6
situated cognition, theories of 22–3
situationism 46
skills: intercultural 1, 2, 124; (I)SL 2, 68–9, 76–8, 124, 134–5; learning theory 16, 24; Liverpool Hope University 88; problem-solving 68, 75, 165–6; tacit knowledge 32, 34; transformative learning, model of 191, 194, 196; virtue ethics 40–1
social capital 69, 184
social transformation 4, 20, 81, 156, 199
social virtue 46, 57, 126, 129
solidarity 2–3, 74, 127, 132, 156, 168, 190
SOS Children Sri Lanka 86–7
SOS Children's Villages 86–7, 93–6, 138, 157, 163, 176
'soul work' 25, 39
South 71, 75, 80–1, 89, 175, 201 *see also* North
spirit/spirituality: higher education 61, 75–6, 87; (I)SL, understanding of 6, 8, 61, 68, 70, 183, 186; learning 19, 24–5; student experience, ISL 118–19, 121, 149, 197; transformative learning, model of 192–3, 196–7; worldliness 60–1; *see also* faith; religion
Step up to Serve (UK) 69

stereotypes: challenging 164, 175, 184, 202; perpetuating/reinforcing 71, 112, 158–60, 175–7, 185, 198, 202–3
St. Katharine's College 86
storge (familial love) 87
student-tutor relations 100, 135–7, 139, 143, 152, 194
study abroad 72, 73
subsidiary, the 32–4, 114
Sullivan, John 80
supremacy, cultural 76
surface learning 16, 22–3
sustainable development 3, 174, 188, 198
Sustainable Development Goals 3

Taylor, Charles 56, 59, 116–17, 142, 149, 195
Taylor, Edward W. 19, 35, 181, 185
techne 37, 40
telos 40
Thayer-Bacon, Barbara 37
theological virtues 39–40, 87; *see also* virtue
Theory U 31–2, 109
Threshold Concepts, theory of 39
Tibetan Children's Villages 86–7, 144; Choglamsar, Ladakh, India 93–6, 144
Tisdell, Elizabeth 19
To Kill a Mockingbird (Lee) 192
Tolliver, Denise 19
Tosey, Paul 23
tourism 2, 71, 89, 94, 96–7, 153, 162–3
Toynbee Hall, London 75
transformation: concept of 15–16; conditions for 183–8; epochal 38, 105; incremental 38; personal 15, 18–20, 73, 133, 199; social 4, 20, 81, 156, 199
transformative learning: conceptual framework 91–2, 103–4, 195, 204; definition 24, 48; Mezirow 15–19; reconceptualization 4–5 *see also* ethical ecology
Transformative Learning Centre, Toronto 24
trust 35, 40, 146–7
tutors 105, 117, 142, 143, 166, 186, 190; relations with students 100, 135–7, 139, 143, 152, 194

uncertainty 21, 32, 39, 56, 111
United Nations Economic Commission for Europe (UNECE) 188

United Nations Educational, Scientific and Cultural Organisation (UNESCO) 3–4, 188
unity: experience (Dewey) 30, 55, 58, 92, 194; human life (MacIntyre) 42, 56
universalism 203 *see also* cosmopolitanism
universities: global citizenship 5–6; idea of (Newman) 60, 79–80, 182, 197; service-learning, growth of 5–6; social problems 59; *see also* higher education; Liverpool Hope University
unpredictability 110–11, 114–15, 120, 123, 199, 110
USA: inequalities 2; (I)SL 68–9, 72, 75, 80
utility 39, 193

values: alignment with action 59, 117, 120, 127, 128, 143, 189–90, 198; orientation, recognising 186–8; *see also* ethics; ethos; morality
virtue: agency and social change 45–6; authenticity and selfhood 56–7, 108, 126, 128–9; cosmopolitanism 156, 177; epistemic 40, 156; ethics 39–43, 136, 193; Service-Learning and faith-based education 79; social 46, 57, 126, 129; tacit knowledge 33; transformative learning, model of 188–9, 190, 193–4, 197–8
virtues, epistemic 40, 156
virtue ethics 39–43, 136, 193
Voluntary Service Overseas 189
Volunteers to Serve America 68
'voluntourism' 72
Vorhandenheit see presence-to-hand
Vygotsky, Lev Semyonovich 35, 46

Walker, Melanie 43, 45–7, 75, 81
Wallace, James 177
Warrington Training Institution 85
Watson, Lilla 73
Wenger, Etienne 22–3, 42, 46
West: capability approach 46; hegemony 20, 158, 160, 170–3; learning theory 18, 24–5; 35
World Education Forum (South Korea, 2015) 3
worldliness *see* cosmopolitanism (worldliness)

zone of proximal development 46
zuhandenheit see readiness-to-hand